THOMAS JEFFERSON ARCHITECT

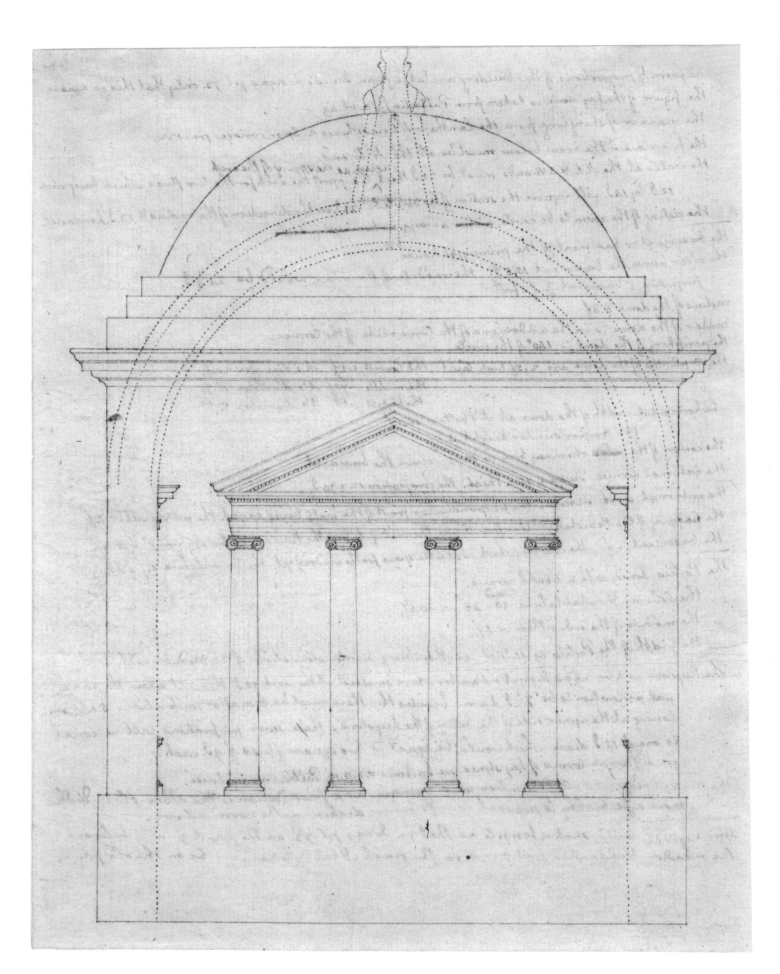

THOMAS JEFFERSON ARCHITECT

Palladian Models,
Democratic Principles,
and the Conflict of Ideals

Lloyd De Witt
and Corey Piper

CHRYSLER MUSEUM OF ART, NORFOLK

IN ASSOCIATION WITH YALE UNIVERSITY PRESS, NEW HAVEN AND LONDON

This book is published in conjunction with the exhibition *Thomas Jefferson, Architect: Palladian Models, Democratic Principles, and the Conflict of Ideals*, presented at the Chrysler Museum of Art from October 19, 2019, to January 19, 2020.

The exhibition and catalogue have been realized with generous support from:

DOMINION ENERGY

NATIONAL ENDOWMENT FOR THE ARTS
NORFOLK SOCIETY OF ARTS
WYETH FOUNDATION FOR AMERICAN ART
EMBASSY OF ITALY IN WASHINGTON, DC

Joan P. Brock
The Goode Family Foundation
Peggy and Conrad Hall
Pamela and Bob Sasser
Susan and Dubby Wynne
Jim Hixon
Penny and Peter Meredith
Ashby and Joe Waldo
Duff Kliewer and Bruce Pensyl
Harry T. Lester
Charlotte and Gil Minor
Lelia Graham and Randy Webb
Meredith and Brother Rutter
Beth and Paul Fraim
Carolyn and Dick Barry
Virginia and John Hitch
Pam and Pete Kloeppel
Suzanne and Vince Mastracco
Patt and Colin McKinnon
Dixie and Jim Sanderlin
Ashlin and Wayne Wilbanks

Programming for the exhibition was made possible in part by Virginia Humanities, Susan and Norman Colpitts, Kirkland Kelley, and the Docent Council of the Chrysler Museum of Art.

Published in 2019 by the Chrysler Museum of Art, Norfolk

in association with Yale University Press,
New Haven and London

Yale

yalebooks.com/art

Designed by Catherine Mills
Set in Walbaum Pro by Monotype
Printed in Canada by Transcontinental

Library of Congress Control Number: 2019939497
ISBN 978-0-300-24620-9

A catalogue record for this book is available from the British Library.

The paper in this book meets the requirements of ANSI/NISO Z39.48-1992 (Permanence of Paper).

10 9 8 7 6 5 4 3 2 1

Jacket illustrations: (*front*) Benjamin Tanner, engraver, *University of Virginia* (detail), 1826 (from an 1824 drawing) (see Nelson, fig. 1); (*back*) Benjamin Henry Latrobe, *View of Richmond from South Side of James River Showing Capitol from Bushrod, Washington*, 1796 (see M. Wilson, fig. 17)

Frontispiece: Thomas Jefferson (American, 1743–1826), Ionic portico and dome, Monticello, probably 1778. Pen and ink. Coolidge Collection of Thomas Jefferson Manuscripts, Massachusetts Historical Society, N91; K62

Page 8: Jacob Caleb Ward, *View of the Natural Bridge, Virginia* (detail), c. 1835 (see plate 13)

Pages 118–19: Benjamin Henry Latrobe, *View of the City of Richmond from the Bank of the James River* (detail), 1798 (see M. Wilson, fig. 1)

CONTENTS

FOREWORD

The exhibition *Thomas Jefferson, Architect: Palladian Models, Democratic Principles, and the Conflict of Ideals* pays tribute to the unique, long-standing ties and friendship between Italy and the United States as well as to our shared values. This common identity dates back to a time when our two nations had not yet been born: its roots can be found in the legacy of the Florentine Renaissance. It developed in the arts, sciences, and political thought as well as through the lives and ideas of great men such as Andrea Palladio and Thomas Jefferson, Benjamin Franklin and Gaetano Filangieri, Giuseppe Garibaldi and Abraham Lincoln.

A native of my own Veneto, Andrea Palladio is recognized as one of the most influential individuals in Western architecture, also owing to the publication, in 1570, of his architectural treatise, the *Quattro libri dell'architettura* (Four books of architecture). In acknowledgment of his important legacy, the Palladian villas of the Veneto are listed by UNESCO, alongside the city of Vicenza, as a World Heritage Site. Indeed, his ideals of proportion, beauty, and classicism, inspired by classical Roman architecture, strongly influenced the development of architectural and urban design, giving rise to a distinct architectural style, Palladianism, which quickly spread to Europe and to North America—as we can see close at hand both in Virginia and the nation's capital. Most significantly of all his many accomplishments, Palladio enabled us to better understand the roots of Italy's own national identity, from ancient Rome to the Renaissance.

Jefferson—thinker, architect, founding father—truly embodies the spirit of the Italian Renaissance, another inexorable link between our great countries. The third president's attachment to Palladio is clearly visible in his creative endeavors, as is his wish to reinterpret the designs of this Italian architect of the Renaissance for his own time and place. Jefferson's plans for Monticello, his Neoclassical mansion in Virginia, and his unfulfilled drawings for the White House deeply reflect Palladio's ideas and artistic concept, and set a new standard for America, conveying the ideals of liberty and democracy through the architecture of some of the most important and significant buildings of the young nation. The goal of the exhibit, and the beautiful accompanying catalogue, is in fact twofold: while it aims to provide US audiences with a better understanding of the influence of Palladio on Jefferson, it also highlights Jefferson's will to use architecture for the new republic that would reflect its spirit and political values.

This exhibition is the result of a joint effort of the Chrysler Museum of Art in Norfolk, Virginia, and the Museo Palladio in Vicenza, Italy, supported by the Embassy of Italy in Washington, DC, and represents a welcome addition to the strong bond between our nations. My sincere appreciation goes to the director of the Chrysler Museum, Erik H. Neil, and to the curators, Lloyd DeWitt, Corey Piper, and Seth Feman, as well as to the director of the Museo Palladio, Guido Beltramini, for making this exhibition possible, and for offering a new perspective into a man, a master of the arts, who played such an important role in the history of both our countries. ❧

Armando Varricchio
Ambassador of Italy to the United States

INTRODUCTION

ERIK H. NEIL

S ince the founding of the United States, Thomas Jefferson has been a
topic for examination by travelers, journalists, critics, political philosophers, and historians (fig. 1). Today there is a small industry of
publications on Jefferson, his family, and his many pursuits.
Undoubtedly architecture was at the top of the list of his preferred activities,
aside from his service in government and agriculture. Strictly speaking, he
was not a professional architect like his contemporary Benjamin Henry
Latrobe, but he was also much more than an amateur. Biographers inevita-
bly comment on Jefferson's home at Monticello as a building inextricably
linked to its builder, to a degree not found in Washington's Mount Vernon
or Madison's Montpelier. Jefferson's engagement with contemporary architectural theories and practices conveniently matched his interest in
advanced political philosophies. He was a critical agent in shaping an architectural language suitable to the ideals of the new republic. His accomplishments in both arenas are still impressive today, even as scholars present a
more complex and contradictory image of the man.

I.

Monticello is a singular architectural achievement, and Jefferson would be
lauded if that were his only significant endeavor in construction. Along with
this famous residence and agricultural complex, he also designed or influenced the design of the Virginia State Capitol, the University of Virginia, the
urban plans for Richmond and Washington, DC, and courthouses in Virginia (fig. 2). He designed country houses like Barboursville and Poplar
Forest, and consulted in one fashion or another on many others. His architectural activities are recorded in a large number of drawings housed primarily in Boston, Baltimore, and Charlottesville. The very existence of this
corpus is a remarkable indicator of the extent and complexity of Jefferson's
architectural activity. He was an earnest but not fluid draftsman, especially
when compared to a formally trained architect like Charles-Louis Clérisseau, his collaborator for the Virginia State Capitol.

Fig. 1. Mather Brown (American, 1761–1831),
Portrait of Thomas Jefferson, 1786. Oil on
canvas. National Portrait Gallery, Smithsonian
Institution, Washington, DC, Bequest of Charles
Francis Adams, NPG.99.66

Fig. 2. Thomas Jefferson (American, 1743–1826), Monticello, Charlottesville, Virginia, 1769–1809. Thomas Jefferson Memorial Foundation at Monticello

Fig. 3. Junius Brutus Stearns (American, 1810–1885), *Washington as a Farmer at Mount Vernon*, 1851. Oil on canvas. Virginia Museum of Fine Arts, Richmond, Gift of Edgar Williams and Bernice Chrysler Garbisch, 50.2.4

Jefferson amassed a very important library of architectural treatises that he mined for ideas as well as practical solutions. A great deal of attention has been paid to his use of treatises, especially in reference to specific details. This is understandable in that these citations are verifiable, and Jefferson obviously loved his books. But the reliance on such citations may also obscure other experiences and practices that defined Jefferson's activity. For instance, when given the opportunity, he traveled extensively to see both modern and ancient monuments. He evinced a special interest in the houses and gardens of the aristocracy. He conversed with other men in Europe and America who shared his passion for architecture. He was also immersed in a society that gave great value to landholders and agrarian ideals. He was raised and operated within a system that depended on an enslaved workforce. All of these factors combined to form his architectural vision.

Jefferson was a tastemaker who was especially concerned about a built environment that would be suitable for free white men like him. Like many of his American peers, he valued sobriety and eschewed excessive ornament in architecture. Taken together, his various projects gave definition to the spaces where his peers and their offspring would live, study, work, govern, and relax. Each ambient was linked in some way to the other in the course of a man's life.

The houses Jefferson designed, beginning with his own, were moderate in scale, especially when compared to many of the royal or aristocratic estates he visited in Europe. They reveal a sensibility for terrain that might be expected from the son of a surveyor, as Jefferson was. Typically they used the language of classical architecture, columns, capitals, and the array of appropriate details replete with associations to the Renaissance and ancient Rome as well as the salons of late-eighteenth-century Paris and the estates of English gentlemen. He favored ideal shapes—squares, circles, and octagons—as the basis for interior spaces. These were model structures fashioned from a coherent set of rules drawn from the authorities of architecture beginning with Vitruvius, Andrea Palladio, and Vignola. Paradoxically, these exemplary residences were reliant upon slaves for their construction and operation. Indeed, plantation houses, with their balanced designs and pleasing proportions, became the locus for the mythology of a well-ordered and tranquil society based on agricultural production with slavery as an intrinsic element. Country houses or plantations like George Washington's Mount Vernon became the emblematic structures for the ruling class of the American South (fig. 3).

It is a well-established fact that Jefferson held a particular affection for Palladio (fig. 4), although he never actually visited a structure built by the Renaissance master. Palladio's lasting influence was due above all to the success of his *Quattro libri dell'architettura* (Four books of architecture), first published in Venice in 1570, with many further editions in the following centuries. Jefferson owned multiple copies. The publication is notable for its clarity in both word and image and the general reliability of its recommendations. Palladio was adept as a translator of the language of antiquity into that of the landholders of the Veneto in the sixteenth century, offering clear rules that any literate man could follow and providing abundant practical advice on how to build for the proper operation of a household and an agricultural estate. Even as architectural tastes and styles changed, the *Quattro libri* maintained its authority, finding renewed importance in England in the eighteenth century, as well as in the English colonies in America. Perhaps the affiliation with Venetian nobles and British aristocrats added to its luster in the New World, offering landowners seeking to re-create the European social order a useful manual.

As the essays in this catalogue attest, however, Jefferson went well beyond Palladian models in his thoughts about architecture. The opportunity to view firsthand a few intact monuments that had survived from the era of the Roman Empire was of special importance as Jefferson became involved in the design of the new Virginia State Capitol in Richmond. In Paris around 1785, Jefferson became familiar with Charles-Louis Clérisseau, who had published an impressive volume on ancient Roman architecture in France, and in particular the so-called Maison Carrée in the southern city of Nîmes (fig. 5). Clérisseau would have been for Jefferson an important conduit to the most advanced thinking about the relationships among antiquity, archaeology, and contemporary architecture. He had

Fig. 4. Giacomo Leoni (Italian, 1686–1746), portrait of Palladio, in *The Architecture of A. Palladio in Four Books* (London: Watts, 1715). University of Zürich Libraries

Fig. 5. Charles-Louis Clérisseau (French, 1722–1820), Maison Carrée, Nîmes, in *Antiquités de la France, première parti: Monumens de Nîsmes* (Paris: Pierres, 1778), plate 2. National Gallery of Art, Washington, DC, Mark J. Millard Architectural Collection, 1985.61.476

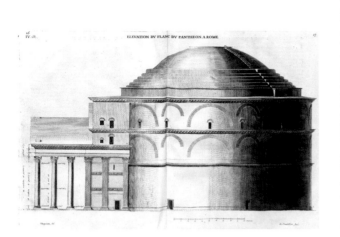

Fig. 6. Antoine Desgodetz (French, 1653–1728), Pantheon, side elevation, in *Les édifices antiques de Rome, dessinés et mesurés très exactement* (Paris: Coignard, 1682), plate 4. Bound volume. Library of Congress, Washington, DC, NA311.D4 1774, NA311.D4 1779, held in Sower by 4198 Jefferson Coll fol. (LCCN 82466699)

Fig. 7. William Goodacre (English, 1803–1883), *Capitol of Virginia, Richmond* (with cartouches of *The Slave* and *The Planter*), c. 1830s. Engraving, watercolor, ink, paper. Chrysler Museum of Art, Gift of Mrs. Robert B. Tunstall, 66.9

spent decades in Italy and had direct relations with prominent architects and theorists such as Giovanni Battista Piranesi, Johann Joachim Winckelmann, William Chambers, and Robert and James Adams. Earlier French architects such as Germain Boffrand and Antoine Desgodetz also influenced his ideas (fig. 6). Jefferson's interaction with Clérisseau is an indication of the widening of his frame of reference and the expansion of his experiences. He made the effort to travel to Nîmes himself to see the Maison Carrée, which served as the model for the new state capitol. Modeling a new building directly on an ancient temple had considerable currency in France during the era of Jefferson's sojourn, as exemplified in the project for the church of Ste-Geneviève by Jacques-Germain Soufflot or the later designs for La Madeleine.

The choice of the ancient temple rather than a model like the palace of Versailles may seem obvious, given the American discomfort with royal authority and the subsequent proliferation of the form in state houses across the new republic, but it was an inspired innovation. It encapsulated the idea that the legitimacy of the government of Virginia rested on ancient pre-Christian and democratic principles rather than on the divine right of kings. Paradoxically, the capitol later became a potent symbol for the distinctly undemocratic institution of slavery and the Confederacy as a whole. The citation of classical precedents was not an infrequent tool of southern apologists for slavery, as evidenced in the figures of the slave and master flanking Jefferson's capitol in William Goodacre's 1830s engraving, for example (fig. 7). However, the shift in emphasis largely occurred in the generations after Jefferson's death.

Upon his return to the United States, throughout the 1790s and until the end of his term as president in 1809, Jefferson was involved with various projects that helped establish the identity of the young republic. Chief among these were the layout of Washington, DC, the creation of a residence for the president, and the construction of the Capitol (fig. 8). Although he could not always play the decisive role, Jefferson's influence was undeniable.

For the residence of the president, Jefferson even submitted his own design, clearly indebted to the ideas of Palladio and Lord Burlington, with details recalling innovations he had seen in Paris (fig. 9). His project, which was not selected, reflected his sense that the buildings in the capital city should represent an ideal. Palladio's Villa Capra "La Rotonda" in Vicenza was an apt model for several reasons. It is situated adjacent to the city rather than in the countryside, and so does not require a range of agricultural out-buildings. The original patron had dedicated his career to government service, albeit in the Vatican as an adviser to the pope. The exterior has a simple grandeur without excessive ornamentation, while the interior layout is essentially a circle within a square, which in three dimensions becomes a sphere within a cube. The pure geometric shapes aspire to perfection just as the new government aspired to a higher ideal.

Fig. 8. Pierre-Charles l'Enfant (French, 1754–1785), *Plan of the City Intended for the Permanent Seat of the Government of the United States* (Washington, DC: US Coast and Geodetic Survey, 1791). Library of Congress, Geography and Map Division

Fig. 9. Designed by Simone Baldissini, constructed by Ivan Simonato, scale model of Thomas Jefferson's entry for the 1792 White House design competition (1:66), 2015, detail. Wood, resin, and tempera. Palladio Museum, Vicenza

II.

The scholarly investigation of Thomas Jefferson's architectural practice began in earnest in the second decade of the twenti-eth century, coinciding with the spirit of the Colonial Revival as well as the dawn of the field of art and architectural history in the United States. The most significant publication of the era was Fiske Kimball's impressive monograph *Thomas Jefferson, Architect*, first published in 1916.[1] Kimball made a thorough study of the drawings and placed them in a coherent order that highlighted the most significant projects. He recognized Jefferson's connection to Palladio and Palladianism. To a great extent his work, along with a few subse-quent articles, established the parameters of Jefferson architectural studies for many decades. The primary questions asked centered on issues of chronology, authorship, and sources, especially printed sources, for various motifs. The landmark exhibition and catalogue *The Eye of Thomas Jefferson* organized by William Howard Adams for the US Bicentennial in 1976 expanded our understanding and appreciation of Jefferson's activities in the arts, including architecture, and may be seen as the culmination of the project set forth by Kimball.[2] For the 250th anniver-sary of Jefferson's birth in 1993, Susan Stein and her colleagues at Monticello mounted an impressive exhibition, *The Worlds of Thomas Jefferson at Monticello*, with a detailed catalogue that further emphasized the breadth of Jefferson's interest in the arts and sciences.[3]

In the years following these exhibitions and publications, it gradually became evident that other questions needed to be asked as well. For example, Jefferson's engagement with botany, agriculture, gardens, and landscape architecture has developed into a field unto itself that largely falls outside the scope of this project. As a whole the collection of essays presented here tends to place Jefferson in a broader historical and intellectual context that, while recognizing his accomplishments and rare set of gifts, also frames him in a less heroic light. His interest in Palladio, in books, and in travel generally was not so unusual for a European landholder of his era. He was very much a man of his time and place.

Changes in approach within the fields of American history and architectural history reflected growing interest in the topic of slavery and the complexities of race relations as reflected in the built environment, with attention to the ways spaces were created and used. Scholars like Dell Upton and others employed close analysis of the landscape to tell different stories.[4] The work of Annette Gordon-Reed and others on the Hemings family was transformational.[5] These scholars were able to mine the rich archival holdings of Jefferson's payment books and letters to understand the central role of slaves and slavery in his personal and professional life. Two essays in our collection consider more deeply the context, conception, and building history of Jefferson's architecture as it relates to slavery.

Today a visitor to Monticello, Poplar Forest, Montpelier, or the University of Virginia will be presented with a more serious and prominent interpretation of the spaces of slavery than had been the case even five years ago. Because of new research, spurred by new ways of looking, we recognize that many of the people who built these Jeffersonian structures and fashioned their architectural details were enslaved. We see also that Palladio's observations regarding the quality of persons who should build a villa might have been just as attractive to Jefferson and his peers as the discussions of ideal proportions and classical precedents. In a slave society, Palladio's prescriptions for the creation of spaces in attics, mezzanines, and basements for servants and service functions had a special resonance.

Jefferson's plan for an "academical village" was visionary (fig. 10). He recognized that the new republic would need thoughtful and wise leaders and sought to create a place where they could be educated. The value he placed on learning remains appealing. Less appealing is the fact that inherent in the construction and operation of the university was the expectation of an enslaved workforce (see M. Wilson essay, fig. 16). The design of the new university reinforced and reified the unjust system of slavery. This was also the case at Monticello, Poplar Forest, and all the other country houses. As Kimball noted more than a century ago, with a shortage of skilled craftsmen, Jefferson needed to train his own slaves to do the specialized work he required.[6]

Jefferson on more than one occasion professed his distaste of slavery and acted to curtail the slave trade, yet he also depended on the institution for his well-being. He wrote "All men are created equal" but also held and published unsavory opinions about racial superiority. A significant section of his *Notes on the State of Virginia* is an elaborately reasoned justification for racial discrimination. Similarly, though his architecture embodied ideals of democracy, beauty, sobriety, and functionality, it was conceived and constructed with the understanding that enslaved people would be at the ready for his needs. A full appreciation of these facts presents a dilemma. We are left with the difficult task of recognizing and reconciling the contradictions of Thomas Jefferson and his architecture. 🍂

NOTES

1. Fiske Kimball, ed., *Thomas Jefferson, Architect: Original Designs in the Collection of Thomas Jefferson Coolidge, Jr.* (Cambridge, MA: Riverside Press, 1916).

2. William Howard Adams, ed., *The Eye of Thomas Jefferson* (Washington, DC: National Museum of American History, 1976).

3. Susan R. Stein, *The Worlds of Thomas Jefferson at Monticello* (New York: Harry N. Abrams, 1993).

4. Dell Upton, "White and Black Landscapes in Eighteenth-Century Virginia," *Places* 2, no. 2 (1984): 59–72.

5. Annette Gordon-Reed, *The Hemingses of Monticello: An American Family* (New York: W. W. Norton, 2008).

6. Kimball, *Thomas Jefferson, Architect*, 85.

THOMAS JEFFERSON, THE MAKING OF AN ARCHITECT

HOWARD BURNS

Thomas Jefferson was engaged with architecture throughout most of his adult life. He bought, read, and used many architectural books, visited buildings, and made notes and sketches of them. He designed for himself and his friends, gave advice, and offered projects for public buildings. He mastered construction techniques and invented structural innovations and labor-saving domestic devices. He personally acquired manual skills and taught them to others. His engagement with architecture continued even through the momentous years of the struggle for American independence, and in his subsequent demanding career as governor of Virginia, American minister in Paris, secretary of state, vice president, and two-term president. His involvement with architecture is documented in hundreds of surviving drawings and pages of notes on architectural and building matters as well as in his vast correspondence, in which references to columns, capitals, and bricks appear frequently.[1] Designing for himself and others and giving advice on architectural matters was a pleasurable and relaxing occupation and part of his private, social, and political way of life. The buildings he visited had an enduring emotional and sentimental resonance for him, bridging that tightly defended divide between the sides of his personality that he characterized in a famous letter as the "Heart and the Head."[2]

Though he never presented himself as a professional architect, or earned a living by designing, Jefferson became a central figure in the development of residential and public architecture in the new America as well as the creator of the American university campus—an architectural type later imitated throughout the world. He was an important protagonist in the architectural scene of the later eighteenth century and early nineteenth century, even though his production was far less and his design

Fig. 1. Tuckahoe, Goochland County, Virginia. Vintage photograph. Carnegie Survey of the Architecture of the South, Library of Congress

skills more limited than that of contemporaries elsewhere who contributed substantially to transforming the architecture of the countries in which they worked, like John Soane in England or Giacomo Quarenghi in Russia. England and Russia, however, were old nations, seeking to modernize with the help of a new architecture and new building types, whereas Jefferson sought to define an architecture for a country that was new, even in its declared values and constitution, and moreover lacking in resources. Jefferson's architectural activity parallels and is connected with his strategic intellectual and political contribution to the principles and institutions on which the new nation was to be built. He saw the connection between nation building and designing for public buildings and universities. In the preface to his *Defence of the Constitutions of the United States* of January 1, 1787, Jefferson's then friend and subsequently predecessor as president John Adams referred to the parallel between framing a constitution and designing a building, probably on the basis of conversations with Jefferson during his visit to London and nearby country houses from March 12 to April 26, 1786: "Called without expectation, and compelled without previous inclination . . . to erect suddenly new systems of laws for their future government, [the founding fathers] adopted the method of a wise architect, in erecting a new palace for the residence of his sovereign. They determined to consult Vitruvius, Palladio, and all other writers of reputation in the art; to examine the most celebrated buildings, whether they remain entire or in ruins; [and] compare these with the principles of writers."[3] For Jefferson, architecture was a lifelong passion that emerged well before he was engaged in constructing a new country. This contribution will consider the phases of his involvement with architecture over a career of more than half a century, and indicate how Jefferson, on the basis of his reading, travel, the new challenges he faced, and his growing experience of building and design, constantly revised his architectural preferences and in consequence also constantly transformed his own house, Monticello.

Jefferson's interest in houses and buildings probably began at home. Much of his childhood was spent at Shadwell, the house of his father, Peter, a plantation owner, Virginia politician, and surveyor. This comfortable house had a study where Peter Jefferson kept his books and instruments; a simple portico ran across the front.[4] Shadwell, however, was not the only house the young Jefferson knew. In thinly populated Virginia, visiting friends and relations usually meant staying with them. While his earliest experiences of the houses of his parents' acquaintances are not documented, it is known that the Jeffersons lived for some years at Tuckahoe, a striking house with a regular H-shaped plan and fine interior workmanship (fig. 1).[5] Jefferson in 1814 recalled that "the town of Beverley was laid off on the 6th of June 1751. . . . I was a boy of about 8. years age, living with my father at Tuckahoe, . . . *and well remember* [my emphasis] his going to Westham to lay off the town."[6] Thus Jefferson when still a child would have seen his father laying out a new settlement and using drawing instruments to trace its plan. Tuckahoe would have shown Jefferson that houses could be interestingly different from one another, and its unusual plan would have reinforced this impression.

In Jefferson's Virginia, the houses of leading plantation owners were key points of reference. His house-and-hospitality view of social life and obligations remained strong throughout his life. In 1807 Jefferson writes to Anne-Louise-Germaine Necker about her son, "If he wishes to know the nation, it's occupations, manners & principles, they reside not in the cities; he must travel through the country, accept the hospitalities of the country gentlemen."[7] His Williamsburg college years would have reinforced his sense of the connection between fine houses and social prominence, laying the basis for his desire to build impressively at Monticello. As a maturing student and politically ambitious young lawyer, Jefferson knew that house design was important not only to offer comfort and convenience but as an indication of (and launching pad for) social and political importance.

Early Virginia letters and diaries document the connection between house and status and the importance of having a house that was both visible and commanded a view. This was easier to achieve in plantation houses near water, but the hilltop site of Monticello, his own house, allowed it to enjoy an extensive view and be seen from a distance, a requisite of houses of important persons from Renaissance times onward, including Palladio's Villa Capra "La Rotonda" (designed in the mid-1560s), Vincenzo Scamozzi's Rocca Pisana (of the mid-1570s), or even a huge Venetian palace like the Palazzo Corner on the Grand Canal.[8] Even Jefferson's former slave Isaac, who regularly accompanied his master, was house-conscious, recalling Colonel Edward Carter's Blenheim as "a low, large wooden house, two stories high."[9] As a student traveling between Williamsburg and Shadwell, Jefferson saw— and stayed in—architecturally important houses. College friend John Page, for example, hosted him at his plantation house Rosewell (fig. 2).[10] Jefferson's interest in this impressive but now-ruined mansion was evident in an early note concerning Monticello, where he recorded the precise dimensions of Rosewell's bricks.[11] With Monticello, thanks to its visible, elevated site and a knowledge of architecture based on Palladio's *Quattro libri dell'architettura* (Four books of architecture) and recent English architectural publications, Jefferson advertised himself as belonging to Virginia's elite, even before his political activity had confirmed this position.

Fig. 2. Rosewell Plantation, Virginia.
Vintage photograph

LASTING ARCHITECTURAL MEMORIES

Familiarity with Virginia plantation houses gave Jefferson a first idea of architectural variety. Williamsburg, despite his later criticism of its architecture, provided the start for his architectural formation. The old capitol there, with its pedimented two-level portico, anticipated a similar feature in the first version of Jefferson's Monticello (1771–75), and probably had also inspired the porticoes added to Shirley Plantation House, another important house he would have known (figs. 3, 4).[12] Similarly the octagonal powder magazine in Williamsburg possibly had an early fascination for him, laying the basis for his later love of octagonal structures, though the youthful Jefferson may have been more impressed by its explosive content than by its form (fig. 5).

The handsome house of Jefferson's law professor and then friend George Wythe on the Palace Green in Williamsburg offered a model for an elegant house, with its regular plan, alignment of doors and windows, and dignified facade (figs. 6, 7). He was probably impressed too by the Governor's Palace, which dominated the impressive, long, grass-covered and tree-lined space known as the Palace Green. From 1757 to 1768 the Governor's Palace was the residence of the cultivated acting English governor Francis Fauquier. Fauquier knew and had probably been a friend of the famous English architect James Gibbs.[13] He possessed a large library, and Jefferson, who often dined with him, may have had his first access to a range of architectural books in the Palace itself.

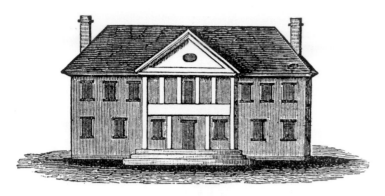

The Palace Green, terminated by the Governor's Palace and flanked by substantial houses, including that of George Wythe, anticipated and probably inspired the underlying formal and functional arrangement of Jefferson's "academical village" in Charlottesville: a long, broad, grass-covered space, flanked by substantial houses and terminated by a monumental building (fig. 8). Along the University of Virginia Lawn all the houses were those of professors, just as in Williamsburg on the Palace Green, one belonged to Jefferson's own former professor. Thus a deep memory of the Palace Green probably sharpened Jefferson's attention to similar layouts that fed into his design for his new college, including the Château de Marly near Paris, which he visited in 1784 and 1786, where pavilions also flank an elongated space terminated by a monumental building.

Fig. 3. Old capitol, Williamsburg, Virginia, destroyed 1832, in Henry Howe, *Historical Collections of Virginia* (Charleston, NC: Babcock & Co., 1845), 42.

Fig. 4. Shirley Plantation House, Virginia

Fig. 5. Octagonal powder magazine, Colonial Williamsburg, Virginia

PALLADIO: CUTTING AND PASTING THE "BIBLE"

Jefferson's architectural expertise first emerges in early notes and drawings for Monticello. They show his familiarity with the books of Robert Morris, James Gibbs, and Palladio, and reveal a judicious and selective way of using his sources. In one of his notes Jefferson cites both Giacomo Leoni's English translation of Palladio's *Quattro libri* (as *The Architecture of A. Palladio in Four Books*) and Gibbs's *Rules for Drawing the Several Parts of Architecture*, writing, "Decoration of paper machee for a ceiling 14 f. 4 I. sq. Divided into 6 + 2 compartments and resembling as much as may be Gibbs' rules for drawg. pl. 58. upper figure, & Palladio B. 4. Pl. 26. fig. C.D.F."[14] Jefferson was referring to a ceiling design in which he wanted to combine motifs present in two different plates in books that he owned, plate 58 in Gibbs's *Rules for Drawing* and plate 26 in book 4 of Leoni's translation of Palladio's *Quattro libri*, a detail of the coffering of the vault of the Temple of Venus and Rome. He wanted his design to resemble these models "as much as may be." As they differ from one another, and perhaps did not even follow the desired overall layout ("Divided into 6 + 2 compartments"), he would have had to combine and adjust them.

Another note refers to three more plates in Leoni's edition of Palladio, and also involves incorporating elements from more than one model in his

Fig. 6. George Wythe House, Colonial Williamsburg, Virginia, 1930. Library of Congress

Fig. 7. Palace Green, Colonial Williamsburg, Virginia. Aerial photograph. Colonial Williamsburg

design for a door (fig. 9).[15] Jefferson wanted to combine the layout of six panels (three for each half of the double door) in the still extant so-called Temple of Fortuna Virilis (the Temple of Portunus) in Rome with a proportional relationship between a door and its architectural frame based on the one between the stone frame and the door opening of the famous round temple at Tivoli.[16] He furthermore cites Palladio's plate showing details of the Pantheon portico "for moulding on edge of border"—presumably for the outer molding of the door frame. In his notes he neglects to identify the molding to which he is referring, because he knows which one it is.[17]

A similarly eclectic approach is at work in the main elevation of Jefferson's first design for Monticello. After initial experimentation, he decided to create a two-story building, higher in the middle than at the sides, with facades based on Palladio's villa designs.[18] But rather than simply replicating a Palladio facade, he combined two different villa elevations: the front facade of the Villa Cornaro at Piombino Dese, with its two-story projecting portico flanked by lower side wings surmounted by an attic level, is fused with the facade elevations of the Villa Pisani at Montagnana, where there are four portico columns at each level, and the orders are Doric and Ionic (figs. 10, 11).[19]

As the rear portico at Montagnana is set into the building, Jefferson instead followed the projecting portico of the Villa Cornaro, reducing the number of columns from six to four, as at the Villa Pisani. The corner columns in Jefferson's design are freestanding, however, as in Roman temples or innumerable English Palladian houses. In fact, in this regard Palladio himself was not a strict Palladian; in all his villas except the Villa Foscari he attached the outer columns of his porticoes either to piers or to walls.

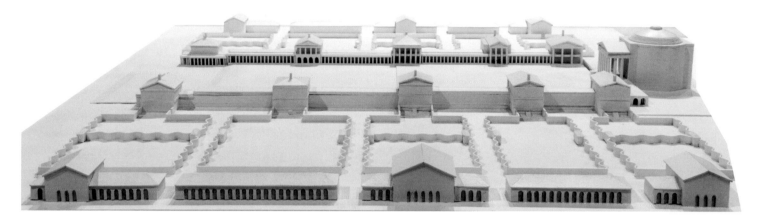

Fig. 8. Designed by Simone Baldessini, constructed by Ivan Simonato, scale model of the University of Virginia (1:350), 2015. Wood, resin, and tempera. Palladio Museum, Vicenza

Fig. 9. Giacomo Leoni (Italian, 1686–1746), details of doors, in *The Architecture of A. Palladio in Four Books* (London: Ward, 1742), book 4, plates 36, 72, and 60. ETH-Bibliothek, University of Zürich, Rar 2443

Fig. 10. Andrea Palladio (Italian, 1508–1580), Villa Cornaro at Piombino Dese, 1552

Fig. 11. Designed by Andrej and Ewa Soltan, constructed by "Ballico-Officina Modellisti," wooden model of Palladio's Villa Pisani at Montagnana (c. 1552), 1974/75. Palladio Museum, Vicenza

Fig. 12. Thomas Jefferson (American, 1743–1826), elevation drawing for the first version of Monticello. Pen and ink. Original manuscript from the Coolidge Collection of Thomas Jefferson Manuscripts, Massachusetts Historical Society, N48; K23

The well-known elevation drawing for the first Monticello was thus the result of a mental and graphic cut-and-paste operation whereby the elevations of the two villas were combined and spatially manipulated (fig. 12). The starting point was the lower level of the facade of the Villa Pisani at Montagnana, plus its pedimented central upper sector. Also from the Villa Pisani comes the extension of the Doric frieze round the building, with the aesthetic function of binding the sides and facades of the structure together. Only the projecting portico and the attics of the low wings derive from the Villa Cornaro. The simplicity of the operation can be illustrated in a montage: every element in it derives unchanged from just two plates in Leoni's *Palladio*.[20] Details are not precisely defined in the small-scale elevations in Palladio's *Quattro libri* or in Leoni's redrawing of them in the first English-language edition (fig. 13). Jefferson therefore turned to Gibbs's *Rules for Drawing* for the two door frames and the windows, which, though he slightly simplified them—the "ears" (projecting lintel portion) are omitted—follow Gibbs in the slenderness of their sills (fig. 14).[21] Always on the lookout for motifs that could resolve a design problem, he wrote on a probable early study for

Monticello, "The flues (two at each end) to be carried along an arch spanning the middle room, and to issue at the top through a stone cut as in Palladio Pl. 49, B. 4." Surprisingly this "stone" is in fact the lantern of Donato Bramante's Tempietto as illustrated by Palladio in book 4 of his *Quattro libri* (plate 49), recycled in Jefferson's mind as a chimney pot.[22]

Jefferson did not merely choose cut-and-paste motifs to create his designs. He was also attentive to basic compositional principles and observed Palladio's design practice attentively. In a note he considers how the details of the architectural orders should be related to the wall that adjoins them: "I do not find that the mouldings of the capital are ever given to the wall, but I observe that the upper mouldings of the base of the shaft, and sometimes a bare zocco [i.e. *zoccolo*, or socle] only are given to the wall of the house and sometimes nothing at all, and qu[ery], which handsomest?" He is also attentive to how Palladio's details are to be constructed, adding, "Have hidden arches over doors and windows to prevent door and window frames from too great pressure."[23] In these notes we see Jefferson, trained in the study of Latin, moving beyond the acquisition of basic vocabulary and teaching himself not only how to read the language but also how to "write" and build the architectural language of ancient Rome.

Fig. 13. Giacomo Leoni (Italian, 1686–1746), Villa Cornaro and Villa Pisani, in *The Architecture of A. Palladio in Four Books* (London: Ward, 1742), book 2, plates 37 and 38. ETH-Bibliothek, University of Zürich, Rar 2443

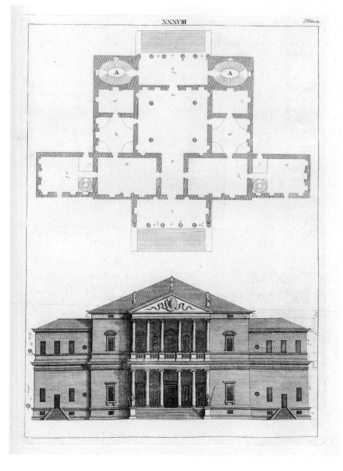

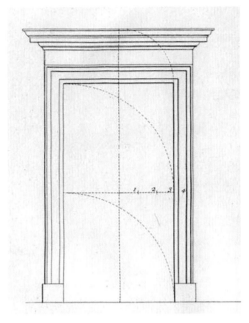

Fig. 14. James Gibbs (Scottish, 1682–1754), *Rules for Drawing the Several Parts of Architecture* (London: Bowyer, 1736), plate 42. ETH-Bibliothek, University of Zürich, Rar 1661: ED.2 GF

Fig. 15. Thomas Jefferson (American, 1743–1826), chapter 2 of *The Life and Morals of Jesus of Nazareth*, c. 1820. Division of Political and Military History, National Museum of American History, Smithsonian Institution, Acc. Nr. 147182, Cat. 158231

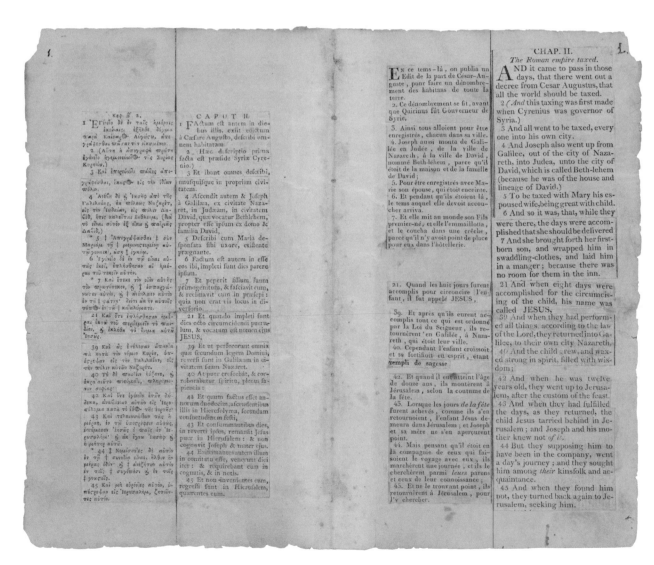

It is striking that from the start Jefferson was not a passive user of Palladio's books. His employment of Palladio's schemes and details was a creative endeavor, involving comparison, choice, combination, and transformation. Instead of simply copying, he used the language of Palladio, and analyzed and observed its conventions. Palladio "was the Bible," Colonel Isaac Coles recalled Jefferson telling him; "You should get it & stick close to it."[24] It is worth noting that Jefferson may have picked up this idea during his travels in England, rather than inventing it himself. John Adams wrote in his diary for July 24, 1786, "We . . . turned out of the Way to see the Seat of Lord Petre at Thorndon. Mr. [Brand] Hollis prefers the Architecture of this House to that at Stow, because it is more conformable to Paladio, his Bible for this kind of Knowledge."[25] While Jefferson was not present on this occasion, he met Hollis in London and subsequently corresponded with him. It is likely that at some point they talked of architecture, given their common interest in it, and that Jefferson too heard him refer to Palladio as the Bible, a role that Palladio already played for Jefferson himself. Once one realizes how creatively Jefferson cut and pasted his architectural bible, one can recall what he did with scissors and paste to the Gospels, as his working copy preserved at the Smithsonian reveals: he maintained the order of the verses but removed those of which he did not approve (fig. 15).[26] Palladio might have been his architectural bible, but the ultimate arbiter of truth and utility was Jefferson himself.

MONTICELLO AND PALLADIO'S VILLA LAYOUTS: TO HIDE OR TO ADVERTISE SERVICE FUNCTIONS?

Jefferson's early overall plan for the house and outbuildings at Monticello inserted the house at the center of service wings that extended from the house and then turned through ninety degrees (fig. 16). This idea was maintained in the final building. In plan the scheme resembled the plan of the Villa Saraceno and its outbuildings published by Palladio (fig. 17).[27] The linking of barns and other service structures, including housing for a manager and/or other staff, places for making cheese or wine, and sometimes the villa kitchen (to keep the main house free of smoke and cooking smells) forms part of Palladio's transformation of the villa complex into a single monumental composition, partly inspired by his reading of ancient Roman temple complexes, like that of Hercules at Tivoli.[28] Jefferson's strategy had the same basic aims as Palladio's: convenience of access and communication, and the desire to link all the functions of the villa in a single monumental design. Both Jefferson and Palladio broke with contemporary practice: in Jefferson's Virginia not only slave housing (which Jefferson does separate from the house complex) but other service structures,

Fig. 16. Thomas Jefferson (American, 1743–1826), overall plan for Monticello. Pen and ink. Original manuscript from the Coolidge Collection of Thomas Jefferson Manuscripts, Massachusetts Historical Society, N61; K34

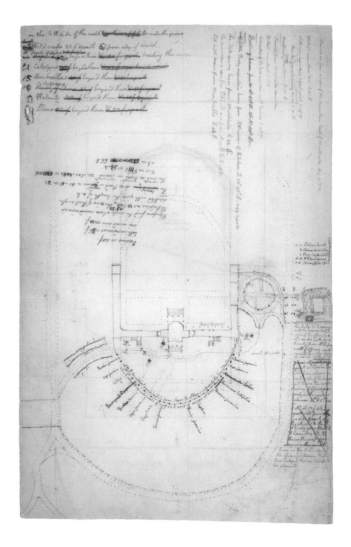

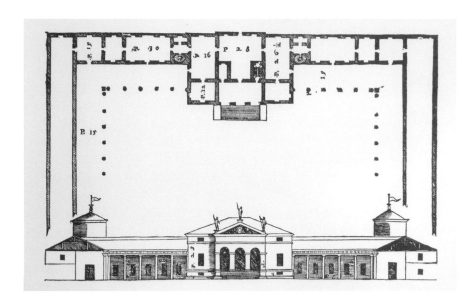

including the kitchen building, were separate from the main plantation house, giving big houses like Shirley or George Washington's Mount Vernon the appearance of a small settlement dominated by the owner's house.

Jefferson's strategy however was not identical to Palladio's. Palladio ennobled and advertised his barns and the outbuildings, signs of wealth and of commitment to the virtuous pursuit of agriculture, beneficial for the individual and also for the Venetian state as it contributed to eliminating dependence on grain imports from the potentially hostile Ottoman Empire. Jefferson in contrast kept the service wings low, and used them to support elegant terraces. Housing for slaves was set apart, at the lower level. Palladio's villa owners, moreover, had free laborers and tenants.

Jefferson's choices were in line with the recommendations of Isaac Ware in his *A Complete Body of Architecture*. Ware recommended placing services at the lower level in town houses and in the wings of country houses. Jefferson at Monticello combined these solutions. He would have noted Ware's distinction between the housing of "upper servants" who "are cleanly and quiet" and have direct contact with their employers, while "on the other hand, the kitchen is hot, the sculleries are offensive, and the servants hall is noisy; these therefore we shall place in one of the wings."[29] Jefferson would have concurred with this advice (obvious to any slaveholder) in organizing the services areas and distinguishing between domestic slaves in constant contact with him and his family, and those responsible for menial tasks.

A further basic difference between Jefferson's country houses and Palladio's villas is that Palladio usually had to insert his villa scheme, with its house, court, farmyard, barns, outbuildings, orchard, and sometimes garden, into a site that was already defined by the presence of earlier structures, orientation needs, roads, and/or a waterway. In contrast, both at Monticello and Poplar Forest, Jefferson could landscape and fashion an open site, modeling the wider setting and creating an extensive garden for the house— and a house for the garden.

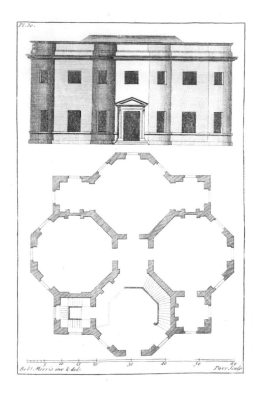

OCTAGONS AND ENGLISH POST-PALLADIAN DESIGN

Jefferson's adherence to Palladio's elevations and orders was not paralleled in his villa plans, which were characterized by a central hall flanked by apartments of two or three rooms of different sizes. By Jefferson's time functional needs and the spaces to satisfy them had evolved, and Palladio's multifunctional chambers no longer would have met the requirements of wealthy families who were beginning to want dining rooms, parlors, places for chance encounters and conversations, bedrooms, libraries, studies, dressing rooms, and closets. Robert Morris's book and the evolving functional conventions of the Virginia house were now more relevant than Palladio.[30] The basic Palladian proportions in fact do not usually appear in Jefferson's plans, nor do Palladio's standard three-room sequences. Morris's plans probably appealed to Jefferson because of their emphasis on economy (Morris estimates the cost of each design) and because of what Morris writes about the views from a house with four octagonal rooms, each with a three-window canted bay: "The situation for this Structure should be on an Eminence whose Summit should overlook a long extended vale, and, if attainable, quite round the Horizon, so that each Room is an easy and quick Transition to some new Object" (fig. 18).[31] The use of the "canted bay," to which Jefferson remained attached throughout his life, reflects not only Morris's book but also recent innovations in English house design represented by smaller houses of the 1760s, like Sir Robert Taylor's Asgill House (1761–64) on the Thames at Richmond (fig. 19).[32]

Important too was Isaac Ware's earlier and larger design for Wrotham Park built in 1754 and published by Ware in his *A Complete Body of*

Fig. 18. Robert Morris (English, 1701–1754), *Select Architecture* (London: Sayer, 1755), plate 30. Getty Research Institute

Fig. 19. Sir Robert Taylor (English, 1714–1788), Asgill House, Richmond, United Kingdom, 1761–64, in Colen Campbell, *Vitruvius Britannicus*, vol. 4 (London: Nicholson, Bell, Taylor and Clemens, 1767), plate 74. ETH-Bibliothek, University of Zürich, Rar 445 fol.

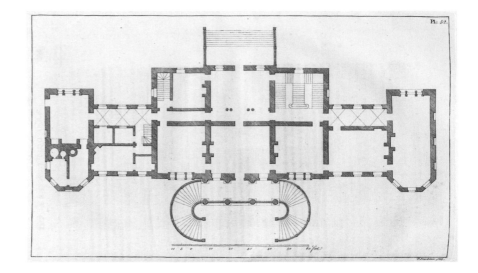

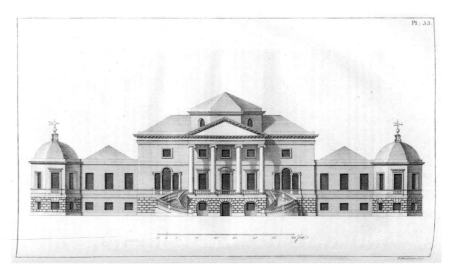

Architecture (1756–57, reissued in 1767; fig. 20).[33] These post-Palladian houses incorporate octagonal rooms and/or canted bays that expand the view and increase the lighting of what otherwise would have been simple square or rectangular spaces. Ware accompanied these designs with explicit criticism of Palladio as the basis for modern house design.[34] Though Morris appears in the 1783 list of Jefferson's books, Ware's bulky treatise is documented as being in Jefferson's possession only at some point from 1815 onward.[35] But even if Jefferson did not own the book before 1815 (which is unlikely), he surely consulted it in the libraries of other architecture enthusiasts.[36] Ware's book was owned by the architect and woodcarver William Buckland, who, after emigrating from England to Williamsburg, moved to Annapolis, whose houses Jefferson had in 1766 considered superior to those of Williamsburg.[37] Annapolis became a center for the propagation of Ware's schemes and the use of the canted bay.[38] James Brice, owner of another important house there, himself purchased a copy of Ware's *Architecture* in 1767.[39] The idea of using canted bays on the front of the wings at Wrotham was copied, presumably by Buckland, from Ware's book, and used both at

Fig. 21. William Buckland (American, 1734–1774), Hammond-Harwood House, Annapolis, Maryland, 1773–78. Photo courtesy of the Hammond-Harwood House

Fig. 22. Thomas Jefferson (American, 1743–1826), Hammond-Harwood House, plan and elevation. Pen and ink. Original manuscript from the Coolidge Collection of Thomas Jefferson Manuscripts, Massachusetts Historical Society, N527; KM10

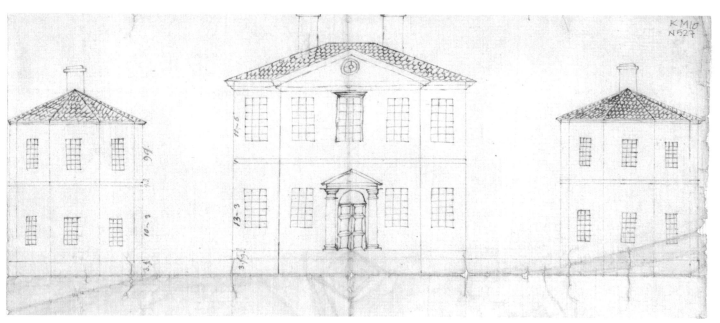

Mount Clare and at the Hammond-Harwood House in Annapolis (figs. 21, 22). Here the trail leads back to Jefferson, who in the 1770s was acquainted with the Maryland capital and its rich and aristocratic house builders. Jefferson made two drawings of the Hammond-Harwood House, probably when he was in Annapolis from late November 1783 to May 1784, each showing the plan and elevation.[40] The drawings probably do not derive from a survey made by Jefferson, though he had the skills necessary to make one. It is more likely that they are copies after Buckland's own drawings.[41] Charles Willson Peale portrays Buckland with the plan and elevation of the house in front of him, and the drawing represented resembles those by Jefferson (see DeWitt essay, fig. 1).[42]

The introduction of an octagonal dome provided an impressive central feature for the southwest facade at Monticello. But unlike the dome of Burlington's Chiswick villa, its presence is not revealed at the main floor level, and the impressive domed space on the upper floor, reached by narrow stairs, is oddly divorced from the rest of the house and its functions (fig. 23). The immediate source for the Monticello dome seems to be Isaac Ware's Wrotham Park, designed in 1754, and published in his *A Complete Body of Architecture*, Colen Campbell's *Vitruvius Britannicus*, and other engraved views.[43] Ware's dome, like that at Monticello, rose unconventionally immediately behind the portico and was lit by round windows. As at Monticello, its octagonal footprint did not reach down to the main floor level—an oddity that perhaps explained its later removal. Jefferson's use of Ware's book also appears in details at Monticello: in the massive and very English, almost Hawksmoorian, arches of the Monticello dining room (fig. 24)—one can compare the interior of Nicholas Hawksmoor's St George's, Bloomsbury— and in the little oval windows in Jefferson's bedroom.[44]

GEOMETRIES, PATTERNMAKING, AND ALTERNATIVES

Use of the books of Palladio, Gibbs, Morris, and Ware gave Jefferson a grasp of the importance of considering and developing alternatives. He also liked geometric patterns and variants on them, as one can see in his designs for railings, in the Poplar Forest plan, and in his combinations of ovals. He inserted three oval rooms in the lower level of the University of Virginia's Rotunda (fig. 25).[45] He also wanted to frame the portraits of "the three greatest men that have ever lived," Francis Bacon, John Locke, and Isaac Newton, each in an oval, contained in a larger oval, a scheme he sketched (fig. 26). John Trumbull's unenthusiastic reaction led him to abandon the idea, though perhaps it lived on in his Rotunda plan, where it would have had (for Jefferson) a private significance, appropriate for a university library.[46] He also deployed ovals in studies for the Capitol in Washington. These oval schemes were probably suggested by the ground-floor plan of the Désert de Retz Column House, which he had visited with Maria Cosway (fig. 27).[47]

The plan of Poplar Forest, Jefferson's remote refuge from the constant stream of visitors to Monticello, has precedents in Gibbs's *Book of*

Fig. 24. Thomas Jefferson (American, 1743–1826), dining room arch, Monticello, c. 1805. Original manuscript from the Coolidge Collection of Thomas Jefferson Manuscripts, Massachusetts Historical Society, N178; K160c

Fig. 25. Thomas Jefferson (American, 1743–1826), first-floor plan of Rotunda, University of Virginia, June 16, 1823. University of Virginia Special Collections, N330r

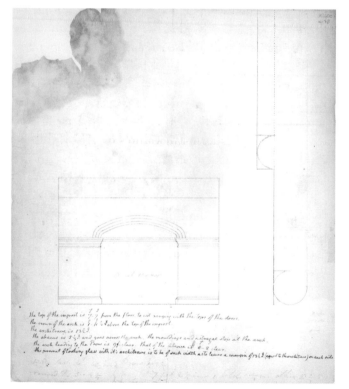

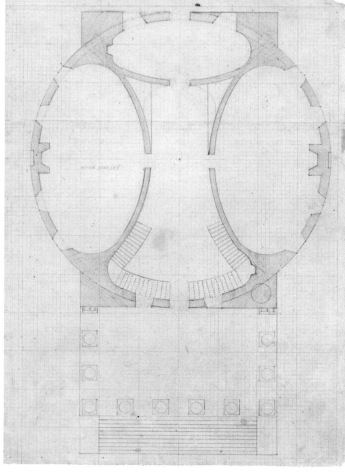

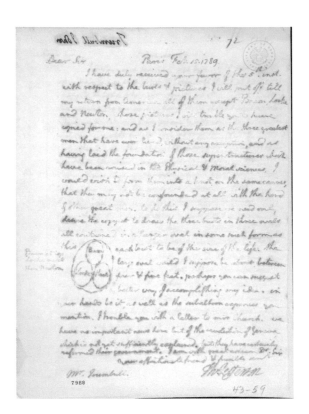

Architecture and Robert Morris. The closest published architectural source, however, has been identified as appearing in *Neue Garten- und Landschafts-Gebäude* (1798–99) by Wilhelm Gottlieb Becker, bought by Jefferson in 1805 (figs. 28, 29).[48] The geometry of the plan, however, also reflects a geometric scheme that appears at Hadrian's villa, in later pavements and tile patterns, in explorations of the octahedron, and in the frontispiece to Vignola's 1562 *Regola delli cinque ordini d'architettura*, which Jefferson owned (fig. 30). The pattern also appears in a vault in Giulio Romano's Palazzo Te, in ceiling designs published by Palladio's renowned predecessor Sebastiano Serlio, and even in the floor and ceiling of the sixteenth-century square ground-floor room of Palladio's Palazzo Chiericati. Almost certainly Jefferson would have noticed the scheme in the books of Serlio and Vignola, though as he famously never visited Vicenza or saw a building designed by Palladio, he would not have known that the Italian architect had actually used this scheme. Jefferson may even have seen the Poplar Forest plan pattern employed in Virginia windows, probably derived from Serlio, as a late-seventeenth-century leaded window incorporating the motif has been excavated in Williamsburg.[49]

ANTIQUE MODELS AND PUBLIC ARCHITECTURE

Until Jefferson was confronted in 1785 with the question of the design of the new state capitol in Richmond, Virginia, he had focused on private rather than public architecture. By 1785 he was familiar with public architecture in Paris, though he had not yet visited London and seen public buildings there like Somerset House or the Royal Hospital at Greenwich, works that he never mentioned, however, and perhaps even disliked. Instead he went directly to the antique, his taste and sympathies probably guided by his classical studies and his attachment to Palladio's *Four Books*, where the whole of the final book concerns ancient Roman temples. His chosen model for the new Capitol was the Maison Carrée in Nîmes, France, which he still knew only from Palladio and from Charles-Louis Clérisseau's 1778 *Antiquités de la France, première parti: Monumens de Nîsmes*, though he was soon to visit it. Jefferson wrote: "The gentlemen had sent me one [design] which they had thought of. The one agreed on here is more convenient, more beautiful, gives more room and will not cost more than two thirds of what that would. We took for our model what is called the Maison quarrée of Nismes, one of the most beautiful, if not the most beautiful and precious morsel of architecture left us by antiquity. It . . . has the suffrage of all the judges of architecture who have seen it, as yeilding to no one of the beautiful monuments of Greece, Rome, Palmyra and Balbec. . . . It is very simple, but it is noble beyond expression, and would have done honour to our country as presenting to travelers a morsel of taste in our infancy promising much for our maturer age."[50] The decision to imitate a well-preserved and beautiful ancient temple approved

Fig. 27. George-Louis le Rouge (French, c. 1712–c. 1790), Désert de Retz Column House, perspective view and ground-floor plan, and front view of the Temple of Repose, in *Treizième cahier des jardins anglo-chinois; Le jardin anglo-chinois* (Paris: Le Rouge, 1776–88), plates 4, 5. Bibliothèque de l'Institut National d'Histoire de l'Art, collections Jacques Doucet, NUM 4 RES 216 (3)

by Palladio rather than to attempt something new is not surprising at a time when ancient architecture was greatly admired. Such a building could be constructed economically, using much cheaper materials than the original; it also would help to form national taste. Jefferson states his ideas on imitation again in a 1791 letter to Pierre-Charles L'Enfant concerning the choice of models for the Capitol and the president's house in Washington: "Whenever it is proposed to prepare plans for the Capitol, I should prefer the adoption of some one of the models of antiquity which have had the approbation of thousands of years; and for the President's house I should prefer the celebrated fronts of Modern buildings which have already received the approbation of all good judges. Such are the Galerie du Louvre, the Gardes meubles, and two fronts of the Hotel de Salm."[51] In his own design for the president's house (1792) Jefferson followed this line, using Palladio's La Rotonda as his model (fig. 31).[52]

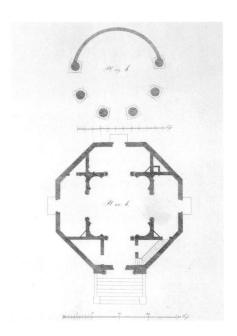

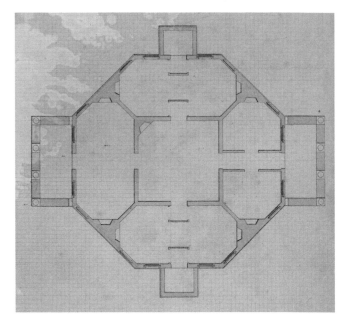

Fig. 28. Wilhelm Gottlieb Becker (German, 1753–1813), *Neue Garten- und Landschafts-Gebäude* (Leipzig: Voss und Compagnie, 1798–99), plate 20b. Universität Heidelberg

Fig. 29. John Neilson (American, c. 1770–1827), floor plan of Jefferson's Poplar Forest, probably 1820. Pen and ink. University of Virginia Special Collections, N-350 K. Pl. 14

Fig. 30. Jacopo da Vignola (Italian, 1507–1573), frontispiece, *Regles des cinque ordres d'architecture* (Paris, 1764). University of Zürich Libraries

JEFFERSON AND THE MODERN ARCHITECTURE OF HIS TIME

Jefferson much admired ancient Roman architecture, which he knew from books and his visit to Nîmes. He was also particularly impressed by the Hôtel de Salm in Paris, designed by Pierre Rousseau and completed in 1787, when Jefferson was still in Paris. The exterior, with its projecting semicircular feature, echoed in the White House, is impressive and elegant. The courtyard, with a larger and a smaller order of columns, recalls Roman frescoes showing monumental colonnades, while the plan recalls features of the Roman baths. It was probably these antique features that most appealed to Jefferson, who seems to have remained unimpressed by the great country houses he saw in England, a lack of enthusiasm perhaps augmented by the huge cost of these buildings, which ruled them out as models for new American architecture. Palladio's villas were indeed smaller, simpler, and clearly designed with economy in mind. However, one cannot exclude on Jefferson's part a certain additional antipathy to the buildings and houses of America's recent enemies, and as a corollary, a favorable disposition toward France and the French, whose architecture became familiar to him during his long residence in Paris. No English building, not even Lord Burlington's Chiswick House, ever aroused in him the enthusiasm he expressed for the Hôtel de Salm or the Halle aux Blés (1763–67).[53] He specifically admired the latter's huge dome constructed in 1782–83 of alternating panels of laminated wood and glass, designed by Jacques-Guillaume Legrand and Jacques Molinos, who adapted a roof solution published earlier by Philibert de l'Orme.[54] As one can see from his project for the president's house in Washington, Jefferson himself wished to follow this audacious and luminous solution, with the structural ribs alternating with glass panels (see fig. 31).[55] From France too came Jefferson's radical decision to reconstruct Monticello with only a single main living floor, an approach he also followed at Poplar Forest.

Jefferson proclaims in a March 1796 letter, "I am now engaged in taking down the upper story of my house and building it on the ground, so as to spread all my rooms on one floor. We shall this summer therefore live under the tent of heaven."[56] There is no doubt as to the source of this radical move. In 1797 he writes: "In Paris particularly all the new and good houses are of a single story."[57]

CONCLUSIONS

Jefferson's basic architectural choices show a judicious, systematic approach, also seen in his conduct of public affairs. He took account not only of the immediate site of a building but also the "site" in the widest sense; that is, a still underdeveloped but vast country, lacking in easily available building materials beyond bricks and wood, in architects, skilled craftsmen, and financial resources. He also strongly felt the need to educate an informed public by creating good examples to be followed.

It was not realistic or even possible to replicate the sort of architecture that he had seen in European cities and in the great country houses of England. In Jefferson's America, funds were limited, and the basic building materials were still those of Palladio's time: brick, plaster, and wooden beams, with a restricted use of stone details. He followed and recommended Palladio's effective and economical way of constructing columns of bricks covered in plaster, rather than facing the cost of obtaining stone columns.[58] He strongly disapproved, however, of wood construction, which he regarded as a false economy.[59] His attachment to Palladio, which reappears vigorously in his design for the new University of Virginia, was thus based on several factors: his admiration for ancient Roman architecture, which Palladio had adapted to modern needs and functions; the beauty of Palladio's

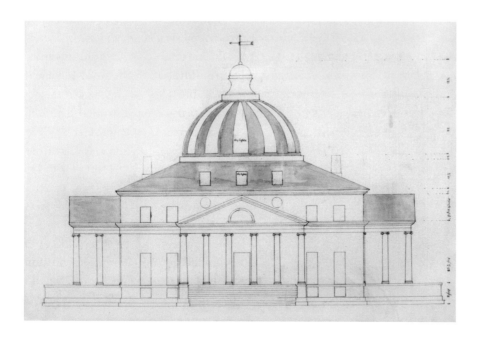

Fig. 31. Thomas Jefferson (American, 1743–1826), elevation for the 1792 White House design competition. Pen and wash. Maryland Historical Society, 1976.88.6, N400; K129

architectural orders; and—one can conjecture—Palladio's concern with a restrained use of ornament and avoidance of excessive expenditure, an attitude that is clear from both the text of his book and his buildings. Palladio was not only a great architect but a great artist in the way in which he modeled his details, elevations, and interior spaces. But his works, at least as Jefferson knew them from editions of Palladio's book, conflicted neither with Jefferson's concern with structural innovations, like terrace floors that would not leak, nor with his later enthusiasm for houses with only one main floor, like several of Palladio's villas. Palladio did not inhibit Jefferson's inventiveness, nor excessively underline his lack of ability to invent complex and eloquent elevations, where the details and placing of doors, windows, and other details declared the character of the building and its owner. He knew he did not possess this art of architectural performance, invented in the Renaissance, as he shows when he modestly asks more professional architects than he was, namely Benjamin Henry Latrobe and William Thornton, for elevation sketches for the houses on the University of Virginia's Lawn. The fact that he had not acquired the ability to invent details and their combinations as the brilliant architects of Europe had done in the previous three hundred years was not, however, only because he was not very good at freehand architectural drawing: it was because this sort of architecture represented the world against which he had so successfully taken a stand, the world of kings and of immensely rich aristocrats, of government of but not by the people, and of those vast differences between rich and poor that he had observed and lamented in France. Jefferson is easy to criticize for his awkward quick sketches or for the fact that he never moved, publicly or privately, against slavery, an institution that he knew to be in conflict with his own moral and political principles. But his limitations do not cancel out his enormous achievements, as statesman, as principal author of the Declaration of Independence, and also as architect of Monticello and the University of Virginia campus, as well as that extraordinarily original and lucid masterpiece, Poplar Forest, where the centrally placed square dining room confounds our expectations, its skylight providing lighting that outshines the rooms surrounding it, which give directly on to the exterior and the future. ❦

NOTES

I would like to thank the friends and colleagues who have helped or guided me in the exploration of the architecture of Thomas Jefferson, in particular Guido Beltramini, Giusi Boni, Leslie Greene Bowman, Cammy Brothers, Bruce Boucher, Lloyd DeWitt, Gardiner Hallock, Susan Kern, Ann Lucas, Takehiko Nagakura, Erik Neil, Gabriele Rausse, Susan R. Stein, Daniel and Joanne Tsai, and Richard Guy Wilson.

1. See, for example, Thomas Jefferson to Benjamin Henry Latrobe, Washington, February 28, 1804, http://tjrs.monticello.org/letter/1821.

2. "From Thomas Jefferson to Maria Cosway, 12 October 1786," *Founders Online*, National Archives, last modified June 13, 2018, http://founders.archives.gov/documents/Jefferson/01-10-02-0309. [Original source: *The Papers of Thomas Jefferson*, vol. 10, *22 June–31 December 1786*, ed. Julian P. Boyd (Princeton, NJ: Princeton University Press, 1954), 443–55.]

3. *The Political Writings of John Adams: Representative Selections*, ed. George Peek (Indianapolis: Hackett, 2003), 117–18.

4. Susan Kern, "The Material World of the Jeffersons at Shadwell," *William and Mary Quarterly* 62, no. 2 (April 2005): 230–34; Susan Kern, *The Jeffersons at Shadwell* (New Haven: Yale University Press, 2010).

5. Henry S. Randall, *The Life of Thomas Jefferson*, vol. 1 (New York: Derby & Jackson, 1858), 11.

6. "Thomas Jefferson to Thomas Taylor, 28 December 1814," *Founders Online*, National Archives, last modified June 13,

2018, http://founders.archives.gov /documents/Jefferson/03-08-02-0145. [Original source: *The Papers of Thomas Jefferson*, Retirement Series, vol. 8, *1 October 1814 to 31 August 1815*, ed. J. Jefferson Looney (Princeton, NJ: Princeton University Press, 2011), 169–71.]

7. "From Thomas Jefferson to Anne-Louise-Germaine Necker, Baronne [de] Staël-Holstein, 16 July 1807," *Founders Online*, National Archives, last modified June 13, 2018, http://founders.archives .gov/documents/Jefferson/99-01-02-5977.

8. Jack McLaughlin, *Jefferson and Monticello: The Biography of a Builder* (New York: Henry Holt, 1987), 35–36.

9. James Adams Bear, *Jefferson at Monticello* (Charlottesville: University of Virginia Press, 1967), 5, 17.

10. "Indeed I should be much happier were I nearer to Rosewell and Severn hall," Jefferson wrote to Page; ". . . I reflect often with pleasure on the philosophical evenings I passed at Rosewell in my last visits there." "From Thomas Jefferson to John Page, 21 February 1770," *Founders Online*, National Archives, last modified June 13, 2018, http://founders.archives.gov/documents /Jefferson/01-01-02-0023. [Original source: *The Papers of Thomas Jefferson*, vol. 1, *1760–1776*, ed. Julian P. Boyd (Princeton, NJ: Princeton University Press, 1950), 34–37.]

11. Thomas Jefferson, "Memorandum Books, 1767," *Founders Online*, National Archives, last modified June 13, 2018, http:// founders.archives.gov/documents /Jefferson/02-01-02-0001. [Original source: *The Papers of Thomas Jefferson*, 2nd ser., *Jefferson's Memorandum Books*, vol. 1, ed. James A Bear Jr. and Lucia C. Stanton (Princeton, NJ: Princeton University Press, 1997), 3–43.]

12. Jefferson visited Shirley on June 20, 1773, and several other occasions. "Memorandum Books, 1773," *Founders Online*, National Archives, last modified June 13, 2018, http://founders.archives.gov /documents/Jefferson/02-01-02-0007. [Original source: *The Papers of Thomas Jefferson*, 2nd ser., *Jefferson's Memorandum Books*, 1:301–54.]

13. McLaughlin, *Jefferson and Monticello*, 45.

14. Jefferson, "Memorandum Books, 1767."

15. Ibid.

16. The door design in Leoni's plate does not correspond to that published by Palladio in the 1570 edition of his *Quattro libri dell'architettura* (Venice: Domenico de'Franceschi, 1570), 3.50. Isaac Ware, in his 1738 and 1755 editions of Palladio, reproduces the door faithfully.

17. Most probably it is the molding at the top of one of the three architraves illustrated.

18. Gene Waddell suggested that this scheme could have been influenced by the building with a central tower that Jefferson's hero Francis Bacon describes in his 1625 essay *On Building*. Waddell, "The First Monticello," *Journal of the Society of Architectural Historians* 46, no. 1 (1987): 16.

19. Giordano and Beltramini note the dependence of the elevation of the first Monticello on those of Villa Pisani and Villa Cornaro. Ralph G. Giordano, *The Architectural Ideology of Thomas Jefferson* (Jefferson, NC: McFarland, 2012), 48–49; and Guido Beltramini, *Jefferson e Palladio: Come costruire un mondo nuovo* (Vicenza, Italy: Marsilio, 2015), 29.

20. The existence of an elevation drawing (K19; N41), showing only the lower level, could represent an unfinished earlier stage in Jefferson's fusion of the two elevations; another elevation drawing (N47) defines the overall scheme but does not show the windows or doors, probably because Jefferson had not yet turned his attention to their design.

21. For other cases in which Jefferson made notes relating to his sources, see Beltramini, *Jefferson e Palladio*, 31–33.

22. Thomas Jefferson, *Sketch for Monticello*, Massachusetts Historical Society (K29; N54).

23. Jefferson, "Memorandum Books, 1767."

24. "Isaac A. Coles's Account of a Conversation with Thomas Jefferson, [before 23 February 1816]," *Founders Online*, National Archives, last modified June 13, 2018, http://founders.archives.gov/documents /Jefferson/03-09-02-0336. [Original source: *The Papers of Thomas Jefferson*, Retirement Series, vol. 9, *September 1815 to April 1816*, ed. J. Jefferson Looney (Princeton, NJ: Princeton University Press, 2012), 500–502.]

25. The phrase occurs in John Adams's diary for Monday, July 24, 1786, http://www .masshist.org/digitaladams/archive /doc?id=D45.

26. Thomas Jefferson, *The Life and Morals of Jesus of Nazareth*, The Thomas Jefferson Papers at the Library of Congress ser. 7, vol. 9 (Washington, DC: Library of Congress, 1904).

27. Palladio, *Quattro libri*, 2.57.

28. Ibid., book 4, 52.

29. Isaac Ware, *A Complete Body of Architecture* (London: Osborne and Shipton, 1756), 413.

30. See Mark R. Wenger, "Town House & Country House: Eighteenth and Early Nineteenth Centuries," in *The Chesapeake House: Architectural Investigation by Colonial Williamsburg*, ed. Cary Carson and Carl R. Lounsbury (Chapel Hill: University of North Carolina Press, 2013), 120–55.

31. Robert Morris, *Select Architecture . . .* (London: Robert Sayer, 1757), 5.

32. For the introduction of octagons and canted bays into English country house designs, see James Steven Curl, *Georgian Architecture in the British Isles, 1714–1830* (London: English Heritage, 2011), 193–94. On the house designs of Sir Robert Taylor, see Richard Lea, Chris Miele, with Gordon Higgott, *Danson House, The Anatomy of a Georgian Villa* (Swindon: English Heritage, 2011). The sources of this new plan type are not entirely clear. The full octagon form was well known in England from its use by Burlington at Chiswick; protruding canted window bays were a feature of Tudor and Jacobean architecture. It is possible that Jefferson was also influenced by the projecting semicircular apses that Robert Castell inserts into his reconstructions of Pliny the Younger's villas (Jefferson probably owned Castell's *Villas of the Ancients* by 1785) but modifies them into half octagons, a form easier to execute, following Ware and echoes of Ware in Annapolis houses.

33. See Eileen Harris, assisted by Nicholas Savage, *British Architectural Books and Writers, 1556–1785* (Cambridge: Cambridge University Press, 1990), s.v. "WARE."

34. On Ware's attitude to Palladio, see Harris, *British Architectural Books*, 472–73.

35. See William Bainter O'Neal, *Jefferson's Fine Arts Library: His Selections for the University of Virginia Together with His Own Architectural Books* (Charlottesville: University of Virginia Press, 1976), 374.

36. For ownership of architectural books in Virginia, see Carl L. Lounsbury, "The Design Process," in Carson and Lounsbury, *The Chesapeake House*, 81–84. Lounsbury refers to the books owned by the architect William Buckland. For the inventory of Buckland's estate, sworn December 19, 1774, see Rosamond Randall Beirne and John Henry Scarff, *William Buckland, 1734–1774: Architect of Virginia and Maryland* (1958; repr., Baltimore: Maryland Historical Society, 2011). Buckland owned at least fourteen architectural books, including works by Batty Langley, William Salmon, Robert Morris, Abraham Swan, and Isaac Ware. Lounsbury mentions the borrowing by the Annapolis cabinetmaker John Shaw of a copy of Ware's book from James Brice, who had a new brick house (1766–73) built in Annapolis, with a five-bay facade and low side wings; Lounsbury, 413. Http://mht.maryland.gov/nr /NRDetail.aspx?NRID=39. See also Orlando Ridout IV, *Building the James Brice House, 1767–1774* (Baltimore: Maryland State Archive, 2013).

37. "Thomas Jefferson to John Page, Annapolis, May 25, 1766," *Founders Online*, National Archives, last modified June 13, 2018, http://founders.archives.gov /documents/Jefferson/01-01-02-0012. [Original source: *The Papers of Thomas Jefferson*, vol. 1, *1760–1776*, ed. Julian P. Boyd (Princeton, NJ: Princeton University Press, 1950), 18–21.]

38. For houses in Annapolis influenced by Robert Morris, Sir Robert Taylor, and Isaac Ware, and the buildings connected with William Buckland, see Mario Di Valmarana, ed., *Building by the Book II* (Charlottesville: University Press of Virginia, 1986). The pertinent contributions are by Trostel, Allston Brand, and Binney.

39. Ridout, *Building the James Brice House.*

40. Thomas Jefferson, *Hammond-Harwood House*, 2 drawings, pen and ink, Massachusetts Historical Society, N1; K107, and N527; M10. The overall facade scheme may have been influenced by the elevation in Palladio's *Quattro libri* of the Villa Pisani at Montagnana, and was certainly indebted to Ware's book. On Jefferson's visit, see Edith Rossiter Bevan, "Thomas Jefferson in Annapolis, November 25, 1783–May 11, 1784," *Maryland Historical Magazine* 41, no. 2 (1946): 115–24.

41. W. H. Adams, ed., *Eye of Jefferson*, exh. cat. (Washington, DC: Museum of American History, 1976), 18, cat. 22.

42. For Buckland's portrait (1774, reworked 1789) at the Yale University Art Gallery, see http://artgallery.yale.edu/collections /objects/6359.

43. Ware, *A Complete Body*, pls. 52–53; Colen Campbell, *Vitruvius Britannicus; or, The British Architect . . .*, V (London: Bell, Taylor and Smith, 1715), pls. 45–46.

44. See Ware, *A Complete Body* V, pls. 70, 71.

45. There are two drawings for the Washington Capitol on both sides of one sheet (N388.1, N388.2), held at the Massachusetts Historical Society, of a circular plan subdivided into five oval rooms. "Washington: Capitol (studies), verso, [1792], by Thomas Jefferson. N388" [electronic edition], *Thomas Jefferson Papers: An Electronic Archive*, Massachusetts Historical Society, Boston, 2003, http:// www. thomasjeffersonpapers.org/.

46. "Thomas Jefferson to John Trumbull, February 15, 1789," *Founders Online*, National Archives, last modified June 13, 2018, http://founders.archives.gov /documents/Jefferson/01-14-02-0321. [Original source: *The Papers of Thomas Jefferson*, vol. 14, *8 October 1788–26 March 1789*, ed. Julian P. Boyd (Princeton, NJ: Princeton University Press, 1958), 561.]

Trumbull replies, "The blank spaces between the three ovals will have a very awkward look. Besides that the whole will be unwieldy either to transport or to hang." "To Thomas Jefferson from John Trumbull, 10 March 1789," *Founders Online*, National Archives, last modified June 13, 2018, http://founders.archives .gov/documents/Jefferson/01-14-02-0383. [Original source: *The Papers of Thomas Jefferson*, vol. 14, *8 October 1788–26 March 1789*, ed. Julian P. Boyd (Princeton, NJ: Princeton University Press, 1958), 634–35.] See also Susan R. Stein, *The Worlds of Thomas Jefferson at Monticello* (New York: H. N. Abrams, 1993), 128–29.

47. William Howard Adams, *The Eye of Thomas Jefferson*, exh. cat. (Washington, DC: National Gallery of Art, 1976), 507 (catalogue entries by F. Nichols and R. Watson). The visit to the Désert de Retz is mentioned in the "Heart and Head" letter; see note 2.

48. Wilhelm Gottlieb Becker, *Neue Garten-und Landschafts-Gebäude* (Leipzig: Voss, 1798–99), pl. 20b. This source was noted by C. Allan Brown, "Thomas Jefferson's Poplar Forest: The Mathematics of an Ideal Villa," *Journal of Garden History* 10, no. 2 (1990): 117–19; see also the richly documented study by S. Allen Chambers Jr., *Poplar Forest and Thomas Jefferson*, 2nd ed. (1993; Bedford, VA: The Corporation for Jefferson's Poplar Forest, 1998), 32–36. Jefferson bought *Plans d'architecture par Becker 4. Cahiers* in June 1805: see "List of Books Ordered from Philippe Reibelt, 21 June 1805," http://founders.archives .gov/documents/Jefferson/99-01-02-1935. ["This is an Early Access document from PJefferson. It is not an authoritative final version."]. The work was among those which Jefferson sold to the Library of Congress in 1815. The structure published by Becker resembles Poplar Forest only in plan; Becker's central room is covered by a dome.

49. I. N. Hume, *Here Lies Virginia* (Charlottesville: University of Virginia Press, 1994), fig. 22.

50. "From Thomas Jefferson to James Madison, with Account Enclosed, 20 September 1785," *Founders Online*, National Archives, last modified June 13, 2018, http://founders.archives.gov /documents/Jefferson/01-08-02-0416. [Original source: *The Papers of Thomas Jefferson*, vol. 8, *25 February–31 October 1785*, ed. Julian P. Boyd (Princeton, NJ: Princeton University Press, 1953), 534–37.]

51. "XII. Thomas Jefferson to Pierre Charles L'Enfant, 10 April 1791," *Founders Online*, National Archives, last modified June 13, 2018, http://founders.archives.gov /documents/Jefferson/01-20-02-0001-0015. [Original source: *The Papers of Thomas Jefferson*, vol. 20, *1 April–4 August 1791*, ed. Julian P. Boyd (Princeton, NJ: Princeton University Press, 1982), 86–87.]

52. See Beltramini, *Jefferson e Palladio*, 24–26.

53. "Cheswick. Belongs to D. of Devonshire. Garden about 6. acres. The Octagonal dome has an ill effect, both within and without; the garden shews still too much of art; an obelisk of very ill effect. Another in the middle of a pond useless." "Notes of a Tour of English Gardens, [2–14 April] 1786," *Founders Online*, National Archives, last modified June 13, 2018, http:// founders.archives.gov/documents /Jefferson/01-09-02-0328. [Original source: *The Papers of Thomas Jefferson*, vol. 9, *1 November 1785–22 June 1786*, ed. Julian P. Boyd (Princeton, NJ: Princeton University Press, 1954), 369–75.]

54. Philibert de l'Orme, *Inventions pour bien bastir et a petits fraiz, trouvees n'agueres* (Paris: Federic Morel, 1561).

55. Thomas Jefferson, *Proposed sketch for the President's House*, elevation. White House Competition drawing, elevation, 1792. Pen and wash. Maryland Historical Society, 1976.88.6 (N400; K129).

56. "From Thomas Jefferson to Benjamin Hawkins, 22 March 1796," *Founders Online*, National Archives, last modified June 13, 2018, http://founders.archives .gov/documents/Jefferson/01-29-02-0026. [Original source: *The Papers of Thomas Jefferson*, vol. 29, *1 March 1796–31 December 1797*, ed. Barbara B. Oberg (Princeton, NJ: Princeton University Press, 2002), 42–44.]

57. "Thomas Jefferson to John Brown, 5 April 1797," *Founders Online*, National Archives, last modified June 13, 2018, http://founders.archives.gov/documents /Jefferson/01-29-02-0271. [Original source: *The Papers of Thomas Jefferson*, vol. 29, *1 March 1796–31 December 1797*, ed. Barbara B. Oberg (Princeton, NJ: Princeton University Press, 2002), 345–46.]

58. Travis McDonald, "The Brickwork at Poplar Forest: Mr. Jefferson Builds His Dream House," *APT Bulletin* 27, no. 1 (1996): 42–43.

59. Thomas Jefferson, *Notes on the State of Virginia*, 1785, MS, Coolidge Collection, Massachusetts Historical Society, 91–92.

THE PALLADIANS

GUIDO BELTRAMINI

There is no such thing as Palladianism, only Palladians. There is no one story, but many stories of architects or groups of architects who have dialogued with Palladio. In narrating these stories, however, we have to tackle two measures of distance: between how Palladio designed his own afterlife and how architects have adopted his lessons, and between our own age and the remote past. We look to that past, knowing that each given experience of space corresponds to a given experience of the world, to different social practices and different—often unconscious but crucial—metaphysical outlooks. Historically speaking, the more often the Palladians' lives and works are interwoven with specific contexts, the more the relationship with the model emerges in all its complexity and true consistency, revealing unique rather than recurring features.

The term *Palladianism* is handy but loose. In Palladio's lifetime, Vincenzo Scamozzi embarked on a reinterpretation of Palladio's language in real time and adapted it to changed economic, social, and political conditions. The visionary invention of Palladio's Villa Capra "La Rotonda" in Vicenza (1566) has the magnificence and abstraction of a celestial dwelling: a cube surmounted by a hemisphere, with four identical porches (fig. 1). The exceptional nature of La Rotonda was immediately grasped by Palladio's contemporaries. In a sonnet, his friend Giambattista Maganza speaks of wonder, envy, and amazement at beholding the most stunning project that Palladio had ever designed, superlative precisely because its patron, Paolo Almerico, had given Palladio freedom to create; specifically he was given "free rein to his brain" ("briglia sciolta al suo cervello").[1] But La Rotonda can hardly be made to meet the needs of our everyday reality: its construction costs quadrupled (at least for the facades), the internal organization is not efficient, and the central *sala* is poorly lit, with only one oculus at the apex of the dome. Scamozzi's Villa Rocca Pisana,

Fig. 1. Andrea Palladio (Italian, 1508–1580), Villa Capra "La Rotonda," Vicenza, 1566. Mediateca del Centro Internazionale di Studi di Architettura Andrea Palladio, Vicenza

Fig. 2. Vincenzo Scamozzi (Italian, 1548–1616), Villa Rocca Pisana, Lonigo, Italy, 1576. Mediateca del Centro Internazionale di Studi di Architettura Andrea Palladio, Vicenza

built in 1576, on the other hand, has an impeccable internal organization because the central *sala* is a hub, providing radial access to all the rooms, and natural light, scientifically studied with optical diagrams, permeates the whole building (fig. 2).[2]

Scamozzi probably worked for Palladio, and certainly inherited many of his contacts, such as Marcantonio Barbaro or Vettore Pisani, as well as several projects requiring completion, such as La Rotonda itself, Palazzo Porto in Piazza Castello, and the Teatro Olimpico. In terms of architectural language, Palladio was always Scamozzi's primary reference point. However, in pursuing his own path, Scamozzi went back to the models that had influenced Palladio, such as the designs of Sebastiano Serlio. From there he started to develop a personal interpretation of the elements of the classical architectural orders, the rhythm of the facades, and the building types. What changes even more radically is Scamozzi's approach to designing. Having trained in libraries rather than, as Palladio had, on building sites, he began by creating a primarily theoretical system for his work as an architect, starting from the Vitruvian phrase "architectura est scientia." Accordingly, the architect should proceed not by "inventing" but rather by offering precise solutions to the various problems, solutions based on solid theoretical premises and the result of a rational design process. This rationality implies an attention to purpose, to the efficiency of the building as a machine for living, to practical construction solutions, and to controlled costs. Scamozzi thus turned Palladio's poetry into prose, facilitating its translation in distant countries and different contexts.[3]

Indeed, it was Palladian-Scamozzianism that conquered northern Europe and then crossed the oceans in the wake of the British Empire. The exterior of Lord Burlington's Chiswick House was the result of his studying the "Vicentine school": the facade comes from Palladio's Villa Foscari, and the rear was inspired by one of his drawings (RIBA XVII/15*recto*), but the sides are from Scamozzi's Villa Molin and the dome emulates the cupola of the Rocca Pisana (fig. 3). The strength of Chiswick, however, lies not in citations but in the unexpected variety of its interiors (an innovation on the Palladian-Scamozzian models) and the startling inversion of the dimensions of elements that were normally subordinate, making them large and dominant, such as the external staircase or enormous obelisk chimney stacks. As Howard Burns has remarked, this artistic feel was fueled by a love of music and a passion for Alexander Pope's witty verse.[4]

The genealogical tree of eminent Palladians starts with two of his "children," Scamozzi and Inigo Jones. These men continued the master's research, assimilating his method and knowledge of the antique. Jones met Scamozzi and studied his architecture during his trip to Italy and the Veneto in 1613–14. He visited several of Palladio's buildings, recording his

impressions in a copy of Palladio's *Quattro libri dell'architettura* (Four books of architecture), still in the Worcester College Library. He may well have taken a large number of drawings by Palladio back to England, where for centuries they would be the "gold reserves" of architecture in that country.

Jones had a more eclectic approach than Scamozzi. His models, alongside Palladio, are the ancient and contemporary Roman architecture of his time. Significantly, however, in one major project, the Banqueting House in London, he actually constructed what was a piece of "paper architecture," bringing to life the fantastic Egyptian Room published by Palladio in the *Quattro libri* but never built (figs. 4, 5). In this case Palladio is to Jones exactly what Vitruvius was to Palladio. Jones begins with a well-defined type, adapted to his own needs; then, using other Palladian examples, he flexibly solves specific problems without losing sight of the initial model. In this way he achieves an unprecedented result: a personal, original development of the chosen model.[5]

Another figure of great importance in this first generation of Palladians was not an architect but a theoretician: Henry Wotton, the English ambassador to Venice and early collector of Palladio's drawings. His 1624 essay "The Elements of Architecture" shaped a new Italophile architectural culture in Britain and Holland.[6] Constantin Huygens, another cosmopolitan intellectual, this time Dutch, had visited the buildings of Palladio and Jones, and with the architect Jacob van Campen triggered an architectural revolution inspired mainly by Scamozzi.[7] In Britain, John Webb, to whom Jones entrusted his Palladio drawings, was a link between the generation of natural or adoptive sons and the grandchildren, dominated by Lord Burlington, who came to Italy and discovered yet more Palladian drawings.[8] Burlington supported architects like William Kent and promoted publications, including the complete English translation of the *Quattro libri*.[9] By the second half of the eighteenth century, Palladio was a British product,

Fig. 4. Andrea Palladio (Italian, 1508–1580), "Reconstruction of an Egyptian Hall after Vitruvius," *Quattro libri dell'architettura* (Venice: Domenico de' Franceschi, 1570), book 2, page 42. Mediateca del Centro Internazionale di Studi di Architettura Andrea Palladio, Vicenza

Fig. 5. Inigo Jones (English, 1573–1652), Royal Banqueting House, Whitehall, London, 1622. Mediateca del Centro Internazionale di Studi di Architettura Andrea Palladio, Vicenza, F0013740

even when in demand in Catherine II's Russia, where Charles Cameron and Giacomo Quarenghi worked.[10] Meantime, the first books of broader surveys of buildings published by Francesco Muttoni and Ottavio Bertotti Scamozzi arrived from Italy, spreading knowledge of new buildings and drawings not included in the *Quattro libri*.[11] Lastly, Thomas Jefferson, the third president of the United States and an ingenious amateur architect, was to make Palladio the foundation of New World architecture.[12]

Palladio was important for Jefferson in many ways. Although he was certainly a key model among Jefferson's references, he was far from being the only one, given the equally important influence of American vernacular traditions and of British and French eighteenth-century architecture. Certainly, unlike many Palladians, Jefferson did not just "look at the illustrations" of the *Quattro libri* but also read the text very carefully, and in Italian too, given that he consciously borrowed the name Monticello, which Palladio had used to describe the small hill where La Rotonda stands.[13] Reading the *Quattro libri*, Jefferson grasped that the real purpose of the Palladian *barchesse* (adjoining outbuildings) was to meet the requirements of farm work (sheds for carts and implements, animal stalls, and wine cellars). We also find these uses in Monticello, unlike other neo-Palladian British or American buildings, where the *barchesse* are simple covered passages joining various parts of the house.[14] Likewise, by reading the description of the Villa Cornaro at Piombino Dese, Jefferson could check out a practical example of the concatenation of individual elements and rooms in a sequence of ratios—a founding element in Palladio's architectural system.[15]

Moreover, Jefferson turned to Palladio as the architect who made available ancient Roman architecture for contemporary use: we might say that Palladio translated "architectural" Latin from the dead language of the ruins of the Roman Empire into a living language for architects. In the early years of his career, when he had not yet left America, Jefferson knew about and had used the language of ancient Roman buildings through the surveys published in the third and fourth books of Palladio's *Quattro libri.* In his Parisian years (1784–89), Jefferson became familiar with the world of archaeologists and antiquarians and through them formed a more accurate, analytic view of the reality of the ruins. Yet when he came to design the Rotunda at the University of Virginia, he chose Palladio's version of the Corinthian-ordered Pantheon for a model, not the one unearthed and described by the new science of archaeology: "I have examined carefully all the antient Corinthians in my profession, and observe that Palladio, as usual, has given the finest members of them all in the happiest combination" (fig. 6).[16]

The Palladians were usually educated gentlemen or scholarly architects, at times both, rarely neither. Their tool of knowledge and action was not only the drawing table but also the book. Palladio's autograph drawings, brought to England by Jones in the early seventeenth century, were the keystone of the new culture. Their style was imitated and they were handed from one architect to another, expanded, and made available through publications. Some Palladians, like Vincenzo Scamozzi, had direct experience of the master's buildings because they grew up with them, or studied them firsthand, like Jones, Burlington, or Quarenghi. Others, like Jefferson, only knew these buildings through the *Quattro libri* and felt no compulsion to visit them on their Italian journeys. Over the centuries, some models were replicated to the letter on the basis of the designs in the *Quattro libri*, such that La Rotonda was repeated in Colen Campbell's Mereworth Castle (1725) and the Palazzo Valmarana in Potsdam's Old Town Hall by Christian Ludwig Hildebrandt (1754).[17] Other copies were based on Palladio's autograph drawings for unbuilt projects, such as General Wade's house by Lord Burlington (1723).[18] Some models were to be as distorted as Jimi Hendrix's "Star-Spangled Banner," as with the buildings designed by Muttoni. Muttoni had a thorough knowledge of Palladio's work, and was in fact responsible for a new edition of the *Quattro libri* in the 1840s. In his own architecture, however, he had a particularly free, creative approach, unique among Palladians. Muttoni always started with a quote from a model by the master: for example, the atrium of his Palazzo Trento Valmarana (1712–17) is an interpretation of the large three-nave atrium of Palladio's Palazzo Barbarano (fig. 7). Muttoni, however,

Fig. 6. Thomas Jefferson (American, 1743–1826), Rotunda, University of Virginia, Charlottesville, 1826. Mediateca del Centro Internazionale di Studi di Architettura Andrea Palladio, Vicenza, F0014503

Fig. 7. Francesco Muttoni (Italian, 1669–1747),
Palazzo Trento Valmarana, Vicenza, 1717.
Mediateca del Centro Internazionale di Studi
di Architettura Andrea Palladio, Vicenza

distorted the Palladian space by compressing it downward, lowering the mighty vaults to make a flat ceiling, and expanding the space out of all proportion. The same is true of his Palazzo Velo (1706), a 2.0 version of Palladio's Palazzo Chiericati, or his church of San Vincenzo in Vicenza (1704), in which the Olympic semicircular screen of columns in the presbytery of Palladio's design for the Redentore church in Venice becomes a tense mixtilinear fragment.[19] In a diametrically opposed approach, the Vicenza-based Ottone Calderari thought that Palladio's architecture was so perfect that new buildings could only be constructed by reassembling parts of them in various combinations, which is what he did in more than a dozen villas and palazzi in the Vicenza area.[20] The Russian architect Ivan Zholtovsky, on the other hand, expressed his love of Palladio in an even more radical way by building perfect copies of Palladio's buildings in Moscow, such as the Palazzo Tarasov, an exact replica of the Palazzo Thiene, or the house on Mokhovaya Street (1932), based on the Loggia del Capitaniato (fig. 8).[21] But for many other Palladians, Palladio was simply the architect who had translated ancient buildings for the modern world, a kind of timeless architectural divinity outside of history.

At the beginning of the second book of the *Quattro libri*, following Sebastiano Serlio's principles, Palladio established a precise relationship between the appearance of buildings and the social rank of the owner, from lords to lawyers and merchants. The specific form of government in Venice until 1797, one of the few republics in a Europe of monarchies, provided a contrast between the courtiers, and a ruling elite made up of *gentiluomini* who built their own palaces without the pomp of princes and lived in the country, where they pursued their interests, led a healthy life, and cultivated their souls by reading the classics. Palladio was their architect, and his villas were the setting for their model of life, obviously inspired by ancient Rome. This certainly did not go unobserved by the liberal British aristocrats in the early eighteenth century, who admired the Venetian constitution, or by Jefferson in his quest for a republican architecture to be adopted as a model for the new United States, which had emerged victoriously from its conflict with monarchical Britain.

Like Leon Battista Alberti and Le Corbusier, Palladio was an architect who wanted to change the world, and wrote a book of instructions on how it was to be done. In the *Quattro libri* he conceived and communicated architecture as a system capable of conveying the mathematics of ancient Roman architecture, made up of construction units (rooms, colonnades, stairs, portals, and windows) bound by rules, types, and ratios. But how many of these elements have stood the test of time? It was not the plans in his books, which were dependent on the uses of the buildings and on the contexts.

In the Veneto tradition before Palladio, houses and villas had a long central hall that developed from the front to the rear with, on either side of it, rooms of equal size facing each other. The new feature of Palladio's plans was that he created "suites" in harmoniously proportioned series of linked rectangular and square rooms of standard sizes (24 by 16, 16 by 16, and 16 by 12 feet; fig. 9).[22] These "molecular" or modular series of basic units are arranged around the central hall, and in general the smallest room is the point of arrival in a sequence of increasingly private rooms. The sequence, however, obliges you to go through all the rooms to reach the last room, with no corridors or lobbies separating them, and therefore with no privacy. This was unthinkable in eighteenth-century Britain, never mind Jefferson's Monticello, in which even the system for conveying food was designed to avoid or minimize contact between the owners and his enslaved black domestic servants.[23]

Fig. 8. Ivan Zholtovsky (Russian, 1867–1959), Palazzo Tarasov, Moscow, 1909. Mediateca del Centro Internazionale di Studi di Architettura Andrea Palladio, Vicenza, F0014276

This explains why Palladio's architectural system was gradually reduced to a language that further boiled down to a statement of belonging to a culture expressed in individual elements, such as the pronaos (porch) on columns on the facade, portals, and Serlian windows. Even the *Quattro libri* were superseded by the pragmatism of pattern books.

Palladio's lesson, however, is like the fossil light of a dead star, which continues

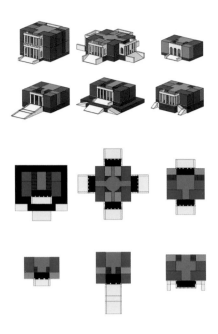

Fig. 9. Palladio's modular system device.
Mediateca del Centro Internazionale di Studi di
Architettura Andrea Palladio, Vicenza

to shine although its source has ceased to exist. One moving example of a tacit memory of Palladio occurred when freed American slaves returned to Africa in the mid-nineteenth century and built from memory the mansions of their former masters using local materials. They rejected the circular plan type of the native dwellings and built houses with rectangular plans, pediments, and front and rear porches, typical of the neo-Palladian mansions on American plantations.[24]

In ancient Rome, Vitruvius pointed to primitive wooden huts as a model for the stone temple. The triangular pediment of a temple was used by Lorenzo the Magnificent and Giuliano da Sangallo to crown the entrance to the villa at Poggio a Caiano in fifteenth-century Tuscany, and this was the first Renaissance building to revive the ancient Roman villa. Seventy years later it became a typical feature of the villas that Palladio designed in the Veneto. In the seventeenth century, the Palladian villa emigrated to the English countryside and then crossed the Atlantic to become plantation houses. From there, the gable went to Africa, and Vitruvius's temple form was a dwelling once more. ❦

NOTES

This text further elaborates and extends the essay "Palladio, Palladianism, Palladians," published in *Palladian Design: The Good, the Bad, the Unexpected*, edited by Marie Bak Mortensen and Charles Hind (London: Royal Institute of British Architects, 2015).

1. Guido Beltramini and Edoardo Demo, "Nuovi documenti e notizie riguardanti Andrea Palladio, la sua famiglia e il suo lavoro," *Annali di architettura* 20 (2008): 130. For La Rotonda, see *La Rotonda* (Milan: Electra, 1988); L. Puppi and D. Battilotti, *Andrea Palladio* (Milan: Electra, 1999), 380–83, 497–98; and Howard Burns, "An Eternal Contemporary," in *Palladio*, ed. Guido Beltramini and Howard Burns (Venice: Marsilio; London: Royal Academy of Arts, 2008), 364–66.

2. Franco Barbieri, *La Rocca Pisana di Vincenzo Scamozzi* (Vicenza, Italy: Banca Popolare di Vicenza, 1985); Charles Davis, "Architecture and Light: Vincenzo Scamozzi's Statuary Installation in the Chiesetta of the Palazzo Ducale in Venice," *Annali di Architettura* 14 (2002): 171–93.

3. Franco Barbieri, *Vincenzo Scamozzi* (Vicenza, Italy: Casa di Risparmio di Verona e Vicenza, 1959); Franco Barbieri and Guido Beltramini, eds., *Vincenzo Scamozzi, 1548–1616* (Vicenza, Italy: Marsilio, 2003); Guido Beltramini, "The Fortunes and Misfortunes of Scamozzi's 'Idea della Architettura Universale' in Palladian Territory," *Annali di Architettura* 18, no. 19 (2007): 199–213; Giles Worsley, "Scamozzi's Influence on English Seventeenth-Century Architecture," *Annali di Architettura* 18, no. 19 (2007): 225–33; Howard Burns, "Note sull'influsso di Scamozzi in Inghilterra: Inigo Jones, John Webb, Lord Burlington," in Barbieri and Beltramini, *Vincenzo Scamozzi*, 129–31; Howard Burns, "Inigo Jones and 18, no. 19 (2007): 215–24.

4. Howard Burns, "Palladio and the Foundation of a New Architecture in the North," and Christy Anderson, "Palladio in England: The Dominance of the Classical in a Foreign Land," in *Palladio and Northern Europe: Books, Travellers, Architects*, ed. Guido Beltramini, Howard Burns, Kurt W. Forster, Werner Oechslin, and Christof Thoenes (Milan: Skira, 1999), 16–55 and 372–83.

5. Rudolf Wittkower, *Palladio and English Palladianism* (London: Thames and Hudson, 1974); John Harris, Stephen Orgel, and Roy Strong, *The King's Arcadia: Inigo Jones and the Stuart Court* (London: Arts Council of Great Britain, 1973); John Harris, *Inigo Jones: Complete Architectural Drawings* (London: Sotheby Parke Bernet, 1989); Charles Hind, "Inigo Jones (1573–1652)," in Beltramini and Burns, *Palladio*, 386–91; Giles Worsley, *Inigo Jones and the European Classicist Tradition* (New Haven: Yale University Press, 2007); Christy Anderson, *Inigo Jones and the Classical Tradition* (Cambridge: Cambridge University Press, 2007); and Edward Chaney, ed., *Inigo Jones' Roman Sketchbook* (London: Roxburgh Club, 2006).

6. Eileen Harris, *British Architectural Books and Writers, 1556–1785* (Cambridge: Cambridge University Press, 1990), 499–503; Gerald Beasley, "Henry Wotton," in *The British Books: Seventeenth through Nineteenth Centuries; The Mark J. Millard Architectural Collection*, ed. Robin Middleton, Gerald Beasley, and Nicholas Savage (Washington, DC: George Brazilier, 1998), 365–68; Howard Burns, "Sir Henry Wotton, 'The Elements of Architecture,' "

in Beltramini et al., *Palladio and Northern Europe*, 62–63; Christy Anderson, "The Learned Art of Architecture: Henry Wotton's Elements of Architecture," in *The Image of Venice: Fialetti's View and Sir Henry Wotton*, ed. Deborah Howard and Henrietta McBurney (London: Paul Holberton, 2013), 124–35.

7. Konrad Ottenheym, "Classicism in the Northern Netherlands in the Seventeenth Century," in Beltramini et al., *Palladio and Northern Europe*, 151–67; Konrad Ottenheym, " 'L'idea dell'architettura universale' in Olanda," in Barbieri and Beltramini, *Vincenzo Scamozzi*, 133–41; and Konrad Ottenheym, "A Bird's-Eye View of the Dissemination of Scamozzi's Treatise in Northern Europe," *Annali di architettura* 18, no. 19 (2007): 187–98.

8. John Bold, *John Webb: Architectural Theory and Practice in the Seventeenth Century* (Oxford: Oxford University Press, 1989); John Harris, *Inigo Jones and John Webb: Catalogue of the Drawings Collection of the Royal Institute of British Architects* (Farnborough, England: Gregg International, 1972).

9. John Wilton-Ely, *Apollo of the Arts. Lord Burlington and His Circle* (Nottingham, England: Nottingham University Art Gallery, 1973); John Harris, *The Palladians* (London: Trefoil, 1981); Jacques Carré, *Lord Burlington, 1694–1753: Le connoisseur, le mécène, l'architecte* (Clermont-Ferrand, France: Adossa, 1993); John Harris, *The Palladian Revival: Lord Burlington, His Villa and Garden at Chiswick* (New Haven: Yale University Press, 1994); Toby Barnard and Jane Clark, *Lord Burlington, Architecture, Art and Life* (London: Hambeldon Continuum, 1996); and Susan Weber, ed., *William Kent: Designing Georgian Britain* (New Haven: Yale University Press, 2013).

10. Dmitrij Svidkovskij, *The Empress and the Architect: British Architecture and Gardens at the Court of Catherine the Great* (New Haven: Yale University Press, 1996);

Howard Burns, "La città bianca: Continuità e innovazione nell'architettura di San Pietroburgo, 1762–1825," in *Dal mito al progetto: La cultura architettonica dei maestri italiani e ticinesi nella Russia Neoclassica*, ed. Andrea Navone and Letizia Tedeschi (Mendrisio, Switzerland: Mendrisio Academy Press, 2004), 454–501; and Federica Rossi, "Giacomo Quarenghi (1744–1817) and Charles Cameron (1746–1812)," in Beltramini and Burns, *Palladio*, 394–97.

11. Franco Barbieri, "Bertotti-Scamozzi Ottavio," in *Dizionario biografico degli Italiani* (Rome: Istituto dell'Enciclopedia Italiana, 1967), 9:632–35; Franco Barbieri, *Illuministi e neoclassici a Vicenza* (Vicenza, Italy: Olimpico, 1972); and Christine Kamm-Kyburz, *Der Architekt Ottavio Bertotti Scamozzi, 1719–1790: Ein Beitrag zum Palladianismus im Veneto* (Bern: Benteli, 1983).

12. Fiske Kimball, *Thomas Jefferson, Architect: Original Designs in the Coolidge Collection of the Massachusetts Historical Society* (1916; repr., New York: Da Capo, 1968), 22–27; James S. Ackerman, "Il Presidente Jefferson e il Palladianesimo americano," *Bollettino del Centro Internazionale di Studi di Architettura Andrea Palladio* 6 (1964): 9–48; James S. Ackerman, *The Villa: Form and Ideology of Country Houses* (Princeton, NJ: Princeton University Press, 1990), 185–211; James Ackerman, "Thomas Jefferson and Italy," in *Origins, Imitation, Conventions: Representation in the Visual Arts* (Cambridge, MA: MIT Press, 2002), 63–91; and Calder Loth, "Palladio's Legacy to America," in *Palladio and His Legacy: A Transatlantic Journey*, ed. Charles Hind and Irena Murray (Venice: Marsilio, 2010), 142–51.

13. Guido Beltramini, "Jefferson, Italy and Palladio," in *Canova's George Washington*, ed. Xavier Salomon (New York: Frick Art Museum, 2018), 114–15.

14. Ackerman, "Il Presidente Jefferson," 41.

15. Guido Beltramini, "Jefferson and Palladio," in *Jefferson and Palladio: Constructing a New World*, ed. Guido Beltramini and Fulvio Lenzo (Vicenza, Italy: Officina Libreria, 2015), 23.

16. "Thomas Jefferson to Arthur S. Brockenbrough, 22 April 1823," *Founders Online*, National Archives, last modified June 13, 2018, http://founders.archives.gov /documents/Jefferson/98-01-02-3471.

17. Kurt Forster and Jorg Bracker, "Palladianism in Germany," in Beltramini et al., *Palladio and Northern Europe*, 168–93.

18. Christy Anderson, "General Wade's House," in ibid., 143.

19. Barbieri, "Bertotti-Scamozzi Ottavio"; Natalia Grilli, *Un archivio inedito dell'architetto Francesco Muttoni a Porlezza* (Florence: La Nuova Italia, 1991); Manuela Barausse, "Muttoni, Francesco," in *Dizionario Biografico degli Italiani* (Rome: Istituto dell'Enciclopedia Italiana, 2012).

20. Barbieri, "Bertotti-Scamozzi Ottavio"; Guido Beltramini, *I disegni di Ottone Calderari al Museo Civico di Vicenza*, exh. cat. (Vicenza, Italy: Marsilio, 1999).

21. Vasilij Uspenskij, "Ivan Zoltovskij, il don Chisciotte del palladianesimo sovietico," in *Russia Palladiana: Palladio e la Russia dal barocco al modernismo*, ed. Arkadij Ippolitov and Vasilij Uspenskij (Vicenza, Italy: L.E.G.O. s.p.a., 2014).

22. Howard Burns, "Making a New Architecture," in Beltramini and Burns, *Palladio*, 258–75, especially 270–72.

23. Robin Evans, "Figures, Doors, Passages," in *Translations from Drawing to Building and Other Essays* (Cambridge, MA: MIT Press, 1997), 54–91.

24. *A Land and Life Remembered: Americo-Liberian Folk Architecture*, photographs by Max Belcher, text by Svend Holsoe and Bernard Herman (Athens: University of Georgia Press, 1988); *Genealogies*, exhibition curated by Guido Beltramini and Giovanna Borasi, Palladio Museum, Vicenza, Italy, October 5, 2012–March 31, 2013.

JEFFERSON AND ENGLAND

RICHARD GUY WILSON

Thomas Jefferson's knowledge of Palladian architecture came through several sources, including books and also firsthand experiences with English buildings inspired by Palladio. His passion for Palladio appears in many letters such as one from 1804: "There never was a Palladio here [in Washington] even in private hands till I brought one."[1] He resided in Europe for five years, and though an avid traveler and tourist, he—oddly—never went to the Veneto, Venice, and Rome. However, he visited England three times: two brief landings—July 25–31, 1784, and October 9–23, 1789—and a longer trip from March 11 to April 27 of 1786. The visits were a result of his appointment as the American minister to the court of Louis XVI in Paris. The impact of the buildings and gardens he saw while in England would be long-lasting and include not only his own houses, Monticello and Poplar Forest, but also some of his designs for friends, such as the Divers at Farmington and ultimately the University of Virginia.[2]

In 1782 Jefferson's wife, Martha, died, and he sought an escape from his life in Virginia. Several of their children had died in infancy, and he had two young daughters. He halted construction on Monticello and contemplated moving abroad. The chance came in 1784 when he was asked by the young American government to go to Paris and take the minister (ambassador) post that John Adams had earlier held.

Jefferson's only book, *Notes on the State of Virginia*, written in 1781–83 and published in Paris in 1785 and in London in 1787 and later, excoriated the state of American architecture and building. "The genius of architecture seems to have shed its maledictions over this land," he exclaimed; ". . . the first principles of the art are unknown, and there exists scarcely a model among us sufficiently chaste to give an idea of them." Bemoaning the American tendency to build in wood, Jefferson argued that such structures lacked permanence, and in another passage he called several of the major public buildings in the colonial capital of Williamsburg "rude, misshapen piles" and "brick-kilns."[3] The buildings he saw and experienced on the Continent and especially in England became part of a major reformation of American architecture.

Jefferson's knowledge of Palladio prior to the English visits came through the books he owned. His architectural library was one of the largest in the young American republic, over time (after the European sojourn) containing about forty different titles.[4] He purchased his first architectural book while a student at the College of William & Mary in Williamsburg from a cabinetmaker outside the gates of the college. The title has been endlessly debated, with claims made that it was a volume of Palladio, or James Gibbs, or Robert Morris, but no matter which it was, it set him on a course of major book purchases in all subjects, including architecture and design. By 1771, as was evident in some architectural drawings, Jefferson owned a copy of Palladio along with treatises by Gibbs and Morris, who were greatly influenced by Palladio. However, for Jefferson his most important source lay with the London-published Giacomo Leoni edition, *The Architecture of A. Palladio in Four Books.*

In the English colonies and the young American republic, the impact of Palladio appeared usually in ornamental details such as door surrounds or fireplace mantels. Only a few buildings existed that demonstrated Palladio's larger vision of the complete structure, such as the Hammond-Harwood House, Annapolis, of c. 1774 by the English émigré architect William Buckland. The house had extended wings with a Palladian touch when Jefferson visited Annapolis in 1782–83 and made a rough sketch of the house. Outside of Charleston, South Carolina, stood Drayton Hall, c. 1750, with a double Palladian portico. But Jefferson never went south of Virginia, and hence it is doubtful he knew of it.

Up north on his way to Boston to sail to France in 1784, Jefferson visited Newport, Rhode Island, where the first American full-temple-fronted portico existed, installed on the Redwood Library and Athenaeum. Designed by Peter Harrison in 1748 and based upon William Kent's designs drawn from Palladio, it was one of the first libraries in the young republic (fig. 1). While Jefferson never commented on the Redwood Library, given his interest in books and also architecture, he undoubtedly went up the hill from Newport Harbor to view it. In New-

Fig. 1. Peter Harrison (American, 1716–1775), Redwood Library and Athenaeum, Newport, Rhode Island, 1748

port he additionally experienced the Market Hall, also designed by Harrison, which drew upon Inigo Jones's Banqueting House (completed in 1622) in London as well as designs by Palladio. Jefferson certainly saw the Banqueting House and other buildings by Jones while in London.

England's connection to Palladio was the deepest of any country/state outside of the Italian Peninsula.[5] Inigo Jones had visited Venice and the Veneto several times and made detailed notes on Palladio's buildings and drawings. In 1615 Jones purchased a huge cache of original drawings by Palladio and his follower Vincenzo Scamozzi and brought them back to London, where they ultimately became

Fig. 2. Giacomo Leoni (Italian, 1686–1746), Moor Park House, remodeling and additions, 1720s, Hertfordshire, United Kingdom

part of the Queen's Collection and made a major impact on English architecture.

Palladio's popularity led to the publication in London of Giacomo Leoni's *The Architecture of A. Palladio in Four Books.* Printed in London in slightly different versions in 1715, 1721, and 1742, Leoni's edition became the standard and was Jefferson's favorite. Leoni redrew all of Palladio's drawings and also changed elements in the text. Born in Venice and a devote of Palladio, Leoni came to England around 1715 and in time changed his first name to James. In addition to translating Palladio, Leoni became an architect and designed numerous buildings with very Palladian features, such as Queensberry House in London as well as several country houses, such as Clandon Park and Moor Park (fig. 2). Jefferson certainly saw some of Leoni's London work, and he visited Moor Park, which he admired, writing in his notes, "The building superb. The principle front a Corinthian portico of 4. Columns."[6] On his various trips he also passed near some of Leoni's other houses, which he might have seen.

Palladianism in England received a major boost in the 1720s and 1730s with the emergence on the scene of Richard Boyle, the third Earl of Burlington. An avid architecture enthusiast, Lord Burlington had traveled in Italy, where he observed Palladio firsthand and acquired some of his drawings. Back in England, with the assistance of William Kent and others, he designed his house and gardens at Chiswick and several other buildings, such as Burlington House in London. He owned an original copy of Palladio's 1570 *Quattro libri dell'architettura* (Four books of architecture), along with some drawings. Feeling that the Leoni edition was "corrupt," as it contained poor illustrations and had other problems, Burlington commissioned Isaac Ware to produce a more accurate edition, initially published in 1738 as *The Four Books of Architecture.* Under Burlington's influence Palladianism effectively became the English style. Jefferson visited Chiswick, and at some point obtained a copy of Lord Burlington's more correct Ware edition of Palladio, but Leoni remained his standard.

During Jefferson's time, and indeed for many years afterward, direct ship routes from the United States to France were rare. Most journeys to the Continent meant stopping and changing ships on England's south coast, at either Portsmouth or the Isle of Wight, and then continuing on to Le Havre or another port. (In the mid-nineteenth century the entry port to England from the United States changed to Liverpool, on the west coast.) Two of Jefferson's visits, in 1784 and 1789, were on the south coast for short periods of time, though he did view some important buildings. On a longer visit from March 11 to April 26, 1786, he made extensive trips to various buildings in the London area and then a six-day journey into the English midlands to visit various towns, country houses, and gardens.

Written records of Jefferson's time in England are mixed, with some listing of expenses, very few letters, and a very brief summary written after his 1786 visit. Whether he knew the architect of each building he visited remains unclear. He did have a guidebook, Thomas Whately's *Observations on Modern Gardening* (1770), which he admired greatly, but it did not list all the designers of the gardens. He purchased a guidebook for the garden at Stowe that listed many of its temples and some of their designers (fig. 3).

The impetus for Jefferson's six-week trip to England in 1786 was the request of John Adams, the American minister to the court of George III. Jefferson, as noted, followed Adams as the American minister to the court of Louis XVI, and the two maintained a close friendship (later they became political adversaries, but they reconciled prior to their deaths, both on July 4, 1826). The stated purpose of the trip was to negotiate a trade treaty with England, which failed, but it gave Jefferson a chance to experience the architecture and gardens of England. While in London he took a house on Golden Square, which was a diplomatic center. Part of his trip included a presentation at the court of George III, which has caused controversy; by some accounts, when the king discovered that it was Jefferson in front of him, he turned his back. In the memoir Jefferson wrote at the end of his life, he recalled that "on my presentation as usual to the King and Queen at their levees, it was impossible for anything to be more ungracious than their notice of Mr. Adams & myself. I saw at once that the ulcerations in the narrow mind of that mulish being left nothing to be expected on the subject of my attendance."[7]

Not every building that Jefferson saw in England was neo-Palladian, but many of the buildings contained elements that could be traced back to Palladio and/or other Italian and classical sources. One example is the Royal Hospital Haslar at Gosport, on the south coast across the bay from Portsmouth, where Jefferson landed on July 25, 1784 (fig. 4). Jefferson spent several days in Portsmouth and would have observed the substantial naval barracks and other structures there. An acquaintance from Virginia, Elizabeth Thompson, had moved to the town of Titchfield on the other side of the bay, and Jefferson went to visit her. In crossing the bay he would have seen the relatively new Royal Hospital, a monumental three fronts

Fig. 3. B. (Benton) Seeley (English, fl. 1744–1776), *Stowe: A Description of the . . . House and Gardens of . . . Earl Temple* (Buckingham, 1777). Library of Congress

Fig. 4. Theodore Jacobsen (English, d. 1772), Royal Hospital Haslar, Gosport, Hampshire, United Kingdom, 1753

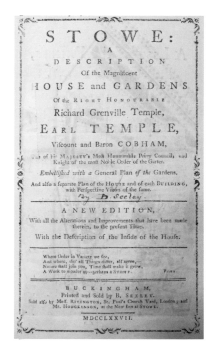

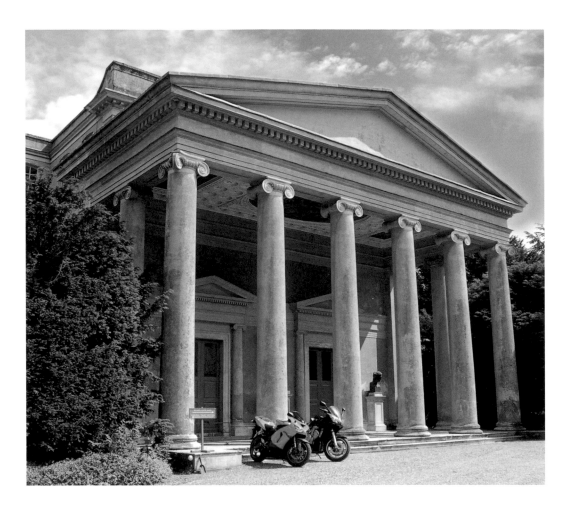

Fig. 5. Nicholas Revett (English, 1721–1804), additions to West Wycombe House west front, 1770s, Buckinghamshire, United Kingdom

on a quad complex of red brick designed by Theodore Jacobsen. Jacobsen also designed the Foundling Hospital in London (1742–52), of which Lord Burlington was a founder. At the Haslar hospital, the three-sided form, the open arcades on the ground floor, and the tall pediment of the central structure have some similarities to Jefferson's much later design for the University of Virginia.

Jacobsen's design for Haslar was certainly inspired by Sir Christopher Wren's Royal Hospital (1682–89) in the Chelsea area of London. Wren's Royal Hospital, one of the largest structures in London during the eighteenth century, is a three-front quad red-brick structure with arcades at the ground floor and, at the center, an imposing temple portico of the Roman Doric order. Jefferson undoubtedly saw this building on his rambles about the city in March–April 1786. Scholars have noted the possible influence of eighteenth-century English and French hospital designs on Jefferson's scheme for the University of Virginia.[8]

Whether inspired directly by Palladio or by other classical sources, Jefferson constantly saw full temple-fronted porticoes on the newer grand buildings in England, as well as the garden follies and structures he and Adams saw on their tour of the Midlands and country mansions such as Claremont House, Stowe, and Blenheim.

West Wycombe House, which Jefferson and Adams visited on April 9, 1786, was a grand house to which numerous full columned porticoes had been added over the years. It was the residence of Sir Francis Dashwood, who organized the Hellfire Club, which celebrated debauchery with its male gatherings, both in London and in a nearby grotto on the property.[9] Benjamin Franklin was a friend of Dashwood and had belonged to the Hellfire Club, but no evidence exists that Jefferson and Adams attended any Hellfire events. On the west front of West Wycombe House, which served as the approach, a new six-columned Ionic portico had been added in 1770, after designs by Nicholas Revett (fig. 5). Drawn from the Greek temple of Bacchus at Teos, the design is one of the earliest examples of what later came to be called Greek Revival in England. Jefferson also saw James "Athenian" Stuart's Greek temple at Hagley. Revett and Stuart had produced the first recorded drawings of Greek architecture, published in *The Antiquities of Athens* (three volumes, published 1762, 1790, and 1795). Jefferson knew of the book and probably acquired the first volume during his time in England.[10]

While in England in 1786 Jefferson spent considerable time observing the new English style of landscape gardening at Stowe, Kew, Esher, Hagley, and several more country estates (fig. 6). These revolutionary gardens, sometimes labeled "picturesque," "romantic," and "Jardin à l'anglaise," were the main subject of the only notes Jefferson made during the English visit. About them, Jefferson wrote, "The gardening in that county, is the article in which it surpasses all the earth. I mean their pleasure gardening. This indeed went beyond my ideas."[11]

In his notes Jefferson also mentioned "a tour to some of the gardens in England described by Whateley in his book on gardening. . . . I always walked over the gardens with his book in my hand, examining with attention the particular spots he described, found them so justly characterized by him as to be easily recognized . . . as might enable me to estimate the experience of making and maintaining a garden in that style."[12] In a six-day trip with John Adams, who also had a copy of Whately, he visited at least twenty different houses and landscapes, along with numerous towns and cities such as Oxford.[13] The curving pathway and landscaped vistas he encountered in so many of these gardens made an impact on his later schemes for Monticello.

From the Palladian perspective, the important element Jefferson observed in addition to the houses were the numerous garden follies and

Fig. 6. William Chambers (English, 1723–1796), plans, elevations, sections, and perspective views of the gardens and buildings at Kew in Surrey (London, 1763). The Royal Collection Trust

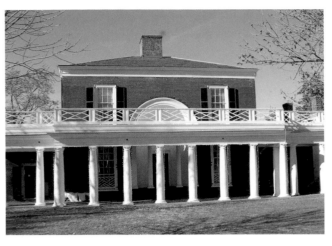

Fig. 7. William Kent (English, 1685–1748), Stowe, Temple of Venus, Buckinghamshire, United Kingdom, 1731

Fig. 8. Thomas Jefferson (American, 1743–1826), Pavilion IX, front view, University of Virginia, Charlottesville, 1819

temples, many of them based upon elements in the various Palladio books. At Hagley, in addition to Stuart's Greek Revival temple, he saw an Ionic eight-columned rotunda built in 1748–49. At Hagley and other locations Jefferson encountered some "sham" ruins, but they made little impact on him.

At Stowe, which was perhaps the most elaborate and extensive "picturesque" garden in England, Jefferson saw at least twenty different temples, follies, sculpture groupings, grottoes, and other creations. One was the 1734 Temple of British Worthies, which contained sculptural busts of notable individuals, all in political sympathy with Stowe's owner. From this, Jefferson may have gotten his ideas for the busts he would later install at Monticello. The Temple of Liberty (later called the Gothic Temple) of 1741–48 at Stowe, a Gothic Revival structure by James Gibbs, made no impact upon him, but there were many others such as the Palladian Bridge of 1742 and the Temple of Friendship of 1737, also by Gibbs, which were fully Palladian. William Kent—Lord Burlington's partner in a number of designs—contributed several structures at Stowe, such as the Temple of Venus of 1731 (fig. 7). At the center of the temple's two extended wings stood a pedimented structure with a large recessed niche, and a row of columns across the front. This form would reappear in Pavilion IX on the Lawn at the University of Virginia (fig. 8). Kent, with Giovanni Battista Borra, a sculptor, also created a ten-columned Ionic rotunda structure in Stowe's gardens.

Probably the most famous English Palladian house, Chiswick, is also noted as playing a role in Jefferson's later architectural development. Jefferson visited Lord Burlington's creation outside London in Richmond, near the Thames River, on April 2, 1786. In his notes he records paying the servant/groundskeeper for entry, writing "Chiswick, Belongs to D. of Devonshire. Garden about 6. acres. The Octagonal dome has an ill effect, both within and without; the garden shews still too much of art; an obelisk of very ill effect. Another in the middle of a pond useless."[14]

The Chiswick that Jefferson described had been designed and built in the 1720s by Lord Burlington with the help of others, including William

Kent, who also worked on the garden's layout and follies (fig. 9). The house known as Chiswick was actually an addition to a much earlier Jacobean structure on the site, since torn down. Burlington's intention with the classical/Palladian addition was to create a party house and an art gallery. While inspired by Palladio's Villa Capra "La Rotonda" outside Vicenza, it was not a copy in any way (fig. 10). Burlington owned many architecture books, and the result was that Chiswick contained Palladian elements, but it also drew from the work of other Italian architects such as Vincenzo Scamozzi, as well as making references to ancient Roman ruins. Burlington died in 1753, and soon thereafter Chiswick passed into the Duke of Devonshire's family, becoming known in the 1770s and 1780s as one of the centers of the Whig Party. On either side of the front of the house, on the exterior, stood two life-size statues: Andrea Palladio and Inigo Jones, indicating Burlington's sources of inspiration.

Chiswick's gardens, initially designed by Burlington, with the assistance of William Kent and also Charles Bridgeman, encompassed about sixty acres (today much reduced) and were one of the earliest English "picturesque" terrains, filled with follies, statues, grottoes, water features, and other elements. One of the most prominent features was a domed structure with an Ionic portico standing at the end of a pond near the house. From the center of the pond rose an obelisk that, as noted, Jefferson condemned.

The center of Burlington's Chiswick was the central two-story domed octagonal space, where busts of noted individuals, both recent and from the antique past, stood, and major paintings adorned the walls. Surrounding the central space on the main floor was a series of rooms, square, octagonal, and rectangular, with open sight lines though them.

As apparent in his notes, Jefferson went into Chiswick, where he castigated the dome as having "an ill effect, both within and without."[15] While his criticism may make some sense—the dome on the exterior is perhaps a bit small in relation to the building mass below (Chiswick's chimney stacks also mar its appearance)—the building nevertheless made a strong impact on him. His own dome at Monticello is only visible from the southern side, and on its interior it has no relation to the main floor (of course Jefferson's experience in Paris with the Hôtel de Salm played the pivotal role in Monticello's design). The full temple-fronted portico on Chiswick's main facade may also have influenced Jefferson's porticoes. The room shapes and sight lines of Chiswick's interior also reappear at Monticello.

Jefferson saw and experienced an incredible number of buildings—from full-scale Palladian-inspired structures to odd garden follies based on

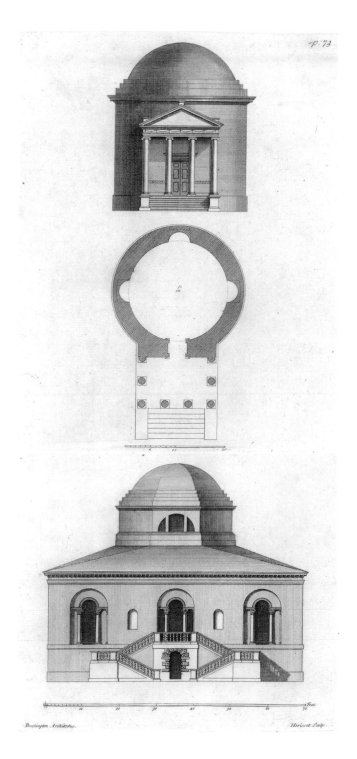

Fig. 9. William Kent (English, 1685–1748), Chiswick House, in *The Designs of Inigo Jones Consisting of Plans and Elevations for Publick and Private Buildings* (London: William Kent, 1727), plate 73. University of Wisconsin Libraries

Fig. 10. Richard Boyle, third Earl of Burlington (English, 1694–1753), Chiswick House, West London, 1729

the medieval past—landscapes, and gardens in England. On the exact role that each would play in his architectural endeavors of the next nearly forty years, however, we can only speculate. What we see and experience enters our minds at the moment, but how it manifests itself over time can range considerably. What is apparent is that Jefferson gained a much larger vision of architecture and landscape design through his English travels, and that the many English interpretations of Palladio's works played a key role in his architectural thought. ☙

NOTES

1. Thomas Jefferson to James Oldham, December 24, 1804, University of Virginia Library, Special Collections.
2. Scholarship on Jefferson's time abroad can be found in George Green Shackelford, *Thomas Jefferson's Travels in Europe, 1784–1789* (Baltimore: Johns Hopkins University Press, 1995); William Howard Adams, *The Paris Years of Thomas Jefferson* (New Haven: Yale University Press, 1997); and Ross Watson, "Thomas Jefferson's Visit to England, 1786," *History Today* 27 (January 1977). His correspondence from this time is in Douglas L. Wilson and Lucia Stanton, eds., *Jefferson Abroad* (New York: Modern Library, 1999).
3. Thomas Jefferson, *Notes on the State of Virginia*, ed. by William Peden (Chapel Hill: University of North Carolina Press, 1955 [1781, 1787]), 152–53.
4. See William B. O'Neal, *Jefferson's Fine Arts Library: His Selections for the University of Virginia Together with His Own Architectural Books* (Charlottesville: University Press of Virginia, 1976).
5. Rudolf Wittkower, *Palladio and English Palladianism* (London: Thames and Hudson, 1985); John Harris, *The Palladian Revival: Lord Burlington, His Villa and Garden at Chiswick* (New Haven: Yale University Press, 1994); and Robert Tavernor, *Palladio and Palladianism* (London: Thames and Hudson, 1991).
6. Jefferson, "Notes," in Wilson and Stanton, *Jefferson Abroad*, 69.
7. Jefferson, "Autobiography," in *The Writings of Thomas Jefferson*, ed. Merrill Peterson (New York: Library of America, 1984), 57.
8. Mary N. Woods, "Thomas Jefferson and the University of Virginia: Planning the Academic Village," *Journal of the Society of Architectural Historians* 44 (1985): 266–83.
9. Evelyn Lord, *The Hell-Fire Clubs: Sex, Satanism and Secret Societies* (New Haven: Yale University Press, 2008).
10. O'Neal, *Jefferson's Fine Arts Library*, 343.
11. Jefferson to John Page, May 4, 1786, in Wilson and Stanton, *Jefferson Abroad*, 73. Also see Edward Dumbauld, "Jefferson and Adams' English Garden Tour," in *Jefferson and the Arts: An Extended View*, ed. William Howard Adams (Washington, DC: National Gallery of Art, 1976), 137–57.
12. Jefferson, "Notes of a Tour of English Gardens," in Wilson and Stanton, *Jefferson Abroad*, 65.
13. Adams's copy of Whately, with some annotations, is in the Boston Public Library.
14. Jefferson, "Notes of a Tour of English Gardens."
15. Ibid.

WHAT HE SAW

Thomas Jefferson's Grand Tour

LLOYD DEWITT

When Thomas Jefferson traveled to Italy in 1787, he did not visit a single building designed by the Renaissance architect Andrea Palladio. Though Jefferson had pondered Palladio's *Quattro libri dell'architettura* (Four books of architecture) since his college days and had already visited Palladian-modeled houses such as the Hammond-Harwood House in Annapolis, designed by William Buckland (fig. 1), and the Redwood Library and Athenaeum in Rhode Island, built by Peter Harrison, he passed up the chance see the villas, palaces, and churches whose designs he had admired at length in Palladio's book. Over time, Jefferson had become so devoted to the designs of Palladio that this omission remains one of the enduring mysteries about his trip through Europe that year.

In 2008, to mark the five hundredth anniversary of his birth, the US Congress declared Andrea Palladio the Father of American Architecture, mainly on the strength of his impact on the buildings of Thomas Jefferson, and in spite of the fact that Palladio's designs were never joined to the reality of the Italian originals in Jefferson's own experience. Some have speculated that Jefferson felt sufficiently mature and independent in his architectural thinking that a special pilgrimage to see Palladio's buildings in the flesh held no appeal. In fact, Jefferson did value the study of architecture through visiting Roman ruins and examples he admired. He wrote to James Adams that architecture, both modern and classical, deserved the "great attention" of American travelers.[1] This he repeated in a report to his secretary William Short, sent during his journey to the South of France, noting that "architecture, painting, sculpture, antiquities, agriculture, the condition of the laboring poor fill all my moments."[2] But here he also hints at a reason why the Palladian buildings were neglected in his travels: Jefferson's own Grand Tour was utilitarian, intended to be restorative as well as useful to him in his role as statesman, and therefore was consciously devoid of the tourism and pilgrimage typical of a gentleman's grand tour.

Fig. 1. Charles Willson Peale (American, 1741–1827), *William Buckland*, 1774, reworked 1789. Oil on canvas. Yale University Art Gallery, Mabel Brady Garvan Collection, 1934.303

Fig. 2. Luigi Schiavonetti (Italian, 1765–1810), after Richard Cosway, *Portrait of Maria Cosway*, c. 1791. Etching and engraving and stipple printed in brown ink in chalk manner. Philadelphia Museum of Art, Muriel and Philip Berman Gift, acquired from the John S. Philips bequest of 1867 to the Pennsylvania Academy of the Fine Arts, with funds contributed by Muriel and Philip Berman, gifts (by exchange) of Lisa Norris Elkins, Bryant W. Langston, Samuel S. White 3rd and Vera White, with additional funds contributed by John Howard McFadden, Jr., Thomas Skelton Harrison, and the Philip H. and A.S.W. Rosenbach Foundation, 1985-52-21185

Jefferson sought to elevate the practice of architecture in Virginia, and was blunt in his critique of the state's existing buildings, claiming of the old capitol in Williamsburg,

> The College and the Hospital are rude, mis-shapen piles, which but that they have roofs, would be taken for brick-kilns. There are no other public buildings but churches and court-houses, in which no attempts are made at elegance. Indeed, it would not be easy to execute such an attempt, as workmen could scarcely be found here capable of drawing an order. The genius of architecture seems to have shed its maledictions over the land. Buildings are often erected, by individuals, of considerable expence. To give these symmetry and taste, would not increase their cost. It would only change the arrangement of the materials, the form and the combination of the members. This would often cost less than the burden of barbarous ornaments with which these buildings are sometimes charged. But the principles of the art are unknown, and there exists scarcely a model among us sufficiently chaste to give an idea of them.[3]

Jefferson made a bold statement by building his own villa, one based on designs in Palladio's *Quattro libri*, on a mountaintop outside Charlottesville. The current, second version of the house, Monticello, bears little resemblance to that first, book-derived home. The trip to Europe he took between the two phases of building the house shows that his Grand Tour had indeed elevated his own architectural practice.

Jefferson was able to travel to Europe after the conclusion of hostilities with Great Britain in 1783. After the death of his beloved wife, Martha Skelton Jefferson, in 1782, Jefferson was ready for a new situation, and he accepted the invitation to serve as treaty commissioner to France.[4] He embarked from Boston in July 1784, with duties as statesman and as father to young girls that would allow him only limited time for exploration and travel, which he tended to apply to the needs of the new republic. During his stay in Europe he took a separate trip to the South of France in the spring of 1787, following the route to Aix-en-Provence and Marseilles.

Jefferson had broken his right wrist on September 18, 1786, while enjoying the sights of Paris in an otherwise entrancing week-long dalliance with the remarkable Maria Cosway, the Italian-English artist (fig. 2). In a letter to James Monroe on December 18, 1786, Jefferson announced, "I am now about setting out on a journey to the South of France, one object of which is to try the mineral waters there for the restoration of my hand, but another is to visit all the seaports where we have trade, and to hunt up all the inconveniencies under which it labours, in order to get them rectified. I shall visit and carefully examine too the Canal of Languedoc."[5] These goals were all practical and sensible as well as useful to his country.

Jefferson's letters and account books provide a wealth of detailed information about this journey to the healing waters of the south. With his own experiences still fresh in his mind, Jefferson penned a short "Hints to Americans Travelling in Europe" on June 19, 1788, just after his return to Paris, for his protégé and secretary William Short and Short's two companions Thomas Lee Shippen and John Rutledge Jr. For reasons of practicality alone, he recommended to them "architecture worth great attention. As we double our numbers every 20 years we must double our houses. Besides we build of such perishable materials that one half of our houses must be rebuilt in every space of 20 years. So that in that term, houses are to be built for three fourths of our inhabitants. It is then among the most important arts: and it is desireable to introduce taste into an art which shews so much."[6] The utilitarian tendency in this passage directed Jefferson's own travel planning toward the goal of improving architecture in the new republic.

When he traveled south, Jefferson went alone. Not required to accommodate others nor depending on a tour guide, he was thus free to follow his own path, declaring that "one travels more usefully when alone, because he reflects more."[7] On occasion he hired valets when he stopped, but otherwise he depended on his classical education and on his chosen guidebooks. He also left Sally and James Hemings, his servants brought from Monticello, where they were enslaved, behind in Paris, and with them, his connection to slavery. Ironically, he consistently observed and carefully noted the happiness or oppression of the "laboring poor" he encountered as a function of the freedom (or tyranny) under which they lived, untroubled by his own dependence back home on the "peculiar institution" of human bondage.

Jefferson departed for Provence from Paris on February 28, 1787. It was a journey that took him through Dijon, Avignon, and Marseilles. At that point he decided to continue eastward, again for practical reasons (to study agriculture), crossing into Italy on April 10. There he visited Turin, Milan, and Genoa but not Rome, Venice, or Vicenza, before returning to France on May 2. He typically visited the main sights of towns he passed through, like the Gothic cathedral of Sens, the palace of the dukes of Burgundy in Dijon in Burgundy, and the cathedral of Milan. He would sometimes climb a church tower to give himself the broadest vista of the place and bought maps and city plans that would help him in planning cities in the United States.[8] His route south followed a trail of the best-preserved Roman buildings in France, from Lyons to Fréjus on the Mediterranean.

Jefferson's choice of this itinerary betrayed the influence of Claude-Louis Clérisseau. Because of the accomplished Parisian draftsman and architect's great understanding of ancient Roman architecture, Jefferson had engaged Clérisseau in August 1786 to help design the new capitol building in Richmond, Virginia, one that would "unite economy with elegance and dignity." Jefferson had difficulty identifying an architect aligned with his classical tastes: "I was a considerable time before I could find an architect whose taste had been formed on a study of the antient models of this art, the styles of architecture in this capital being far from chaste."[9] His quest met with success, however: "I at length heard of one, to who I immediately addressed myself, and who perfectly fulfills my wishes. He has studied 20 years in Rome, and has given proofs of his skill and taste by a publication of some antiquities of this country."[10] Jefferson had decided by September 1785 to model the new Virginia capitol after one of the antiquities published in that book, one he knew from Palladio, who had also published in chapter

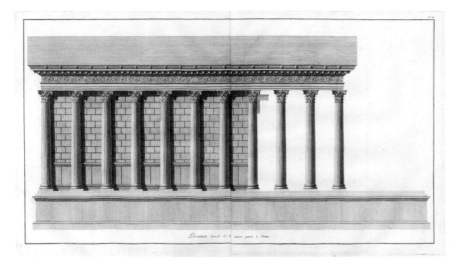

Fig. 3. Charles-Louis Clérisseau (French, 1722–1820), Maison Carrée, side elevation, in *Antiquités de la France, première parti: Monumens de Nîsmes* (Paris: Pierres, 1778), plate 3. University of Zürich

Fig. 4. Richard de Bas à Ambert d'Auvergne, watermark (papermaker), ruled paper, 1782. 35.9 x 47.6 cm. Thomas Jefferson Memorial Foundation at Monticello, Nr. 1962-1-53

28 of the last of his *Quattro libri* a plan of the Maison Carrée ("Square House," completed c. AD 2), or more accurately, the Temple to Caius and Lucius Caesar, Augustus's deified grandsons and presumed heirs. Jefferson reasoned to the directors of the building project, James Buchanan and William Hay, that this temple was "the most perfect and precious remain of antiquity in existence" and "has pleased universally for 2000 years . . . noble beyond expression, and would have done honour to our country as presenting to travelers a morsel of taste in our infancy promising much for our maturer age," a model approved by "the suffrage of the world."[11] Jefferson thus designed the new "temple to democracy" from a Roman model as published in Palladio's books, adapted with the help of a master draftsman, before even having seen the Maison Carrée himself. Both Palladio and Clérisseau helpfully published the Maison Carrée, along with the second-century Temple of Diana in Nîmes (actually the library of a grotto complex around a sacred spring), as reconstructions and models. Jefferson acquired Clérisseau's 1778 *Antiquités de la France, première parti: Monumens de Nîsmes*, which included these monuments and more, from its author in Paris just before his departure south to Provence (fig. 3), and it clearly guided his travel plans.[12]

Jefferson was a true amateur architect, never having trained as a builder. He relied on architects like Clérisseau and other builders to execute his sketches and designs, which he often plotted on graph paper, an aid he discovered in Paris (fig. 4). While his father, Peter Jefferson, had been a surveyor and cartographer—most remembered today for the definitive map of Virginia published with Joshua Fry in 1753 (plate 12)—Thomas Jefferson studied and practiced law, with architecture remaining a kind of pastime. He drew on his considerable library of architecture books to learn principles of design. He began collecting architecture books while still a law student at the College of William & Mary with the acquisition of Giacomo Leoni's 1715 English edition of *The Architecture of A. Palladio in Four Books* and James Gibbs's 1738 edition of *Rules for Drawing the Several Parts of Architecture* (fig. 5). Jefferson's Grand Tour transformed him from a "talented provincial to travelled sophisticate," but more than simple sophistication, his travel resulted in the continual elevation of his own practice through the incorporation of ancient models that expressed his ideals.

In his letter of March 20, 1787, to his friend Madame de Tessé, grande *saloniste* and aunt by marriage to the Marquis de Lafayette, Jefferson waxed poetic about all the ancient monuments that "nourished me from Lyon to Nimes," but wrote that the Maison Carrée "was the best morsel of antient architecture now remaining" and that he had spent an entire day gazing at it "like a lover at his mistress." He felt "immersed in antiquities from morning to night . . . for me, the city of Rome is actually existing in all the splendor of its empire."[13] A week later he wrote to his secretary William Short that "the remains of antiquity . . . are more in number, and less injured by time than I expected, and have been to me a great treat. Those at Nismes, both in dignity and preservation, stand first."[14] Jefferson also visited the arena of Nîmes and the nearby Pont du Garde, key elements of a Roman town, which no doubt added to his intense appreciation of the site.

One of the most well-preserved Roman sites that Jefferson saw in the South of France was the city of Orange, whose immense theater remained intact, as did its triumphal arch of Marius.[15] Any intrusions into what for Jefferson was a vision of perfection provoked him to irritations that he expressed to Tessé. Upon discovering that the "Praetorian Palace" of Vienne (the first-century Temple of Augustus and Livia) had been "defaced" by "Barbarians," transformed into a church through the stripping of Corinthian columns in order to add a Gothic window, he wrote to Tessé, "you would have seen me more angry than I ever hope you will see me" and was further horrified that local officials did not prevent the arena at Orange from being dismantled for paving material (fig. 6).[16]

Jefferson could not, however, depend on local craftsmen to produce temples like those he encountered in his travels or in the books of Palladio and Clérisseau, and had to make adjustments to his design for the Virginia State Capitol, exchanging the Maison Carrée's Corinthian order for the Ionic "on account of the difficulty of the Corinthian Capitals."[17] Other changes were called for as well: he reduced the Maison Carrée's porch from three rows of columns to two so as not to "darken the apartments," and exchanged the fluted half-columns of the Nîmes building for flat walls animated by three stories of windows and panels containing garlands. These adjustments are visible in the 1:60 scale plaster model produced by Jean-Pierre Fouquet that Jefferson ordered in December 1786 to guide the workmen in Richmond, who, Jefferson feared, were "not very expert in their art" (fig. 7).[18] The finished building nevertheless deviated

Fig. 5. James Gibbs (Scottish, 1682–1754), frontispiece, *Rules for Drawing the Several Parts of Architecture* (London: W. Bowyer, 1732). Library of Congress, NA2841.G5 Pre-1801 Coll: fol 1753 (3rd ed.)

Fig. 6. Temple of Augustus and Livia, Vienne, France, 1st century AD

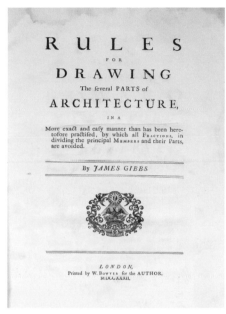

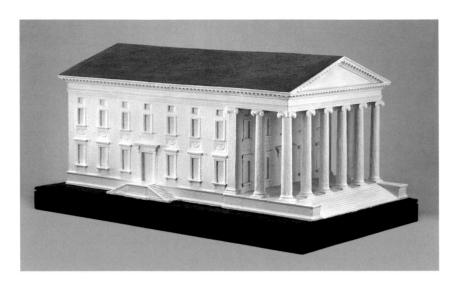

Fig. 7. Jean-Pierre Fouquet (French, 1752–1829), plaster model (1785–86) for Virginia Capitol (completed 1788). Collection of the Virginia State Library and Archives, Richmond, Courtesy of the Virginia General Assembly

markedly from the model. The manufacture of the capitol was not all of stone but partially of its imitation in brick, wood, and stucco, much the way Palladio's own projects were constructed. Jefferson also deferred "with reluctance" to Clérisseau's preference for Vincenzo Scamozzi's design for Ionic capitals with diagonal volutes, as published in book 6 of the 1615 *Dell'idea dell'architettura universale*, rather than "the more noble capital of antiquity" with parallel volutes (fig. 8, plate 18).[19] Not only the classical orders and materials but also the situation of the building were adjusted in the transposition to America; Jefferson placed his version of the Maison Carrée, designed to dominate a public square of a Roman forum, on a hill in a still-untamed natural setting overlooking the James River (see M. Wilson essay, fig. 1).

The pseudo-peripteral Maison Carrée and the Richmond capitol imitated in their gabled roofs standard rectangular Greek peristyle temples like the Temple of Theseus. Jefferson knew this temple from his copy of Julien-David Le Roy's 1758 *Les ruines des plus beaux monuments de la Grèce* (fig. 9). Unlike the Parthenon, however, the Maison Carrée also stood on the high base typical of Roman temples, as advocated by the Roman architect Vitruvius. Like Palladio and other devotees of Vitruvius, Jefferson preferred the Roman imitation to the Greek original. Not until the Greek War of Independence of 1832 gave access to that country's antiquities to tourists did a wave of neo-Hellenism take hold more generally in architecture and taste. Benjamin Henry Latrobe, the architect commissioned by Jefferson to complete the US Capitol in Washington, represented a new generation whose preference was tilting toward the original Greek designs. As Latrobe himself stated emphatically, "I am a bigoted Greek in the condemnation of the Roman Architecture of Baalbek, Spaletro, Palmyra and of all the buildings erected subsequent to Hadrian's reign."[20] Latrobe's student, the architect Robert Mills, described Jefferson, in contrast, as "altogether Roman in his taste for architecture."[21]

Leaving Nîmes on March 24, Jefferson continued south and visited the ancient site of Glanum near Saint-Remy. There he saw the Tomb of the Julii and the adjacent triumphal arch, and later acquired a landscape print of the site (fig. 10).[22] After Glanum, he reached one of the goals of his trip, Aix-en-Provence and its healing mineral waters. He took the treatment there for his right wrist, but wrote Short that "having taken 40. douches there without any sensible benefit," he judged the waters ineffective and would discontinue the treatments, which he did not repeat during the return journey.[23] He then continued to Marseilles, where he learned about rice production in France, a crop whose cultivation he sought to improve in the United States. What he learned there apparently served as adequate

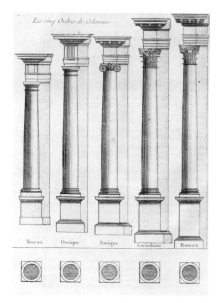

Fig. 8. Vincenzo Scamozzi (Italian, 1548–1616), *Les cinq ordres*, in *Oeuvres d'architecture de Vincent Scamozzi* (Paris: Jombert, 1764). Washington University, NA2812.S57 1764

Fig. 9. Julien-David Le Roy (French, probably 1724–1803), Temple of Theseus, Athens, in *Les ruines des plus beaux monuments de la Grèce* (Paris: Guérin and Delatour, 1758), plate 11. National Gallery of Art, Washington, DC, Mark J. Millard Architectural Collection, 1985.61.2497

Fig. 10. Abbé Bernard Lamy (French, 1640–1715), *Description de deux monuments antiques qui subsistent près la ville de Saint-Remy en Provence* (Paris: Pasquier, 1779), fold-out illustration. Österreichische Nationalbibliothek

pretext to visit Piedmont, Italy, to learn yet more about growing rice, which was a closely guarded secret there.[24] Moving toward the Italian frontier, he stopped to see ruins at Fréjus, another ancient Roman site. The remains of the aqueduct, theater, amphitheater, and harbor beacon all drew his admiration there, but in the end none of the other ruins had the impact of those at Nîmes.

Jefferson complained to his old professor George Wythe that his "time allowed me to go no further than Turin, Milan and Genoa; consequently I scarcely got onto classical ground." He wrote to Maria Cosway that his short Italian stay, from April 10 to May 2, 1787, only gave him a "peep into Elysium"[25] because he felt bound to focus on practical and patriotic pursuits. He

Fig. 11. Milan Cathedral, Italy. Gelatin silver stereograph card, published by J. F. Jarvis, 1897. Chrysler Museum of Art, Gift of Mrs. George G. Martin, Jr., O.6137

had declared to William Short that his only objective in Italy was witnessing the growing and cleaning of rice and that he anticipated going no farther east than Turin, where he spent some time and visited key Baroque monuments. However, he did continue east from Turin, visiting Vercelli to closely examine rice production and clandestinely procure, at considerable risk to his life, seed rice that he eventually smuggled to planters in South Carolina.[26] He then went yet farther east, to Milan, where he apparently bypassed Leonardo's *Last Supper* in favor of the city's immense Gothic cathedral, where his bias against Gothic architecture was especially pronounced (fig. 11). In his "Hints to Americans Travelling in Europe," he wrote, "The Cathedral of Milan is a worthy object of philosophical contemplation, to be placed among the rarest instances of the misuse of money. On viewing the churches of Italy, it is evident without calculation that the same expense would have sufficed to throw the Appenines into the Adriatic and thereby render it terra firma from Leghorn to Constantinople." In this, he merely echoed his guidebook, Joseph Addison's 1705 *Remarks on Several Parts of Italy*, which noted, "This profusion of stone, though astonishing to strangers, is not so wonderful in a country that has so many veins of it running through its bowels."[27] Jefferson continued in his letter to Cosway, "I entered [Elysium] at one door, and came out at another. . . . I calculated the hours it would have taken to carry me on to Rome. But they were exactly so many more than I could spare. Was not this provoking? In thirty hours from Milan I could have been at the espousals of the Doge and the Adriatic, but I am born to lose everything I love."[28] His regret surfaces again in his "Hints to Americans Travelling in Europe": "When you are doubting whether a thing is worth the trouble of going to see, recollect that you will never again be so near it, that you may repent the not having seen it, but can never repent having seen it."[29]

In the few words he left behind about what the brevity of his stay in Italy caused him to miss, however, Jefferson never mentioned Palladio. Instead of visiting Palladio's buildings, Jefferson was led by recently published guidebooks. To Jefferson, guidebooks written by kindred spirits freed one from depending on others and also helped guide memory: "Before entering Italy buy Addison's travels," he advised. "He visited that country as a classical amateur, and it gives infinite pleasure to apply one's classical reading on the spot. Besides it aids our future recollection of the place."[30] Addison stood out as "classical" in Jefferson's outlook, someone who would connect the landscape to the kinds of education that he, Short, and Short's fellows had enjoyed and that motivated them to seek out traces of antiquity in their European travels.

Jefferson spent three precious days in the republic of Genoa, which boasted no ruins of ancient Rome but many stately homes.[31] It was in Genoa that he ordered stone mantelpieces for Monticello from Antonio Capellano, following his own sketched designs.[32] In Genoa he encountered the square court of the Doria Palace, a structure he recommended Short and his friends visit, and likely himself used as a model for the initial design of the University of Virginia. Genoa was the only republic Jefferson had visited thus far, and he noted that freedom of citizens did not proceed from or depend on material wealth or trade but was a function of government. He frequently noted the freedom and prosperity of the peasants along the way on his travels, a habit he also recommended to Short in his "Hints to Americans Travelling in Europe": "Examine their [rulers'] influence on the happiness of the people: take every possible occasion of entering into the hovels of the labourers, and especially at the moments of their repast, see what they eat, how they are cloathed, whether they are obliged to labour too hard; whether the government or their landlord takes from them an unjust proportion of their labour; on what footing stands the property they call their own, their personal liberty &c."[33] Jefferson's eye was as much on models of government, and their improvement, as on architecture.

At this point, instead of continuing on to Rome, Vicenza, or Venice, Jefferson crossed back into France. Some have speculated that it was Clérisseau's influence that dissuaded him from visiting Vicenza and Venice. Clérisseau had himself visited Vicenza during long years of working with the renowned British Neoclassical designer and architect Robert Adam, who criticized Palladio's villas as "pondersome" and "disgustful" and further berated Palladio as a "fortunate genius who purchased a reputation at an easy rate," whose plans and elevations were "ill-adjusted."[34] It is doubtful, however, that such views reached or affected Jefferson through Clérisseau, who seems to have encouraged the American instead to do as both he and Palladio had done: experience the buildings of Roman antiquity.

Decades later, in 1816, Jefferson's friend Isaac A. Coles testified to Jefferson's enduring attachment to Palladio, writing to a friend that Jefferson recommended Palladio's *Quattro libri* to him in a now-famous quote: "Palladio he said was the Bible. . . . You should get it & stick close to it."[35] One of Jefferson's builders, Thomas Blackburn, literally enacted this advice in his elaborate copies after key pages in the *Quattro libri*. Blackburn's subsequent Neoclassical buildings in Virginia show Jefferson's success in

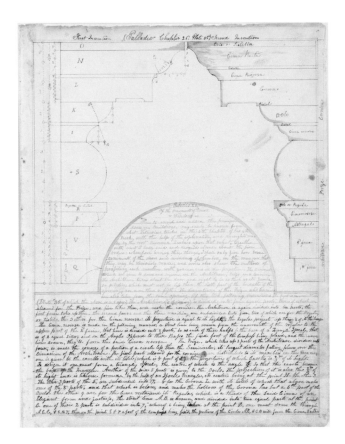

Fig. 12. Thomas R. Blackburn (American, 1795–1867), copy after Palladio's *Quattro libri*, chapter 26, on the ornamentation of doors and windows, in *Architectural Drawing Books*, c. 1825–58, 1:19. Virginia Museum of History and Culture, Mss 5:10 B5628:1

Fig. 13. Designed by Andrej and Ewa Soltan, constructed by "Ballico-Officina Modellisti," model of Palladio's Tempietto di Villa Barbaro, Maser, 1971. Wood, plywood, and porcelain. Palladio Museum, Vicenza, M.AP.08

Fig. 14. Robert Turnbull Macpherson (Scottish, 1814–1872), *The Pantheon, from the Piazza della Rotonda*, 1858. Albumen print from wet collodion negative. Chrysler Museum of Art, Museum purchase, in memory of Alice R. and Sol B. Frank, 2018.3

inculcating his classicizing taste in a new generation of builders (fig. 12). Thus Jefferson profoundly changed the course of American architecture, just as he had set out to do. Jefferson never wrote a book on architecture. Instead he built the University of Virginia, partly as a means to teach classical architecture and realize his hope that the architecture of America would be elevated by the following of these models. Each pavilion represented a different classical order, while the Rotunda echoed both Palladio's Tempietto di Villa Barbaro in Maser and its model, the ancient Pantheon in Rome (figs. 13, 14).

On his return journey through France, Jefferson did not attempt another treatment of his wrist at the mineral springs, but he did return to Nîmes and revisit its ancient sites. He then continued west to Montpellier before arriving at the head of the Canal du Midi at Sète. The canal was of great interest to Jefferson because the United States had need of canals, and moreover this ingenious canal passed through mountains and a division of water direction, unlike those in the Low Countries, for example. It remained in use nearly year-round, linking the Mediterranean with the Atlantic and thus allowing trade to proceed unimpeded by such perils as pirates and storms. Such a grand project, a model for the Erie Canal and other American ventures, recalled the Roman aqueducts whose remains Jefferson had seen at Nîmes, and was the kind of structure whose design could directly benefit the nascent American republic in increasing trade and agriculture.

Jefferson's next trip, to Holland, was on official business; there he would join John Adams in meetings to renegotiate debts. He departed March 4, 1788, and stayed in Rotterdam, The Hague, and Amsterdam, encountering a number of seventeenth-century buildings designed by Jacob van Campen, the most influential advocate of Palladio's style, which thereby became closely identified with the flourishing of economic and cultural activity during the Dutch Republic's "Golden Age."[36] While he would have encountered nearly every major public building by van Campen, the only one Jefferson noted was the 1641 Mauritshuis in The Hague (fig. 15). Its pedimented façade, like that of van Campen's epic 1648 Town Hall of Amsterdam, closely follows Palladio's facade for the Villa Pisani, and its exposed brick and stone construction, partly a response to the lack of any local source for building stone, may have been for Jefferson, who faced the same problem, an affirmation of the way he had built the exterior of Monticello.[37] Painter Jan van der Heyden also gave voice to Dutch Palladianism in his c. 1670 *An Architectural Fantasy*, in which a Palladian country villa and portal are beautifully situated beside a classical brick-and-stone pavilion that recalls the Mauritshuis (fig. 16).

Fig. 15. Bartholomeus van Hove (Dutch, 1790–1880), *The Mauritshuis in The Hague*, 1825. Oil on panel. Rijksmuseum, Amsterdam, SK-A-1369

Fig. 16. Jan van der Heyden (Dutch, 1637–1712), *An Architectural Fantasy*, c. 1670. Oil on panel. National Gallery of Art, Washington, DC, Ailsa Mellon Bruce Fund, 1968.13.1

One house in Holland was sufficiently notable for Jefferson to capture its design in a sketch, which he almost never did in Europe. That house, Welgelegen, at that moment being completed by the Dutch-American financier Henry Hope for his prodigious art collection, was of Palladian design and featured a dramatic pedimented center pavilion of paired columns (fig. 17). Jefferson regarded it as the finest in Holland, and among the best on the continent. The two wings to the central pavilion, whose "odd but pleasing effect" he noted, have since been taken down.[38] Through the work of van Campen, his acolyte Pieter Post, and David Vingboons, Palladianism became the house style of the Dutch republic. Jefferson arrived in Holland at a peculiar moment, months after the Prince of Orange had staged a Prussian-backed coup and ended centuries of republican government. Jefferson would have been aware that Palladianism had no political identity in Holland, having been employed by the hereditary princes of Orange and the republican burghers of Amsterdam alike.[39]

Jefferson continued from Amsterdam to Utrecht and thence toward Nijmegen, crossing into Germany on April 1, 1788. Near Duisberg, he wrote in his "Hints to Americans Travelling in Europe," he had attempted to inquire about the location of the site of the Battle of the Teutoberg Forest (AD 9), the spectacular defeat of the army of the Roman general Varus that would define the Rhine as the border of the Roman Empire. Jefferson's strong language skills failed him in this instance; he lacked any skill in the German tongue and left without achieving his goal, an episode that demonstrated how narrowly his classical education and modern guidebooks (or, in this case, the lack thereof) guided his travels.[40] His notes were on practical matters such as the production of bread and wine and the source of millstones, but also the contents of art collections and the quality of inns. There were few buildings of note along his route, but the art collection of the elector at Düsseldorf drew his attention. In a letter to Maria Cosway he praised a highly naturalistic painting of *Abraham and Hagar* by the seventeenth-century Dutch artist Adriaen van der Werff, reasoning that "I am but a son of nature, loving what I see & feel, without being able to give a reason, nor caring much whether there be one." Jefferson disparaged the "old faded red things of [Peter Paul] Rubens," that favorite artist of absolute monarchs, a judgment for which he would have to endure the scorn of his own portraitist, John Trumbull.[41] To Madame de Tessé he had confided his great affection for a Baroque sculpture of Diana and Endymion by René-Michel Slodtz he had seen near Paris (fig. 18).[42] Unlike his taste in architecture, Jefferson's taste in art was not rigidly Neoclassical.

Jefferson's travels through France, Italy, Holland, and Germany were by no means a traditional Grand Tour of Europe. Few English and German travelers would have sought out the Languedoc canal or the rice fields of Piedmont, or had their classically trained imagination satisfied with the Roman monuments of provincial Nîmes. Jefferson's goals as he headed south, however, were aligned with the needs of his most important building project: the young American republic. One of these needs was to elevate the republic's architecture by constructing buildings modeled after those of classical antiquity, a goal that was largely addressed by building the Virginia State Capitol after the model of the Maison Carrée in Nîmes, prior to actually encountering the original. Jefferson traveled alone and followed an itinerary of his own devising, taking few notes and making fewer sketches along the way while traveling through Orange, Nîmes, and Fréjus. He was flexible and spontaneous yet rigid about his goals, deciding only in Marseilles to visit Italy for its rice fields and then expressing regret to Maria Cosway about how close he had come to Rome and Venice without being able to visit them. His experiences of Roman architecture in France, which he felt were of value equal to or greater than those in Rome itself, were adequate to nourish his imagination for the balance of his architectural career and have made their impact felt continuously since then. His direct experience of Palladianism all over Europe, and his encounter with ancient Roman buildings in France, all contributed to the development of the mature Jeffersonian style, whose influence has persisted in the United States for centuries.

Fig. 17. Paviljoen Welgelegen, Haarlem, completed 1789

Fig. 18. René-Michel Slodtz (French, 1705–1764), *Diana and Endymion*, 1740. Marble. Private collection, France

NOTES

1. William Howard Adams, *The Paris Years of Thomas Jefferson* (New Haven: Yale University Press, 1997), 108.
2. Ibid., 109.
3. Thomas Jefferson, *Notes on the State of Virginia* (London: Stockade, 1787), nr. 15.
4. George Green Shackleford, *Thomas Jefferson's Travels in Europe, 1784–1789* (Baltimore: Johns Hopkins University Press, 1995), 7.
5. "From Thomas Jefferson to James Monroe, 18 December 1786," *Founders Online*, National Archives, last modified June 13, 2018, http://founders.archives.gov/documents/Jefferson/01-10-02-0465. [Original source: *The Papers of Thomas Jefferson*, vol. 10, *22 June–31 December 1786*, ed. Julian P. Boyd (Princeton, NJ: Princeton University Press, 1954), 611–13.]
6. "Jefferson's Hints to Americans Travelling in Europe, 19 June 1788," *Founders Online*, National Archives, last modified June 13, 2018, http://founders.archives.gov/documents/Jefferson/01-13-02-0173. [Original source: *The Papers of Thomas Jefferson*, vol. 13, *March–7 October 1788*, ed. Julian P. Boyd (Princeton, NJ: Princeton University Press, 1956), 264–76.]
7. Hugh Howard, *Dr. Kimball and Mr. Jefferson: Discovering the Founding Fathers of American Architecture* (New York: Bloomsbury, 2006), 62.
8. Shackleford, *Jefferson's Travels*, 77.
9. Thomas Jefferson to James Buchanan and William Hay, Paris, August 13, 1785, in *The Papers of Thomas Jefferson*, vol. 7, *2 March 1784–25 February, 1785*, ed. Julian P. Boyd (Princeton, NJ: Princeton University Press, 1953), 366; reprinted in J. McCormick, *Charles-Louis Clérisseau and the Genesis of Neo-Classicism* (Cambridge, MA: MIT Press, 1990), 191.
10. Jefferson's enduring affection for Clérisseau was expressed in his acquisition of gifts for the older master. He commissioned a wooden copy of an ancient *askos*, or wine ewer, at Nîmes in 1787, and then had it reproduced in silver for Clérisseau, although the gift was never delivered. A classicizing amphora-like silver coffeepot was fashioned in Paris by Jean-Baptiste-Claude Odiot for Clérisseau as well. Shackleford, *Jefferson's Travels*, 14; McCormick, *Clérisseau*, 197.
11. Thomas Jefferson to James Buchanan and William Hay, Paris, January 26, 1786, *Papers*, 8:366, in McCormick, *Clérisseau*, 191–92.
12. Adams, *Paris Years*, 110.
13. "From Thomas Jefferson to Madame de Tessé, 20 March 1787," *Founders Online*, National Archives, last modified June 13, 2018, http://founders.archives.gov/documents/Jefferson/01-11-02-0229. [Original source: *The Papers of Thomas Jefferson*, vol. 11, *1 January–6 August 1787*, ed. Julian P. Boyd (Princeton, NJ: Princeton University Press, 1955), 226–28.]
14. Howard, *Dr. Kimball and Mr. Jefferson*, 63.
15. Shackleford, *Jefferson's Travels*, 82.
16. Ibid., 108.
17. Jefferson to Buchanan and Hay, January 26, 1786.
18. Jefferson scholar Fiske Kimball posited that these changes, visible in a drawing by Jefferson, corrected by Clérisseau, were adaptations of the pure structure of the original to the style of the modern French architect. McCormick, *Clérisseau*, 197.
19. Ibid., 192; Calder Loth, *Classical Notes: The Scamozzi Ionic Capital*, https://www.classicist.org/articles/classical-comments-the-scamozzi-ionic-capital/.
20. Benjamin Latrobe, *The Journal of Latrobe* (New York: D. Appleton, 1905), 139, viewed on www.questia.com.
21. Howard, *Dr. Kimball and Mr. Jefferson*, 261.
22. Jefferson acquired a landscape print showing the site and monuments at Glanum. It must be that of Abbé C. Lamy, *Description de deux monuments antiques qui subsistent près de la ville de Saint-Remy en Provence* (Paris: Pasquier, 1779); Shackleford, *Jefferson's Travels*, 84.
23. "From Thomas Jefferson to William Short, 7 April 1787," *Founders Online*, National Archives, last modified June 13, 2018, http://founders.archives.gov/documents/Jefferson/01-11-02-0269. [Original source: *The Papers of Thomas Jefferson*, vol. 11, *1 January–6 August 1787*, ed. Julian P. Boyd (Princeton, NJ: Princeton University Press, 1955), 280–81.]
24. Shackleford, *Jefferson's Travels*, 84.
25. Ibid., 89.
26. Ibid., 94–95.
27. Joseph Addison, *Remarks on Several Parts of Italy, &c. in the Years 1701, 1702 and 1703* (London: Tonson, 1705), 27–28.
28. "From Thomas Jefferson to Maria Cosway, 1 July 1787," *Founders Online*, National Archives, last modified June 13, 2018, http://founders.archives.gov/documents/Jefferson/01-11-02-0435. [Original source: *The Papers of Thomas Jefferson*, vol. 11, *1 January–6 August 1787*, ed. Julian P. Boyd (Princeton, NJ: Princeton University Press, 1955), 519–20.]
29. "Jefferson's Hints."
30. Ibid.
31. Giacomo Brusco, *Description des beautés de Genes et ses environs* (Genoa: Gravier, 1768).
32. Shackleford, *Jefferson's Travels*, 100.
33. "Jefferson's Hints."
34. Shackleford, *Jefferson's Travels*, 107.
35. "Isaac A. Coles's Account of a Conversation with Thomas Jefferson, [before 23 February 1816]," *Founders Online*, National Archives, last modified June 13, 2018, http://founders.archives.gov/documents/Jefferson/03-09-02-0336. [Original source: *The Papers of Thomas Jefferson*, Retirement Series, vol. 9, *September 1815 to April 1816*, ed. J. Jefferson Looney (Princeton, NJ: Princeton University Press, 2012), 500–502.]
36. Konrad Ottenheym, "Classicism in the Northern Netherlands in the Seventeenth Century," in *Palladio and Northern Europe: Books, Travellers, Architects*, ed. Guido Beltramini et al. (Vicenza, Italy: Museo Palladio, 1999), 152.
37. Konrad Ottenheym, "Palladio's *Quattro Libri* in Seventeenth Century Holland: Models for Courtier and Citizens," in *Palladio, 1508–2008: Il simposio del cinquecentenario*, ed. Franco Barbieri, Donata Battiloti, and Guido Beltramini (Venice: Marsilio, 2008), 335–37.
38. *Papers* 13, 16, at http://catdir.loc.gov/catdir/toc/becites/main/jefferson/50007486.v13.toc.html.
39. Christa de Jonge, "High-Flown Ideals, Ambitious Stratagems? On the 'Problem' of Palladio's Success in Northern Europe," in Barbieri, Battiloti, and Beltramini, *Palladio, 1508–2008*, 340; Shackleford, *Jefferson's Travels*, 137.
40. "Jefferson's Hints."
41. "Thomas Jefferson to Maria Cosway, 24 April 1788," *Founders Online*, National Archives, version of January 18, 2019, https://founders.archives.gov/documents/Jefferson/01-13-02-0027. [Original source: *The Papers of Thomas Jefferson*, vol. 13, *March–7 October 1788*, ed. Julian P. Boyd (Princeton, NJ: Princeton University Press, 1956), 103–4.]. Shackleford, *Jefferson's Travels*, 141.
42. "From Thomas Jefferson to Madame de Tessé, 20 March 1787," in *Thomas Jefferson Travels: Selected Writings, 1784–1789*, ed. Anthony Brandt (Washington, DC: National Geographic Society, 2006), 171; Shackleford, *Jefferson's Travels*, 79.

BOOKS, BUILDINGS, AND THE SPACES OF DEMOCRACY

Jefferson's Library from Paris to Washington

BARRY BERGDOLL

In Paris, where Thomas Jefferson lived for five years from August 1784 to September 1789, two of the future president's great passions came together: architecture and books. Almost from the moment he arrived "on the vaunted scene of Europe,"[1] Jefferson sought to accumulate direct experiences and knowledge of an architectural history much longer than that of the young American republic. He would, famously, work with the French architect, painter, and cicerone Charles-Louis Clérisseau to adapt the model of the first-century Roman temple known as the Maison Carrée at Nîmes for the new state house of Virginia at Richmond. But his was no mission of historical recovery. Rather, Jefferson was open to the most current thinking about architecture. He was an observer of the building boom during the years that turned out to be the twilight of the reign of Louis XVI, and to the lively discussion of public architecture and monuments in the city that had been slowly gaining force since the 1750s. Jefferson would experience the first dramatic events of the French Revolution in July 1789. He would follow the subsequent debates back at home during the next decade over how a new French national capital could be crafted within the historic fabric of Paris, which would replace Versailles as the seat of power after 1792. His love affair with eternal values, which he believed were represented by ancient architecture and had the capacity to put a young republic on a footing equal to the great nations within the history of civilization, was tempered always by an engagement in the political spectacles of radical regime changes on both sides of the Atlantic.

Books and buildings were, of course, passions for Jefferson from his student days in Williamsburg to his many-faceted public life, with roles in the newly designated Virginia state capital at Richmond, as US minister to France in Paris and Versailles, and then in the US capital, as it moved during his political career from New York to Philadelphia to Washington, one of the last new capitals planned in the eighteenth century. Books and buildings continued to be instrumental, finally, in his planning of the University of

Virginia in the decades after his presidency. He would be involved in selecting and obtaining works for two of the great libraries of the early republic: the new Library of Congress and that for the University of Virginia, for which he drew up buying lists, notably on art and architecture.[2] Jefferson's ability to read English, Italian, and French meant that his European years were ones of reading as much as of looking. He was therefore one of the earliest Americans to understand architecture as not only the science of building but also an intellectual discipline, a body of knowledge and a practice with a role in the formation of citizens in a new form of political life.

Paris was a construction site of monumental stone buildings, most with public functions, a striking contrast with the brick building traditions of the colonial towns of the American East Coast, from Boston to Savannah. "While at Paris, I was violently smitten with the Hôtel de Salm, and used to go to the Thuileries [across the river from the building] almost daily to look at it,"[3] Jefferson wrote to a friend in 1787, explaining his admiration for this monument that changed the very face of Paris along its riverbanks. The Hôtel de Salm was indeed a fascinating building for Jefferson, not only in that it represented a new approach to residential planning and to the very image of a stately house but also because it blurred distinctions between private architecture and the recently emerged ethos of institutional buildings as public monuments. In this regard, the Hôtel de Salm and the nearby building for the surgical faculty, architect Jacques Gondoin's École de Chirurgie, were architectural cousins. One housed a prominent private citizen, while the other served as a monument to the public good of expanding knowledge of medical intervention to promote public health. Both were under construction on the Left Bank during the first two years of Jefferson's sojourn.

The Hôtel de Salm design combined the traditions of French *hôtel* planning with an innovative embrace of the purity of classical architecture, expressed in a great freestanding Ionic colonnade. This stood before the house's forecourt, replete with a porte-cochère as triumphal arch, a motif shared by Gondoin's medical school. Both buildings followed the recommendation of architectural theorist Marc-Antoine (Abbé) Laugier (whose influential 1765 *Observations sur l'architecture* was, surprisingly, missing from Jefferson's library and later book lists) that public space could be increased by allowing a public view into the grand courtyards of buildings, which in the past had been hidden behind walls and grand opaque portals. Architect Pierre Rousseau combined a classical portico and a dome to create a monumental house for Prince Frederich III of Salm-Kyrbourg. Poised on the banks of the Seine, it was not only one of the most significant private undertakings of a period rich in inventive adaptations of classical forms to modern uses but also, famously, to have a very direct effect on the evolving design of Monticello, where over the following decades both Jefferson's private pleasures and his public persona would be accommodated. Begun in 1782, the Hôtel de Salm's construction spanned over five years, so that Jefferson tracked the construction of this monumental and palatial residence in fine-cut masonry until it was finally occupied in 1787. The trip across the river from his residence on the Right Bank became one of his favorite long walks through the capital.

Architectural design and new engineering prowess made possible some of the most ambitious buildings of the day, such as Jacques-Germain Soufflot's great church of Ste-Geneviève (1757–90), already in construction for some two decades before and during Jefferson's residency. Ste-Geneviève provided a compelling demonstration of the progressive interlocking of the aesthetic quest for an architecture that could shape values through spatial experience and the manipulation of light, and the pushing of limits through new engineering forms. Here Soufflot reduced refined structure to its most lucid minimum. He did so while creating an interior that impressed the visitor with the grandeur of its freestanding Corinthian columns holding aloft vaults shaped for efficient direction of structural forces to the columnar supports, as well as with the dramatic play of side and top lighting. The prowess of crowning this very open structure with a complex dome of three interlocking shells made it an object of wonder but also of anxiety, as shortly after Soufflot's death in 1780, structural cracks had already begun to appear. Explaining his method, today too easily pigeon-holed as Neoclassicism, as an act of creative and progressive synthesis, Soufflot's pupil Maximilien Brébion later spoke of "uniting . . . the purity of and magnificence of Greek architecture with the lightness and audacity of gothic construction."[4] In this way French Neoclassicism, as Jefferson experienced it, was anything but a blind revival of archaeological forms. Once he received the six volumes of architect Jean-Baptiste Rondelet's seminal treatise on the foundation of architecture in construction, *Traité théorique et pratique de l'art de bâtir* (1802–3), it would become even clearer to Jefferson how much Soufflot—and Rondelet, who succeeded Soufflot in completing Ste-Geneviève—had depended on an innovative French system of embedding iron supports within the masonry. This technique, a kind of forerunner of today's reinforced concrete, had already been developed in the late seventeenth century for the colonnade that Claude Perrault and Louis Le Vau designed for the east facade of the Louvre, which was lauded over and over again in Jefferson's growing collection of architectural books.

Jefferson would have ample stimulus to think of the way both architects and engineers were transforming Paris, and at the same time of the very notion of architecture. He witnessed the construction of the last of the bridges created by the French engineer Jean-Rodolphe Perronet, which connected the place Louis XV (today's place de la Concorde) to the Left Bank, creating a shortcut between what was then the Tuileries and the Hôtel de Salm. The prowess of French engineering in everything from spanning rivers to the design of towns was visible in the *plans-reliefs*, or city models, selectively on display in the Louvre galleries on the occasion of the annual art salon. These were of vital interest to Jefferson as he thought of the means necessary to unite the territory of the thirteen colonies now amalgamated into the United States. Paris's new architecture, from churches to bridges

INTÉRIEUR DE LA NOUVELLE SALLE DE COMÉDIE FRANÇAISE DE L'ANCIEN PROJET .

Fig. 1. Charles de Wailly (French, 1730–1798), interior of the new hall of the Comédie Française, 1776. Watercolor and graphite on paper, 59.5 x 93.5 cm. Musée Carnavalet, Paris, Acc. Nr. C. 6350

to the trio of great public buildings that restructured the map of the Left Bank—Jacques Antoine's Hôtel de la Monnaie (1767–75), the new Paris mint; the Odéon Theater (1767–83); and the École de Chirurgie—demonstrated the modernization of the city and unification of territory through design, and served equally as new places of public assembly, education, entertainment, and pleasure (fig. 1). The prestige enjoyed by the engineers employed by the crown after graduating from the École Royale des Ponts-et-Chaussées (Royal School of Bridges and Roads), founded in 1747, was to inspire Jefferson in his insistence that the United States needed an organized Army Corps of Engineers.

Jefferson's books were visual sources of models for new architecture. He amassed most of the key English and French plate books on ancient monuments, as well as critical French volumes on the fashionable new Parisian residential architecture, particularly those featuring examples of more modest dimensions that might serve in the New World. The role that his folio volumes played in his detailing of the classical orders or molding profiles in his own architectural designs, from his homes at Monticello and Poplar Forest to the new buildings of the University of Virginia, is well known. But his books also served as both visual and philosophical inspiration for designing public buildings for the United States. It was in these texts that he engaged with the growing philosophy that architecture was not only a record of the historical evolution of humanity but also an agent of progress, even of enlightenment, as he might find in the volumes of Denis Diderot's *Encyclopédie* that he offered to purchase as a key work for James Madison.

Julien-David Le Roy's *Les ruines des plus beaux monuments de la Grèce* (1758; rev. ed. 1770) was a compendium of measured drawings of the most important monuments Le Roy had visited in his pioneering travels to Ottoman-held Greece in the 1750s. It was also a demonstration of how principles of antiquity could be maintained through a chain of development, thus combining notions of absolute beauty with enlightenment notions of progress. This was clearest in Le Roy's plate showing the evolution of the temple, or religious building (fig. 2). In a similar plate created on the occasion of the laying of the cornerstone of Ste-Geneviève, Leroy traced the development of the form from ancient types through to modern churches that combined a basilican floor plan with a great dome, such as St. Peter's in Rome, as well as the two royal churches of Ste-Geneviève and of La Madeleine, under construction in Paris since 1764.

Ste-Geneviève's great dome, completed years after Soufflot's death in 1780 and after Jefferson had returned to the United States, was a major tourist attraction as a construction site. Unfinished and unconsecrated even as the French Revolution unfolded, the building was repurposed and rebaptized by the revolutionary government as the Panthéon, a secular and civic "Temple of Great Men," in 1791.[5] The three days of public mourning decreed by the new French national assembly to mark the passing of Benjamin Franklin, "the illustrious American who could seize both lightning from heaven and the scepter from tyrants," had highlighted the need for a new place of civic celebration, in this instance for a deist born outside the Catholic faith. A ceremony was held in the Halle aux Blés, which was draped in black and featured a sarcophagus serving as a base for a bust of Franklin. Honoré Gabriel Riqueti, comte de Mirabeau, referred to Franklin as the "first apostle of Liberty" in his eulogy, and the marquis de Lafayette spoke of the event as "the first homage solemnly paid to civic virtue."[6] If the French revolutionaries were inspired by the Americans in creating their cult of great men, as exemplars of civic virtue to be housed in the newly created Panthéon, the innovations of French public architecture were in turn to inspire Americans in their search for the forms of democratic polity.

The semicircular anatomical amphitheater of Gondoin's École de Chirurgie was easily accessible to the public and famed for the equality of its sight lines to the central podium for dissection (fig. 3). It later served as the prototype for the halls of legislative assembly in both Washington and in revolutionary Paris in the 1790s. There the egalitarian nature of its seating made the ancient Greek theater form an ideal configuration for those who came together to pass legislation. The semicircular theater form was both a functional and a symbolic spur to democratic debate. Gondoin suggested one way to roof this form, which in ancient Greece had been left open to the elements. Rather than a Roman coffered half dome, it was to the wooden dome developed in 1782–83 by the architects Jacques-Guillaume Legrand and Jacques Molinos to cover the open circular courtyard at the center of

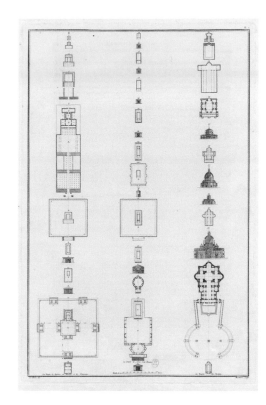

Fig. 2. Julien-David Le Roy (French, probably 1724–1803), the evolution of the forms of the temple, from *Les ruines des plus beaux monuments de la Grèce, considérées du côte de l'histoire et du côte de l'architecture* (Paris: Musier, 1770), plate 1. National Gallery of Art, Washington, DC, Mark J. Millard Architectural Collection, 1985.61.2497

PL. XXIX.

Fig. 3. Jacques Gondoin (French, 1737–1818),
view of the anatomy theater at the École de
Chirurgie, in *Description des écoles de
chirurgie* (Paris: Cellot et Jombert, 1780), plate
29. Bibliothèque Nationale de France,
ark:/12148/bpt6k5688688j

Nicolas Le Camus de Mézières's Halle aux Blés (grain market) of 1763–67 that Jefferson looked for inspiration when remodeling the US House of Representatives chamber in the years after 1803. Legrand and Molinos had transformed a utilitarian building into a place of public assembly by crowning it with a wooden dome, using an innovative interpretation of a French Renaissance system of building the dome in segments. (Jefferson could study this system in his copy of Philibert de l'Orme's 1576 *Nouvelles inventions pour bien bastir et à petits fraiz*, which he acquired in Paris and sold with his library to Congress, a second copy later to be ordered for his university.) The wooden dome in Paris integrated long lozenges of glass between wooden ribs to transform the center of the building into a spectacle of daylight, a form that Jefferson explicitly required Benjamin Henry Latrobe, the new architect of the US Capitol under Jefferson's presidency, to study.

In Paris, Jefferson had witnessed a city in transformation, one in which antique forms were embraced as much for their ability to represent new values and new notions of the public—a word much in debate at the period—as they were as signs of antiquarian erudition. In contrast to the dominant use of brick and wood in American construction from Boston to Savannah, Jefferson was able in Paris to observe the role of fine cut masonry in creating a sense of magnificence, grandeur, and public presence. He also observed a way of structuring a city around landmarks, which was to become a leitmotif of the planning of Washington, DC. The Jardin des Tuileries presented not simply a model of an urban garden and promenade but also one of the first royal spaces open for public use, thus offering a place to reflect on what lessons the urban transformation of a monarchy might offer to the task at home. This was the case in Virginia, but also in the wider evolving debate on where the institutions of the newly minted United States of America might best be achieved, in a newly created city for a new country or in a remodeled urban center such as New York or Philadelphia. Indeed, it was in Philadelphia that the Constitutional Congress had met during the summer of 1787 to draft the Constitution, which became the governing document of the young country a few months after Jefferson's return, when Rhode Island completed the state-by-state ratification of this new architecture for democracy.

Equally, Paris was a center of learning that spread far beyond its famed university into the great private libraries and a lively market for books. "While residing in Paris, I devoted every afternoon I was disengaged, for a summer or two, in examining all the principal bookstores, turning over every book with my own hand, and putting by everything which was related to America, and indeed whatever was rare and valuable in every science,"[7] Jefferson recalled to his friend Samuel H. Smith years later. Forming a library was for Jefferson not merely a stage in his lifelong self-education and engagement with ideas. He was building not simply his private estate but also a new national capital and later a university, the first in the United States to adopt this title instead of the older, more limited term *college*. Shortly after his arrival in Paris, it became clear that books needed to be supplied to those back at home who were directly making the decisions that would build the new republic in everything from its Constitution, adopted in the final moments of Jefferson's sojourn, to its new buildings, to the decision, ultimately made a few years after his return, to lay out a new capital city on the banks of the Potomac. In November 1784 Jefferson wrote to James Madison, "I shall subjoin the few books I ventured to buy for you. I have been induced to do it by the combined circumstances of their utility and cheapness. I wish I had a catalogue of the books you would be willing to buy, because they are often to be met with on stalls very cheap, and I would get them as the occasions should arise. The subscription to the Encyclopédie is still open. Whenever an opportunity offers of sending you what is published of that work (37 volumes) I shall subscribe for you and send it along with other books purchased for you."[8]

Much has been written in the enormous bibliography on Jefferson about the relationship between his architectural designs and the architectural models he found both in his rich collection of illustrated architectural books, such as the multiple editions of Andrea Palladio's 1570 *Quattro libri dell'architettura* (Four books of architecture), and in his copy of Antoine Desgodetz's invaluable compendium of measured drawings of antique monuments, *Les edifices antiques de Rome* (1695). In addition, much has been written not only about what Jefferson saw in Paris and in Versailles and where he went regularly for his governmental duties but also about the tours that took him to London and onward to some of the most innovative new gardens in the English picturesque style. Further travel took him to the Netherlands, the Rhineland, and Karlsruhe, the new radially planned princely capital of the margravate of Baden-Durlach, which embodied notions of power, in this case the divine right of a ruler, in the very layout of a city. In search of the classical, Jefferson would content himself primarily with the ancient remains in the South of France, since his short trip into Italy took him from the Piedmont into Lombardy and from Turin to Milan but, curiously, not on to the Veneto, where he would have encountered Palladio at first hand, nor to Rome. Palladio's influence would remain that of an artist of the page rather than the countryside.

Jefferson's book purchases are very well documented. His engagement with English and French architectural ideas did not stop when he sailed home to the United States. It continued through his active awareness

Fig. 4. Pierre Patte (French, 1723–1814), frontispiece, *Monumens érigés en France à la gloire de Louis XV* (Paris: Patte, 1765). Heidelberg University, T 2337 RES

of the publishing market and his active engagement with the formation of the libraries both of Congress and of the University of Virginia, for which he drew up a wish list of volumes on architecture and art in 1825.[9] What has received considerably less attention is the inspiration Jefferson might have equally taken from the texts of the volumes he collected. These contain many of the most significant discussions of the late-eighteenth-century notion that architecture was not merely the creation of buildings with fine proportions and details but also an agent for developing human sensibilities through the relationship of sensations to knowledge. This key doctrine of sensationalism lay at the core of the philosophy of John Locke, who was additionally an important political referent for the founding fathers. No less important was the growing conviction that spatial arrangements could influence not only human taste and thought but also behavior. This could be effected through everything from the arrangement of debate in a legislative assembly to the ability through the precise design of hospitals and prisons to offer corrections to health and behavior to the layout of universities to foster knowledge, enlightenment, and community. Architecture and matters of state were thus interrelated factors for Jefferson. Architecture was to be not only the ornament of the new nation but an agent in its very constitution.

Some speculation on the role played by Jefferson's acquisition of most of the key works in which French architectural practitioners and thinkers reflected on the concept of the monument should be added to the scholarship on Jefferson's library, and on the role of the monument in shaping civic virtues and public values. These titles included Pierre Patte's *Monumens érigés en France à la gloire de Louis XV* (1765) and Charles-François de Lubersac de Livron's *Discours sur les monuments publics de tous les ages et de tous les peuples connus* (1775), both of which Jefferson acquired during his stay in Paris, and later ordered as well for the university library (see figs. 4, 6). The renowned scholar on Jefferson's architecture Fiske Kimball discovered that after 1792 Jefferson also purchased the transcript of an important address, *Discours sur les monuments publics*, given to the legislative body of Paris in December 1791 by Armand-Guy Simon de Coetnempren, comte de Kersaint. This indicates the extent to which Jefferson followed intertwined debates about the form of government and the shape of buildings and the city that animated the early stages of the French Revolution, culminating in the staging in 1794 of the Concours de l'An II (competitions of the revolutionary year II). These required nothing less than designing all of the public buildings that would be needed for a new democratic society.[10] Jefferson's purchase of Kersaint's compendium would be twinned with the acquisition of J. N. L. Durand's 1800 *Recueil et parallèle des édifices de tout genre, anciens et modernes*, and included in his list of architecture books needed for the University of Virginia's library.

Patte's *Monumens* was not only a record of all of the statuary monuments realized or proposed to celebrate the glory of the reign of Louis XV but also a record of the fact that erecting public monuments was inherently

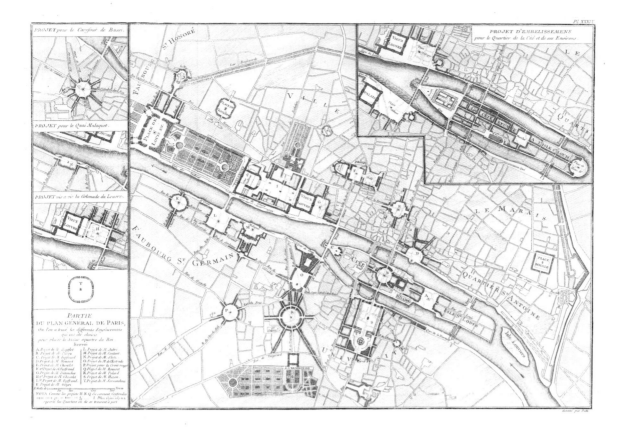

Fig. 5. Pierre Patte (French, 1723–1814), composite map of Paris with rival plans for the place Louis XV, in *Monumens érigés en France à la gloire de Louis XV* (Paris: Patte, 1765), plate 39. Heidelberg University, T 2337 RES

involved in the crafting of public space in the city (fig. 4). In 1748 a flurry of alternatives had been proposed for creating a dignified frame of a public space to provide a setting for the equestrian statue of the king commissioned by the city of Paris from the famed sculptor Edme Bouchardon as a sign of allegiance to the monarch. This continued the creation of *places royales*, or royal squares, that began with the installation of new statues of Louis XIV in cities around France, but Patte was to transform that tradition into a trampoline for a broader discussion of urban form. Nearly two decades after the designs were prepared, Patte recorded many of the individual suggestions of numerous architects for alternative placements in the city, engraving over a score of them on a single map. Most of the designers had argued that the creation of a new royal square could serve double duty to engender much-needed improvements to the city in circulation of river and street traffic, the reorganization of the chaotic central markets, or even the provision of settings for a new city hall or other public buildings. Patte's fictive map of Paris, dotted with royal squares, represented a visual manifesto for a new type of city planning in which open space was a key instrument for both the efficiency and the grandeur of the city (fig. 5). Providing places for people to gather and take respite from the crowded conditions of the public streets implied a new notion of the city as a stage of public life. While the future plan of Washington, DC, drawn up by the French engineer Pierre-Charles L'Enfant took much inspiration from the form of Versailles in its juxtaposition of a grid and radial avenues, the idea of a plan punctuated by

Fig. 6. Charles-François de Lubersac de Livron (French, 1730–1804), frontispiece, *Discours sur les monuments publics de tous les ages* (Paris: Imprimerie Royale, 1775). Bibliothèque Nationale de France, FOL-S-1636

public buildings that structure views and public spaces in a city fabric seems prefigured in the elevation of a sculptural commission into the reconceptualization of the modern city as happened in Paris.

Lubersac de Livron's 1775 *Discours sur les monuments publics de tous les ages*, published on the occasion of the coronation of Louis XVI at Reims Cathedral, was likewise a paean to monarchy, yet it contained a lengthy history of the relationship between public space and the state of society (figs. 6, 7).[11] Lubersac insisted on the interdependence of the embellishment of public space in the city and the demands of public utility. He thus contributed to crafting a notion of the relationship between, as we would say in modern terms, infrastructure and public building. He likewise renewed a decades-old demand that one of the most admired works of architecture in Paris, Perrault's Colonnade at the Louvre, should be given a frame of open space for its admiration, freeing it from the houses and other timber structures that made it nearly impossible to view the building as a whole, a proposal already made by Voltaire nearly twenty years earlier.

Lubersac weaves together a history of the human crafting of space, beginning with a tale of clearing land and foundation to make way for human settlement (which an American reader like Jefferson would immediately connect to the idea of the bounty of the unspoiled American interior) and continuing with a history of France read though the monuments that could be encountered by a traveler. In this case the itinerary is that of an imagined tour of the newly ascended King Louis XVI surveying his domain. Following the progress of the monarch, the reader encounters both the glories and the needs of French towns, culminating in the triumphant entry of the king into his capital of Paris (significantly, not Versailles). Most of the monuments that Jefferson admired on his long walks in Paris are praised and described, even as certain needs are discreetly evoked (see fig. 7).

Not the least is Lubersac's call to resuscitate the ancient Greek notion of the prytaneum, the place where the sacred flame was kept alight, where the keepers of the flame could meet, and where often distinguished visitors could be found. For Lubersac, as for many other theorists of the relationship between the lost civic sphere of the ancient Greeks and the crafting of a civic sphere in a transforming monarchical France, the prytaneum was a "building more august through the inspirations that leads to its construction than necessarily through its architecture" and "served also to house all of those who had rendered service to the fatherland, and they were maintained at state expense. The value that they placed on this honor was such that everyone worked assiduously to merit it." He went on to note that this high civic function was combined with a utilitarian one, since it "was also the public granary, where grains were held in reserve to supplement bad harvests."[12]

The program in fact of the combined granary and of public assembly at the Parisian Halle aux Blés made it a descendant of this idea. In great detail Lubersac describes and lauds the collection of noble new buildings to house public functions, from the Jardin des Plantes (botanical gardens) to the Hôtel de la Monnaie and the École de Chirurgie. He also describes the great resources of the royal library at the Palais du Louvre to make a pointed plea for the transformation of the collections held at the underused palace into a museum that could "become the most interesting museum in the world," and "a new attraction for foreigners whose curiosity brings them to France."[13] Finally he recommends that a city of monuments needs to be organized in such a way that clear sight lines exist from one to another and that axial relationships in the city plan can underscore the relationship between one institution and another. Jefferson translated this notion into the visual relationship between the White House and Congress that would be at the very heart of both the American constitution and the new capital city.

The 1792 arrival in the United States of a copy of Kersaint's *Discours*, originally delivered before a legislative assembly in revolutionary Paris, could not have been more timely. L'Enfant had drawn up a plan for the new federal city. With his dismissal in 1792 by George Washington because of a series of disagreements over a variety of issues, including the demolition of a house that stood in the way of an intended new street, responsibility for developing the plan and the first public buildings, the White House and the Congress, fell to Washington, his secretary of state, Jefferson, and the three federally appointed commissioners for the new city.[14] Jefferson had already made it clear to L'Enfant in a letter of April 10, 1791, that the buildings should be based on "some one of the models of antiquity which have the approbation of thousands of years."[15] Though it would be many years before even the central governmental district was filled in by buildings and activity, Jefferson was eager that the young republic be grounded in associations with ancient architecture, the source for him of many republican ideals. It must have pleased him to be reminded of his old friend, the draftsman and architect Charles-Louis Clérisseau, who had guided him in his transfer of his admiration for the Maison Carrée, which Jefferson famously wrote that he gazed on as at a mistress, into the designing of America's first public building based on ancient forms and images, for the Virginia State Assembly.[16] The title page of Kersaint's *Discours* featured a quote from an ancient text that Clérisseau had included in his great illustrated folio volume *Antiquités de la France, première parti: Monumens de Nîsmes* (1778), a copy of which Jefferson had purchased from the architect/cicerone a year before his own visit to Nîmes (see fig. 10):[17] "It is an honorable task and a perfectly dignified and glorious design to have as goal to preserve for ages to come the monuments which draw admiration. See the Formula for the Institution of Theodoric, King of the Goths and Master of Rome, to his architect, translation by Mr. Clérisseau, *Antiquités de France, First Volume*."[18]

Here, then, it was clear that to emulate the monuments of the ancients was also to recapture the ancient sense that to build a city was to prepare a

Fig. 7. Charles-François de Lubersac de Livron (French, 1730–1804), *Monument à la gloire du roi et de la France*, in *Discours sur les monuments publics de tous les ages* (Paris: Imprimerie Royale, 1775). Bibliothèque Nationale de France, FOL-S-1636

Fig. 8. Armand-Guy-Simon de Coetnempren, comte de Kersaint (French, 1742–1793), *Projet du pritanée à élever sur les ruines de la Bastille*, in *Discours sur les monuments publics* (Paris: Didot l'Aîné, 1792), plate 4. Bibliothèque Nationale de France, ark:/12148/btv1b2100022p

Fig. 9. Armand-Guy-Simon de Coetnempren, comte de Kersaint (French, 1742–1793), *Pritanée de la 1ère Classe*, in *Discours sur les monuments publics* (Paris: Didot l'Aîné, 1792), plate 1. Bibliothèque Nationale de France, ark:/12148/btv1b2100022p

legible monumental landscape for posterity. As Kersaint paraphrased it in his introduction, "Monuments are the irreproachable testimony of history, without their august ruins, all that the Greeks and Romans would have transmitted to us would appear as nothing more than a fable."[19] He went on to say that the new age of liberty would not be an ephemeral event if it paid attention to the need for "a free nation which cherishes glory [that] would live in the future and consecrate the most glorious age of the annals of the human spirit (the triumph of the truth over every sort of prejudice) as a dignified edifice of sublimity as its object. Thus the author thought that the National Palace of a people which bases its freedoms on the eternal rights of man will be constructed of indestructible materials, such as reason, of which it will be the sanctuary."[20]

Kersaint calls for a series of transformations to turn Paris from a city too long neglected by an absent king in his palace at Versailles into the framework for an experiment in shared power between monarch and the people's representatives (fig. 8). But Jefferson and his collaborators could well read the text as a gloss on the task at hand in laying out the city later renamed Washington. Jefferson hired the surveyor Andrew Ellicott in November 1791 to create engraved plans of the new city, published in 1792, long before anything of that plan's translation of the sharing of the powers among the executive, legislative, and judiciary branches inscribed in the constitution adopted five years earlier was visible on the ground. No less would he be fascinated to learn that the French too had appointed by ballot

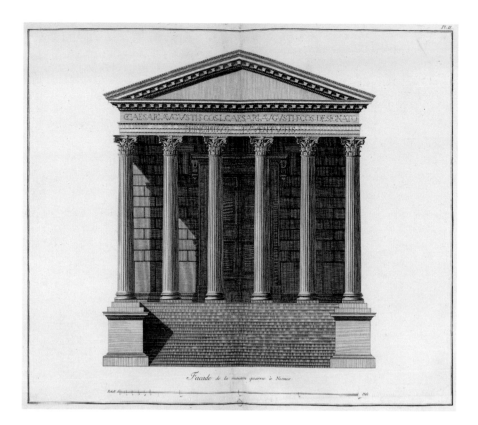

Fig. 10. Charles-Louis Clérisseau (French, 1722–1820), *Antiquités de la France, première parti: Monumens de Nîsmes* (Paris: Pierres, 1778), plate 2. National Gallery of Art, Washington, DC, Mark J. Millard Architectural Collection, 1985.61.476

a group of four men to serve as commissioners for public monuments, by decree of the brand-new French National Assembly. If the very architecture of the American constitution was inscribed in the urban form of Washington, the challenge facing the commissioners in Paris was to make a society of laws adopted through legislation visible in public space. For this, Kersaint turned to the architects Legrand and Molinos, who had transformed the Halle aux Blés with its great skylit dome. They imagined a series of monuments, such as the new interpretation of the ancient prytaneum, not as a singular shrine of the sacred flame but rather as a public system of small monuments (fig. 9). These would hold copies of laws, decrees, and public notices, and each prytaneum would be topped by a Phrygian cap, the veritable symbol of the freed citizen adopted from a belief that such a form had been worn by emancipated slaves of ancient Rome. There would be different types, adapted in scale and style to their local surroundings throughout the country.

Kersaint was confident that architecture could both train citizens and also create respect for the legislators even in the most remote districts of the country. To that end he worked with the architects Legrand and Molinos to develop designs for a "national palace," which they proposed to create on the foundations of the ambitious church of La Madeleine, whose cornerstone had been laid in 1764, but which was far from complete. Its great temple portico facade, ending the axial view up the rue Royale, renamed rue de la Révolution in 1792, would now serve to dignify the work of the legislators who would find their place under a skylit dome where "the representatives of the nation, arranged on the circular tiers of the hall, will all be at an equal distance from the president of the assembly, everyone's attention will be naturally directed toward him, and the speaker could, from the tribune, see all his colleagues."[21]

As he goes on to explain, all the departments—as the territorial units that replaced the traditional provinces would now be called—would be represented by banners around the room so that legislators would not forget the jurisdiction they represented. The problem of creating a national capital in a single location, within a vast territory, over which equality is to reign would play equally into the planning of Washington, DC. There L'Enfant decided that Washington's principal long axial streets would carry the names of the states, thirteen at first, thus evoking a geography of the nation, as one moved from north to south. The fact that Pennsylvania Avenue connects the White House and Congress was intended to recall not only the geographic centrality of the Keystone State but also the fact that the Constitution had been ratified at Philadelphia.

The revolutionary period in Paris and the period of planning the new federal city of Washington were in fact to develop in parallel during the course of the 1790s, even if by the time Jefferson himself finally moved into the recently completed White House, in 1801, things had changed dramatically in France. Negotiations between France and Jefferson's administration over the Louisiana Purchase coincided with Napoleon's declaration of himself as emperor in 1804. Jefferson's views on the political evolution in France, as opposed to his quest to place the new American republic on solid and lasting footing, were perhaps most clearly expressed in a private letter he wrote to Benjamin Rush during the campaign of 1800: "I have sworn upon the altar of God eternal hostility against every form of tyranny over the mind of man."[22] Books for Jefferson were instruments not only for training the mind but also for crafting the places of democracy, from the federal capital to the university that would preoccupy him in his years after his retreat from government. "I cannot live without books; but fewer will suffice where amusement, and not use, is the only future object,"[23] he wrote to his predecessor John Adams in the summer of 1815, just as he prepared to sell 6,700 volumes to the Library of Congress, turning his private sources of reading into the building blocks of the nation. ❦

NOTES

1. "Behold me at length on the vaunted scene of Europe! . . . you are perhaps curious to know how this new scene has struck a savage of the mountains of America. . . . Were I to proceed to tell you how much I enjoy their architecture, sculpture, painting, music, I should want words. It is in these arts they shine." "From Thomas Jefferson to Charles Bellini, 30 September 1785," *Founders Online*, National Archives, last modified June 13, 2018, http://founders.archives.gov/documents/Jefferson/01-08-02-0448. [Original source: *The Papers of Thomas Jefferson*, vol. 8, *25 February–31 October 1785*, ed. Julian P. Boyd (Princeton, NJ: Princeton University Press, 1953), 568–70.]

2. William Banter O'Neal, *Jefferson's Fine Arts Library: His Selections for the University of Virginia Together with His Own Architectural Books* (Charlottesville: University Press of Virginia, 1976).

3. "From Thomas Jefferson to Madame de Tessé, 20 March 1787," *Founders Online*, National Archives, last modified June 13, 2018, http://founders.archives.gov/documents/Jefferson/01-11-02-0229. [Original source: *The Papers of Thomas Jefferson*, vol. 11, *1 January–6 August 1787*, ed. Julian P. Boyd (Princeton, NJ: Princeton University Press, 1955), 226–28.]

4. Brébion to Ch. Cl. de Flahaut de la Billardie, Comte d'Angiviller, October 20, 1780, Paris, Archives nationales, O[1] 1694–[43], as quoted in *Neoclassical and Nineteenth Century Architecture,* by Robin Middleton and David Watkin (New York: Harry N. Abrams, 1980), 22 (author's translation from the original French cited by Middleton).

5. Barry Bergdoll, ed., *Le Panthéon, Symbole des Révolutions* (Paris: Editions Picard, 1989).

6. Mark Deming, "Le Panthéon révolutionaire," in Bergdoll, *Le Panthéon*, 97.

7. Jefferson to Samuel H. Smith, September 21, 1814, in *The Works of Thomas Jefferson*, ed. Paul Leicester Ford, vol. 11 (New York: G.B. Putnam's Sons, 1905), 430, reprinted in Douglas L. Wilson and Lucia Stanton, eds., *Jefferson Abroad* (New York: Modern Library, 1999), ix.

8. Jefferson to James Madison, November 11, 1784, in Wilson and Stanton, *Jefferson Abroad*, 6.

9. O'Neal, *Jefferson's Fine Arts Library*.

10. James Leith, *Space and Revolution: Projects for Monuments, Squares, and Public Buildings in France, 1789–1799* (Kingston, Canada: McGill-Queens University Press, 1991).

11. Charles-François de Lubersac de Livron, *Discours sur les monuments publics de tous les ages* (Paris: Impimerie Royale, 1775).

12. Ibid., 36.

13. Ibid., xxxvii.

14. See Pamela Scott, *Temple of Liberty: Building the Capitol for a New Nation* (Oxford: Oxford University Press, 1995).

15. "XII. Thomas Jefferson to Pierre Charles L'Enfant, 10 April 1791," *Founders Online*, National Archives, last modified June 13, 2018, http://founders.archives.gov/documents/Jefferson/01-20-02-0001-0015. [Original source: *The Papers of Thomas Jefferson*, vol. 20, *1 April–4 August 1791*, ed. Julian P. Boyd (Princeton. NJ: Princeton University Press, 1982), 86–87.]

16. Jefferson to Madame de Tessé, 20 March 1787.

17. O'Neal, *Jefferson's Fine Arts Library*, 73.

18. "C'est un emploi bien honorable et un dessein tout-à-fait digne de gloire, que celui qui a pour but de faire passer aux siècles à venir des monuments qui feront leur admiration. Voyez *Formule d'Institution de Théodoric, roi des Goths et maitre de Rome, à son architecte*, traduction de M. Clérisseau, *Antiquités de France, Iere partie*." Armand-Guy Kersaint, *Discours sur les monuments publics, prononcé au conseil du Département de Paris, le 15 décembre 1791* (Paris: Imprimerie de P. Didot l'Aíné, 1792), title page. All translations from this work are mine.

19. "Les monuments sont les témoins irréprochables de l'histoire; sans leurs ruines augustes tout ce qu'elle nous a transmis des Grecs et des Romains ne nous eût paru qu'une fable." Ibid., vi.

20. "Une nation libre qui chérit la gloire voudra vive dans l'avenir et consacrer les plus glorieuse époque des annales de l'esprit humain (le triomphe de la vérité sur toutes les sortes de préjugés) par un édifice digne de la sublimité de son objet. Ainsi l'auteur a pensé que le palais national d'un peuple qui fonda sa liberté sur les droits éternels de l'homme devroit être construit de matériaux indestructibles, comme la raison dont il sera le sanctuaire." Ibid., vi.

21. "Les représentants de la nation, placés sur les gradins circulaires de la salle, seront presque tous à une égale distance du président de l'assemblée; tous les (64) regards se diregeront naturellement vers lui; et l'orateur pourra, de la tribune, apercevoir tous ses collegues." Ibid., 63.

22. "From Thomas Jefferson to Benjamin Rush, 23 September 1800," *Founders Online*, National Archives, last modified June 13, 2018, http://founders.archives.gov/documents/Jefferson/01-32-02-0102. [Original source: *The Papers of Thomas Jefferson*, vol. 32, *1 June 1800–16 February 1801*, ed. Barbara B. Oberg (Princeton, NJ: Princeton University Press, 2005), 166–69.]

23. "Thomas Jefferson to John Adams, 10 June 1815," *Founders Online*, National Archives, last modified June 13, 2018, http://founders.archives.gov/documents/Jefferson/03-08-02-0425. [Original source: *The Papers of Thomas Jefferson*, Retirement Series, vol. 8, *1 October 1814 to 31 August 1815*, ed. J. Jefferson Looney (Princeton, NJ: Princeton University Press, 2011), 522–23.]

RACE, REASON, AND THE ARCHITECTURE OF JEFFERSON'S VIRGINIA STATEHOUSE

MABEL O. WILSON

While visiting Richmond, Virginia, in 1796–98, newly immigrated British architect Benjamin Henry Latrobe painted two watercolors of the state's new capitol building. His translucent hues in one of the watercolors depicted the stately white stucco-covered brick temple sitting nobly atop Shockoe Hill and overlooking the town's sparsely populated pastoral landscape (fig. 1). One of the earliest examples of American civic architecture, the capitol building was designed by statesman, architect, planter, and slave owner Thomas Jefferson, modeled in part on the Maison Carrée, a first-century Roman temple in Nîmes, France. The new capitol building Jefferson envisioned to house Virginia's governmental functions needed to both symbolize and enable the power of "the people" to govern and adjudicate the laws of the new state. Virginia had drafted and ratified its state constitution in 1776, and Jefferson had been a key author. The Virginia document's organization of various governmental functions would become a model for the organization of the United States government. The self-trained architect intended the Neoclassical state capitol to also serve as a model for civic architecture throughout the thirteen states.

In discussing this period of revolutionary action and postrevolutionary planning, it is important to trace the various rationales conceived to identify who comprised "the people" of Virginia, and by extension "the people" of the United States of America. In other words, who were Virginians or American citizens, endowed with constitutional rights, and which people were noncitizens? A survey of the population of the small bustling port town of Richmond reveals the racial contours of this division. The city's white residents, who were America's newly minted citizenry, staffed and served its government seat, patronized its taverns, shops, stables, and inns, profited from its docks along the James River and its warehouses trading in tobacco and slaves, and lived in the wood-frame houses shown in the foreground of Latrobe's watercolor. Among the several thousand white Americans labored

Fig. 1. Benjamin Henry Latrobe (British, 1764–1820), *View of the City of Richmond from the Bank of the James River*, 1798. Pen, pencil, ink, and watercolor. Maryland Historical Society, 1960.108.12.34

an almost equal population of noncitizens, free and enslaved African men, women, and children. Legally defined as "property," the enslaved served their masters and mistresses to produce the region's great wealth that filled the coffers of the burgeoning nation. A depiction of this slave economy can be found among a later series of watercolors painted by Latrobe, produced while the Englishman traveled north to Fredericksburg. One scene documents a white overseer keeping dutiful watch over two enslaved women, who with hoes raised in mid-air tamed the soil and burned tree stumps to clear the land for either cultivation or new construction (fig. 2). Chattel slavery—believed by some to be a necessary evil—clung as the dark underbelly of America's civilized values of freedom, liberty, and equality, which eventually split the United States in half when the Civil War erupted in 1861.

It is critical to consider that enslaved black people, humans classified as property who lacked the proper political subjectivity to be literally (and legally) self-possessed, built several of the nation's important civic buildings—the Virginia Capitol, the White House, and the US Capitol. Designed by white architects, these edifices stand today as Enlightenment monuments to the power of reason and the virtues of equality, justice, and freedom. One astute deliberation about the moral peril of slavery measured against an exegesis on the natural inferiority of the Negro's mind and body can be found in Jefferson's *Notes on the State of Virginia* (1785), a lengthy assessment of the state's geography, geology, wildlife, human inhabitants,

Fig. 2. Benjamin Henry Latrobe (British, 1764–1820), *An Overseer Doing His Duty near Fredericksburg, Virginia*, c. 1798. Ink on paper. Maryland Historical Society, 1960.108.1.3.21

and political economy. Jefferson wrote and revised *Notes on the State of Virginia* in the same years that he designed Virginia's capitol building.

Born into the wealthy British planter class of colonial Virginia, Jefferson epitomized the consummate humanist polymath. Because his oeuvre encompasses the aesthetic and technical domain of architecture, the political realm of government, and the rational sphere of natural philosophy and history, his works offer an ideal lens through which to understand the intersections of the emerging modern discourses of architecture, nationalism, and racial difference as they coalesced in the late eighteenth century. Analyzing Jefferson's architecture and his writings together with correspondence in this period broadens the social, economic, cultural, and political context in which the first work of American civic architecture—the Virginia State Capitol—was conceived and realized.

RACE, REASON, AND ARCHITECTURE

In the later eighteenth century, slavery was not an odious institution rooted in the remote confines of backwoods plantations. In truth slavery and the slave trade were integral to the formation of the economy, government, and national character of the United States. To be sure many white Americans recognized the enslavement of Negroes, to use a term common of the period, to be undeniably contrary to the nation's founding creed: the "self-evident" truths that "all men are created equal." That equality originated in nature and was necessary for liberty to be achieved were moral principles Jefferson enshrined in the Declaration of Independence (1776). There is, however, an inherent contradiction—some might argue a disavowal—in how the founding fathers constituted a new nation that ensured liberalism's "unalienable rights" to "Life, Liberty and the pursuit of Happiness," while continuing to violently enslave other humans for personal gain.

With nationalism growing in the West in the closing decades of the eighteenth century, Europeans, typically men, continued to conceptualize the racial paradigm of human difference that had emerged from centuries of contact with and colonial expansion into Asia, Africa, and the New World. The inauguration of the transatlantic slave trade in the fifteenth century was critical to the invention of racial hierarchies. During the Revolutionary period and shortly thereafter, "race" had not yet been categorized in terms of biologically verified variations in the human type organized on a hierarchy of mental and physical evolution, as would happen under the disciplines of modern science in the mid-nineteenth century.

As the West shifted from a Judeo-Christian cosmology of heavens and the earth to a humanist worldview, philosophers deployed universal reason to imagine a self-determined and self-conscious moral subject—political Man—who perceived and conceived "the nature of things," including his social relations.[1] Natural rights became foundational for new social formations—nation-states—whose governments, guided by historically derived ideas of democracy, guaranteed freedom for their citizens. At the same time Europeans also invented, to borrow scholar Denise da Silva's term, the "Others of Europe," who were not modern, not rational, not free, not white, and not citizens. These subhumans, often characterized as weak and submissive, labored in the colonies and dwelled in yet to be charted territories.[2] Europeans consigned the moral and physical character of nonwhite people to the bottom of the repurposed Great Chain of Being. Natural historians and scientists developed representations of time and space in the emerging discourses of history and science that placed nonwhite people in prehistory and in regions unexplored on colonial maps. The rendering of nonwhite people as primitive and uncivilized in turn rationalized the conquest of their territories, the expropriation of their land and labor, or their mortal elimination by war or disease. This racial inferiority, particularly the "Others of Europe's" lack of culture, dialectically elevated and affirmed the universality of Man and whiteness as the ideal representation of the human in the West's own imagination.[3]

It is important to keep in mind that from the fifteenth century onward, secular reason also had an impact on European "arts of building," on building's transformation from a medieval trade guild to the modern discipline of architecture.[4] With the rise of academies and learned societies, architectural treatises circulated debates on architecture's appropriate use and proportions of classical elements and the ideal configuration of different building types. New techniques of geometry and cartography influenced modes of architectural representation. The archaeological inspection through drawings of Roman, Greek, and Egyptian ruins and other locales conveyed documentation to amateur architects who could not travel to faraway destinations. A growing interest in mechanics, documented at length in dictionaries and encyclopedias, advanced new construction methods that separated architecture from engineering. In other arenas, natural philosophers explored Man's capacity for aesthetic judgment to assess what ideal forms were visually pleasing. The taxonomic organizational methods used by natural historians to discern speciation, in particular racial differences, were applied to the study of the historical transformation of buildings to determine character and organization. To begin to chart a history of architecture, architects made comparative archeological, ethnographic, and aesthetic evaluations of how far Europe's architecture had advanced beyond the rest of the world's ancient building practices.[5]

These technical and aesthetic developments gave rise to the figure of the modern architect. At first self-taught elites like Jefferson and eventually European apprentice-trained architects like Latrobe were employed by the state and by private citizens to design the government buildings, offices, banks, customs houses, storehouses, libraries, museums, prisons, great houses, and plantations that symbolized regimes of power and organized the territorial dynamic between the metropole and colony. Jefferson's designs for the Virginia State Capitol reveal the mutually constitutive relationship between race, reason, and architecture.

A PERFECT MORSEL OF GOOD TASTE

In 1776, shortly after the newly formed United States had officially declared independence from the British Crown, Jefferson proposed a bill to the Virginia House of Delegates to move its state capital from Williamsburg, the colonial seat since 1699, to Richmond, a fledgling settlement farther up the James River. The bill to move the capital was passed by the House of Delegates in 1779 shortly before Jefferson became governor of Virginia, a post he held for two years.[6] Richmond would be more centrally accessible to the state's citizens and representatives, safe from enemy incursion, and navigable by waterway.[7]

Home to a wealthy planter class who eagerly sought independence in stewarding their own affairs, Virginia was one of the most powerful and prosperous of the thirteen colonies. The growing ranks of the English planter class began assembling large tracts of fertile territory in the late 1600s for the cultivation of the colony's main cash crop and export, tobacco. This territorial expansion, a system of land privatization enabled by patents and headrights awarded by the crown, further encroached upon the communal lands of indigenous people—the tribes of the Powhatan confederacy—and pushed them westward into the lands of the Monacan and Manahoac. By the time the Second Continental Congress met in Philadelphia to declare independence from Great Britain in July 1776, Virginia's free white population had grown substantially, along with its population of enslaved black laborers. The latter had been purchased and imported as a labor force to tend the tobacco fields, and, unlike the earlier colonial workforce of indentured Europeans, could be held in perpetuity.

One criterion for choosing the location of the new capital was that it be along a river. Access to the ports and private plantation docks along Virginia's various rivers—the James, York, Rappahannock, and Potomac—were key for the sale of hogsheads of tobacco and their transport to European markets. These and other raw materials fed manufacturers in the North and Europe, forming the backbone of industrialization, which in turn fed the growing European and American demand for luxury commodities. The waterways were also essential for the importation of goods such as salt, fine cloth, coffee, tea, wine, furniture, books, and black slaves from ports in Europe, the West Indies, Asia, and Africa. This mercantile trade, streams in the transatlantic

slave trade, created the wealth of the great eighteenth-century Virginia planter families, the Wayles, Byrds, and Randolphs, as well as more modest families like the Jeffersons, Washingtons, and Custises (fig. 3).

The bill to move the capital from Williamsburg to Richmond laid out a plan for the new seat of government. Jefferson's scheme for the civic district of Richmond subdivided several blocks into plots, which were sold at auction (fig. 4). To determine the configuration of the governmental buildings, Jefferson executed the first designs for the Virginia state capitol in 1776, the same year that he drafted the state constitution. He revised the drawings in the period from 1779 to 1780.[8] In Jefferson's estimation, to adequately house Virginia's government and growing white population, construction practices needed to evolve beyond the erection of crude wooden structures and awkwardly proportioned brick buildings such as those found in the former colonial seat of Williamsburg. "Architecture," he lamented, "seems to have shed its maledictions over this land."[9] Virginia, however, lacked highly skilled craftsmen and workmen trained to correctly draw and execute the classical orders of entablatures, pediments, and columns. This lack of skilled labor was perhaps an outcome of the fact that one segment of the construction workforce was enslaved. Literacy, especially the ability to write, among the enslaved was discouraged in the pre- and postrevolutionary eras in order to maintain subjugation and suppress revolt.[10]

All the components of the new civic order—executive, legislative, and judicial branches—were accounted for in Jefferson's bill and organized in his initial drawings that placed each branch in its own building on Shockoe Hill. In possession of several key folios of Palladio and other volumes on Greek and Roman antiquities, Jefferson had experimented with Palladian

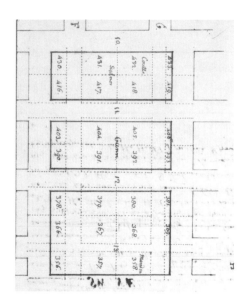

Fig. 3. Edward Savage (American, 1764–1820), *The Washington Family*, 1789–96. Oil on canvas. National Gallery of Art, Washington, DC, Andrew Mellon Collection, 1940.1.2

Fig. 4. Thomas Jefferson (American, 1743–1826), plan of the town, showing 28 lots from which "shall be appropriated ground for the State House, Capitol, halls of Justice, and Prison," 1780. Ink on paper. Huntington Library, CSmH9372

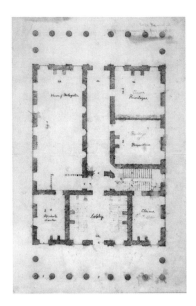 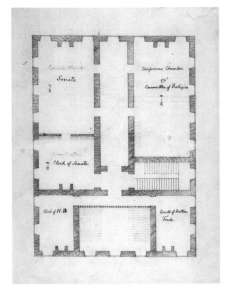 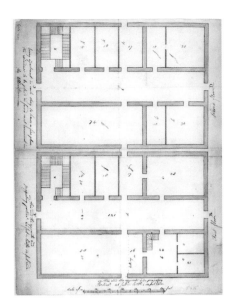

Fig. 5. Thomas Jefferson (American, 1743–1826), first floor of the Virginia State Capitol, 1780. Ink on paper. Huntington Library, CSmH9372

Fig. 6. Thomas Jefferson (American, 1743–1826), second floor of the Virginia State Capitol, 1780. Ink on paper. Huntington Library, CSmH9372

Fig. 7. Capitol, as proposed by the directors, 1785. Ink on paper. Coolidge Collection of Thomas Jefferson Manuscripts, Massachusetts Historical Society, N272; K109

Fig. 8. Charles-Louis Clérisseau (French, 1722–1820), plan of Maison Carrée, Nîmes, in *Antiquités de la France, première parti: Monumens de Nîsmes* (Paris: Pierres, 1778), plate 3. University of Zürich

Fig. 9. Charles-Louis Clérisseau (French, 1722–1820), Maison Carrée, Nîmes, perspective view, in *Antiquités de la France, première parti: Monumens de Nîsmes*, 2nd ed. (Paris: Pierres, 1804), plate 2. Bibliothèque Nationale de France

Neoclassicism mainly at Monticello, his plantation house under construction in the Piedmont and in unbuilt designs for his alma mater, the College of William & Mary.[11] For the state capitol, Jefferson placed the House of Delegates and other offices on the lower level. The Senate chambers, associated clerks, and other legislative functions were located on the upper level (figs. 5, 6). Astutely aware of architecture's ability to project the longevity and stability of the state, Jefferson believed that the new capitol and courthouse buildings should be "built in a handsome manner with walls of Brick, and Porticos."[12] To achieve that desire, he designed Neoclassical exteriors that echoed the Roman republicanism and Athenian democracy that best spoke to the values of liberty and justice.

In 1784 Jefferson was appointed minister plenipotentiary, and the following year he succeeded Benjamin Franklin as ambassador to France, a post he held for four years. During his diplomatic assignment in Paris, where he lived with his two daughters, along with several enslaved Africans he had brought along to tend to their needs, Jefferson was charged with finally completing the plans for the capitol once the land on Shockoe Hill had been claimed by eminent domain.[13] In the spring of 1785 two of the state government's directors of public buildings—James Buchanan and William Hay—sent for review revised plans for the layout of the foundations, as a means of quelling legislative discontent with the choice of the capitol's site (fig. 7). Buchanan and Hay's pragmatic scheme of a series of rooms divided by a long central hallway lacked the aesthetic vision of Jefferson's skillful plans.[14] They informed Jefferson that to limit the expenditure of public monies, the Virginia assembly wanted all of the government departments housed in one building.[15] Governor Patrick Henry wrote to Jefferson in the late summer of 1785 that a cornerstone had been laid and that foundations of brick, their construction overseen by Hay and Buchanan, were out of the ground, based on his earlier drawings.[16]

With construction commencing, Jefferson needed to act quickly to refine and complete his designs. To assist with the preparation of drawings and a model, he secured the talents of French architect Charles-Louis Clérisseau.[17] Jefferson had reviewed drawings of the perfectly preserved Maison Carrée in books and greatly admired Clérisseau's publication *Antiquités de la France, première parti: Monumens de Nîsmes* (1778), which he eventually purchased from Clérisseau while in Paris (fig. 8).[18] A skilled draftsman and archaeologist, Clérisseau, with his meticulous orthographic documentation of the temple's details, proportions, and layout, suited Jefferson, who possessed not only the eye of an architect but also the fastidious gaze of a naturalist (fig. 9).

Because the legislators desired to conduct all of the state's business in one structure, Jefferson with Clérisseau revised the earlier plans to place the General Court across from the state's lower chamber of the House of Delegates on the first floor. At the center of the elegantly proportioned two-story court that connected the two chambers, Virginians planned to erect a statue to General George Washington, a former member of the House of Burgesses, which would aesthetically enhance and elevate the environment for civil debate (fig. 10).[19] The second floor housed the Senate chambers and auxiliary spaces for clerks. The new design took advantage of the basilica form, so that the protocols of assembly, deliberation, and adjudication, adapted from the colonial government, operated smoothly.

In a letter to James Madison, Jefferson expressed his desire that Virginia's new capitol building would become a model of architecture worth emulating throughout the new nation: "How is a taste in this beautiful art to be formed in our countrymen, unless we avail ourselves of every occasion when public buildings are to be erected, of presenting to them models for their study and imitation?"[20] Jefferson told his friend that for many the Maison Carrée was "one of the most beautiful, if not the most beautiful and precious morsel of architecture left us by antiquity" (fig. 11).[21] The monuments of antiquity offered Americans perfectly preserved examples of Greco-Roman classicism, an architecture emblematic of truth, justice, and democracy, one that for Jefferson had not been corrupted by the capricious flourishes of the Rococo that suited the tastes of the French aristocracy. He commissioned model maker Jean-Pierre Fouquet to complete a plaster maquette based on his design (figs. 12, 13). In June 1786, he shipped the model along with Clérisseau's drawings to Hay and Buchanan in Richmond.[22]

The didactic purpose of this novel design for the capitol building, Jefferson wrote to Madison, was "to improve the taste of my countrymen, to increase their reputation, to reconcile to them the

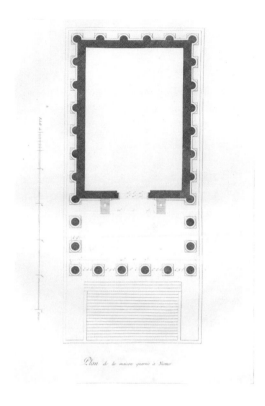

Plan de la maison quarrée à Nismes

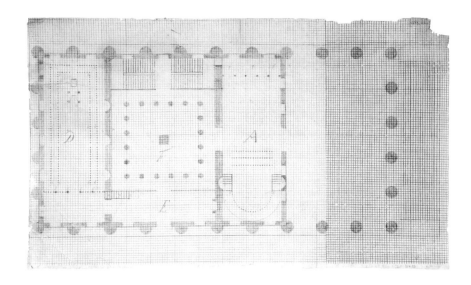

respect of the world and procure them it's [*sic*] praise."[23] In return for erecting a beautiful work of civic architecture, Americans would gain the regard of the world, which for Jefferson meant it would win the admiration of Europeans. The rationale for replicating historical buildings held in high regard was that it was "very simple, but it is noble beyond expression, and would have done honour to our country as presenting to travellers a morsel of taste in our infancy promising much for our maturer age."[24] What he feared most was the prospect of erecting a tasteless "monument to our Barbarism."[25] Jefferson hoped that the new capitol building would be a transformative exercise that would seed a new culture and society in the New World, a fecund American civilization. His proposed designs for the Virginia State Capitol would offer an invaluable public primer on how architecture could represent the virtues of durability, utility, and beauty.

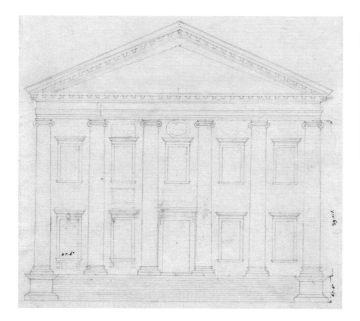

One challenge faced by Virginians and the new union of thirteen states alike was how to cultivate the character of their new political subjects, "the people." In eighteenth-century Europe and its colonies, refined taste, as in a "morsel of taste," in art, dress, architecture, and even food (fueled by the growing appetite for sugar, coffee, and tobacco), became a marker of elevated intellectual and economic status. But this "culture of taste," writes Simon Gikandi, also harbored "repressive tendencies—namely, the attempt to use *culture* to conceal the intimate connection between modern subjectivity and the political economy of slavery."[26] That interdependence between the formation of a new white American culture, one that included the arts of building, and the enslavement of African peoples, justified by their presumed innate mental and physical inferiority, can be found in Jefferson's *Notes on the State of Virginia*, which he wrote in the same period in which he conceived the designs for Virginia's capitol building.

Fig. 12. Thomas Jefferson (American, 1743–1826), Virginia State Capitol, Richmond, end elevation, 1785. Ink on paper. Coolidge Collection of Thomas Jefferson Manuscripts, Massachusetts Historical Society, N279, K116

Fig. 13. Designed by Simone Baldissini, constructed by Ivan Simonato, scale model of the Virginia State Capitol, Richmond (1:66), 2015. Wood, resin, and tempera. Palladio Museum, Vicenza

THE STATE OF VIRGINIA

An esteemed member of the American Philosophical Society and deeply invested in the philosophical tenets and methods of the period, Jefferson took great interest in scientific principles drawn from the careful observation of facts and by the meticulous study of things and phenomena. His command of natural history and natural philosophy birthed *Notes on the State of Virginia*, Jefferson's only published book-length manuscript. He printed a private edition in Paris in 1785 that he gave to friends. A public edition was printed in London two years later.

Notes on the State of Virginia originated as a report prepared in response to twenty-three queries sent to Jefferson in 1780 by French diplomat François Barbé-Marbois, who circulated the survey to gain a better understanding of the geographic and historic character of the newly formed United States. Like his surveyor and plantation owner father Peter

Jefferson, Thomas Jefferson was well versed in the geography, natural resources, populations, and history of the state. Unlike standard European accounts that speculated on the New World based on secondhand observations, Jefferson's book was a comprehensive compendium of life in the Americas that originated in the colonies. *Notes on the State of Virginia* contributed to current debates on political and scientific thought.

In *Notes on the State of Virginia* Jefferson took stock of the state's natural features and human inhabitants. In the first part, his taxonomic assessment of plants, animals, minerals, climate, rivers, mountains, and caves highlighted the state's bountiful resources. He noted that natural laws governed the human species residing within the state's boundaries and divided them into the racial taxonomies: *Homo sapiens europaeus*, *Homo sapiens americanus*, and *Homo sapiens afer*. Concerned with the current state of Virginia, the book also reviewed the state's systems and institutions that organized its society, namely its commerce, manufacturing, government, religion, and civil society. Intimately familiar with Virginia's Constitution, Jefferson outlined the government's branches and duties, noting in detail the rights and laws that adjudicated the legal status and relationships, albeit unequally, between the aforementioned races of Europeans, aboriginals, and Africans.

Jefferson provided evidence in philosophy, war, government, oratory, painting, and the plastic arts to show that "America, though but a child of yesterday, has already given hopeful proofs of genius."[27] America—its politics and culture—as Jefferson had also assessed in his letter to Madison, was still in its infancy. He was confident that the United States would evolve to rival if not surpass Europe, if the minds and tastes of its white citizenry were properly nurtured, for instance, by exposure to tasteful, aesthetically pleasing architecture of the kind exemplified by the Virginia capitol building. Even though he sought to sever ties with what he believed to be a calcifying European aristocratic culture, Jefferson nonetheless preserved its aesthetic values as a means to foster American culture.

One central tenet espoused by the Enlightenment's natural philosophers was that in nature, all races of the human species had been born equal, a view cherished by natural rights advocates such as John Locke, Montesquieu, and the nation's founding patriarchs, who had constituted the new republic according to principles of equality. What mattered most, however, was the difference in how far each race had advanced to become liberal subjects capable of self-governance, a state of enlightenment dependent upon innate faculties of mind and body. Jefferson countered European philosophes like Georges-Luis Leclerc, the comte de Buffon, by arguing that "before we condemn the Indians of this continent as wanting genius . . . we must consider that letters have not been introduced among them." In other words, American Indians had not yet evolved to a rationalized state of civilization.[28] Regardless, almost all philosophers agreed that white Europeans were by far the superior race. They did not agree, however, on Jefferson's rationale that indigenous Americans were superior to enslaved Africans.

The transatlantic slave trade had transported another race to the Americas—*Homo sapiens afer*, Africans or Negroes. For Jefferson, Negroes, because of their naturally inferior faculties, could not be incorporated into the new nation state as citizens.[29] In Query 14, "The Administration of Justice and the Description of the Laws," Jefferson sought a political solution to the problem of what to do with the Negro population living in Virginia, the majority of whom were enslaved. On several occasions Jefferson had proposed language in state legislation and in early drafts of the Declaration of Independence that terminated the importation of slaves into Virginia and the United States. (During his presidency he would succeed in 1808 in abolishing the international slave trade, but not its lucrative domestic market.)

Along with political concerns, Jefferson held "physical and moral objections" to the Negro based on a lifetime of observations of their comportment and character.[30] Because universal reason relied upon experimentation and observation for the validation of truth, Jefferson's conceptualization of the racial paradigm of human difference found one promising register in skin color. He rationalized that what counted as beautiful could be applied to the breeding of animals and also to the human species—where variations in physiognomy, hair texture, and skin color were visible. Out of all these markers, skin color was the most obvious indicator of racial difference. The origins of the skin's coloration for Jefferson, however, could not be discerned by dissection of the epidermal layers or a chemical analysis of blood or bile. He determined skin color as "fixed in nature" and therefore of divine causation. The aesthetics of blackness, the state of being black, both informed the rationalization of the variations in the human species that divided peoples living on the continents of Europe, Asia, Africa, and the Americas and affirmed the superiority of Europeans through their whiteness.

Under Jefferson's probing gaze, the features of the black body were seen as less beautiful in comparison to the symmetry and flowing hair of the white physiognomy. The overall lack of beauty in blackness visually and viscerally appalled Jefferson. He verified this by suggesting that even Native Americans had a preference for whites, much like "the preference of the Oranootan [*sic*] for the black women [*sic*] over those of his own species."[31] To posit black women as subhuman, closer to apes, was based on an early racial theory of polygenesis in natural history, which posited that each race was a different species. This degrading concept had circulated ten years earlier in Edward Long's epic *History of Jamaica*.[32] Blackness signified the Negro's subhumanity and validated her ruthless exploitation.

The Negro's inability to appreciate beauty, except in the most sensual manner, or to create works of true aesthetic value, except out of mimicry, also provided Jefferson with additional evidence of their natural mental inferiority. In Query 14 Jefferson surmised that in their ability to remember, blacks were equal to whites, but in their ability to reason and to comprehend mathematics and sciences, they were certainly inferior. "In their imagination," he wrote, blacks were "dull, tasteless, and anomalous."[33] To affirm the truth of his observations on the inferior minds of the Negro race, Jefferson offered the examples of composer/writer Ignatius Sancho and poet Phillis Wheatley.

Jefferson held nothing but contempt for Sancho, whose "letters do more to honour the heart than the head."[34] Sancho was born on a slave ship en route to the Caribbean and at age two migrated to England with his master. There he cleverly escaped enslavement by entering into domestic service in the households of several aristocratic families. Self-educated, he advocated for the abolition of slavery in a series of letters exchanged with a highly regarded abolitionist that brought him praise. Sancho leveraged his fame to become a well-known actor, playwright, and composer and an acquaintance to many of Europe's political and aristocratic elites. A celebrity in his right, Sancho sat for a portrait by the great painter Thomas Gainsborough (fig. 14). But in Query 14, Jefferson ranked Sancho, who was the first black person to vote in a British election, at the bottom in comparison to contemporary white men of letters. Jefferson suggested that if Sancho's works had any merit at all, it was most likely attributable to a white collaborator rather than to Sancho's own genius.

In Jefferson's mind, Wheatley possessed the inferior traits of both her race and gender. Wheatley was enslaved to a Boston family at age eight. Her owners named her Phillis after the slave ship that had transported her from the Senegambia to the port of Boston. Yet despite her appalling plight as an enslaved servant, she like Sancho learned to read and write at a young age. She was well read in ancient history and, inspired by the verses of Homer and John Milton, she began to write poetry, publishing a collection in 1773 (fig. 15). One of the few eighteenth-century American women to have been published, Wheatley used her public stature to advocate for American independence and for the natural rights of slaves. She was eventually freed by her owners after her first and only volume was published. Despite Wheatley's remarkable achievements under the harshest of circumstances, Jefferson believed her incapable of writing poetry, since love for the Negro could only stimulate the senses but not the imagination. He wrote that her poems were "below the dignity of criticism."[35]

To answer if the Negro, whether enslaved or freed, had a place in America, Jefferson put forward an emancipation scheme in Query 14. He proposed that enslaved children "should continue with their parents to a certain age, then be brought up, at the public expence [sic], to tillage, arts or sciences, according to their geniuses."[36] Once adults, women at age eighteen and men at age twenty-three, they should be colonized to African, Caribbean, or western US territories and supported until they grew in strength.[37] To replace the now absent labor force, Jefferson proposed to send "vessels at the same time to other parts of the world for an equal number of white inhabitants."[38] The arrival of European immigrants would realize Jefferson's vision of a nation composed of white freeholders whose homesteads would expand the nation's boundaries westward.

Fig. 14. Thomas Gainsborough (British, 1727–1788), *Portrait of Ignatius Sancho*, 1768. Oil on canvas. National Gallery of Canada, Acc. 58

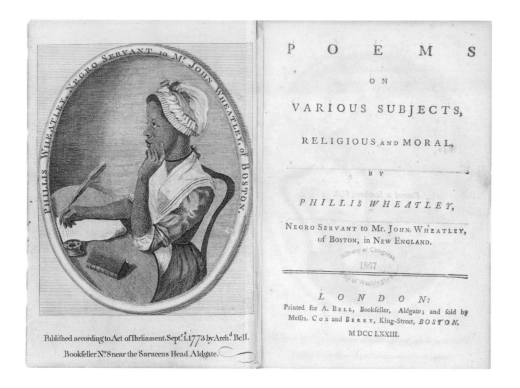

Fig. 15. Engraving after Scipio Moorehead (attributed; American, c. 1750–after 1775), frontispiece to Phillis Wheatley, *Poems on Various Subjects, Religious and Moral* (London: A. Bell, 1773). Library of Congress, PS866.W5 1773

Pragmatically, Jefferson believed that Virginia's history of chattel slavery would prevent black and white races living peacefully together, citing those "deep rooted prejudices entertained by whites; ten thousand recollections, by the blacks, of the injuries they sustained."[39] Emancipation and citizenship for the enslaved could only result in "convulsions which will probably never end but in the extermination of one or the other race."[40] American civilization therefore could not thrive with a free black population. The undesirability of blackness, the "unfortunate difference of color, and perhaps faculty, is a powerful obstacle to emancipation of their people," argued Jefferson in *Notes on the State of Virginia*.[41]

Once enslaved blacks were freed, Jefferson required them to be "removed beyond the reach of mixture."[42] Thus Jefferson feared not only revenge but also miscegenation.[43] These sentiments on the abolition of slavery and the slave trade as well as the resettlement of freed Africans were beginning to circulate widely on both sides of the Atlantic, eventually leading to the formation of the African colonies of Sierra Leone (1808) and Liberia (1822). The conservation of whiteness—symbolically and biologically—was paramount to the formation of the United States' cultural identity.

While emancipation might be desirable for political and moral reasons, the economic realities of how chattel slavery fueled the wealth and maintained the well-being of white Americans made it difficult to terminate an already two-century-long reliance. The enlightened white men who "liberated" the nation espoused the humanistic values of natural rights—Lockean "life, liberty, and property"—yet many were unwilling to part with their human property. Some of Jefferson's generation did manumit their slaves either during their lifetime or upon death, as did George Washington and his heirs. However, Jefferson, who owned up to two hundred slaves

Fig. 16. *Isaac Jefferson*, 1847. Daguerreotype, photographer unknown. University of Virginia Library, Special Collections, Tracy W. McGregor Library, MSS2041

at one time, more than six hundred over his lifetime, freed only seven slaves—two during his lifetime and five upon his death (fig. 16).[44]

In later editions of *Notes on the State of Virginia*, Jefferson records that by 1792 there was almost an equal number of enslaved blacks and free whites living in Virginia. The population of free blacks had grown substantially as slaveholders liberated slaves after the Revolutionary War. But those manumissions began to taper off as the value of slaves increased, with the domestic slave trade prospering as new states and territories in the west opened up due to the demand for vast swathes of land to establish large plantation operations. Slave labor was indispensable for cultivating crops like wheat and cotton, which were becoming more popular because tobacco farming had exhausted the soil in the Tidewater. Slave owners profited from hiring out enslaved blacks to other plantations or to perform unskilled and skilled work in towns and cities. Places like Richmond, where the capitol building was under construction, teemed with enslaved and free black artisans and laborers.[45]

In 1785 Jefferson wrote from Paris to directors Hay and Buchanan that given the scarcity of talented craftsmen in Virginia, it might be wise to hire European craftsmen well versed in wood, stone, and plaster construction techniques. Securing the services of a skillful stonecutter, for example, was desirable because, according to Jefferson, "under his direction, negroes who never saw a tool, will be able to prepare the work for him to finish."[46]

Once construction of the capitol building was under way, enslaved laborers joined the teams of workers that cleared the land, dug foundations, hauled wood, cut lumber, molded and fired bricks, laid bricks, transported stone, painted walls and trim, and removed the waste from Shockoe Hill. While those of Virginia's planter class like Jefferson possessed hundreds of slaves to work their agricultural holdings and small-scale industries like nail manufacturing, it was also common for free white Virginians engaged in business and trade, including construction, to possess a small number of enslaved Africans. While director of public buildings in Richmond, Hay, for example, owned six slaves over the age of sixteen (tax records only make note of those who were taxable, so there could have been others under age twelve).[47] Samuel Dobie, a skilled Richmond builder with working knowledge of classical architecture who executed Jefferson's designs, though not always faithful to the statesman's intent, owned two adult slaves during the time of construction.[48] Enslaved laborers were rented from slave owners such as a Mr. Elliot who loaned his "Negro man" for five days in September 1788 to assist in mixing mortar.[49]

Many of the tradesmen—plasterers, plumbers, and painters—owned several slaves. Edward Voss of Culpeper, a subcontractor and the supplier of the four hundred thousand bricks for the foundations, for example, owned seven slaves. In October 1788 Voss sent an invoice to the directors to pay Robert Goode "the sum of ten pounds 20 shillings for the hire of Negroes to oblige."[50] To perform numerous rough carpentry and woodworking tasks for several years through 1795, Dobie subcontracted Dabney Minor, who lived on a farm in Woodlawn, in nearby Orange, Virginia, where he owned seven slaves and kept ten slaves in Richmond.[51] Minor's arrangement exemplifies the connection between rural regions where raw materials were cultivated and towns where commodities and goods, including slaves, circulated in and out of markets. During the busy year of 1789, Minor's workers erected the interior framing of the courtroom and doorways, laid tongue-and-groove flooring in the courtroom, mounted scaffolding for workers to install pediments and cornices, moved bricks, and cut the wooden templates Voss used to erect the exterior columns—all part of a long list of tasks for which Minor was paid £154 (in 1788 Minor earned £1,004 for work on the site).[52] An advertisement Minor placed in Richmond and Hanover newspapers in 1794 explained that runaway slave Lewis or Lewy had been "employed at the whipsaw, and in rough plaining [sic]," which shows how Minor deployed enslaved workers in the various facets of his construction business.[53]

Because Richmond was a port town, freed black men also worked on the capitol building. A laborer named Fortune, who was known to Hay and Dobie, worked on the construction site for several months in 1788. His tasks included clearing away timber, planks, and rubbish from the yard. Fortune was paid directly, indicating that he might be either a freedman or an enslaved laborer who had some modicum of control over his time.[54] It is unclear from records whether enslaved Africans were rented for long periods of time and hence lived onsite. But given that Richmond was already a busy port town, the enslaved population, including women and children, provided a range of services from cooking to laundering to stabling. Enslaved blacks provided a significant portion of the labor necessary to erect Jefferson's monument to American civic life.

IMMOVABLE VEIL OF BLACK

The second of Latrobe's watercolors of the Virginia State Capitol, whose perspective is taken from across the James River, similarly depicts the civic temple dominating the rustic landscape, much in the same way that Jefferson's Monticello and the University of Virginia (1817–26) commanded their respective sites (fig. 17). In these two other designs, the high ground, both natural and man-made, provided Jefferson with the opportunity to architecturally reconcile the paradox between freedom and slavery by placing the slave dependencies beneath the main living spaces in rooms and passages hidden from view. That way the white-columned Neoclassical buildings appeared to Jefferson and to visitors as idyllic beacons of democratic values overlooking sublime nature, unsullied by the presence of those spaces where unsightly slaves toiled to make the land fertile and the lives of white citizens comfortable.

Fig. 17. Benjamin Henry Latrobe (British, 1764–1820), *View of Richmond from South Side of James River Showing Capitol from Bushrod, Washington*, 1796. Pencil, pen and ink, and watercolor on paper. Maryland Historical Society, 1960.108.1.1.36

Fig. 18. Advertisement for runaway slave, the *Virginia Gazette, Williamsburg*, September 14, 1769. Courtesy of the Virginia Historical Society, Richmond

Blackness was seen as a sublime "eternal monotony," an "immovable veil of black which covers all the emotions of the other race," wrote Jefferson in Query 14.[55] Black bodies and blackness for Jefferson, as for others of his era, proved an impenetrable threshold to reason. They were distasteful. Wielding the tools of enlightenment, Jefferson rationalized the Negro to the back end of the social and political forces that would advance American civilization, in the same manner he designed their spaces of interminable servitude to be placed belowground (fig. 18). While all men were born equal, as natural rights proponents advocated, to Jefferson, the Negro possessed neither the aptitude to reason nor the faculties to appreciate beauty or liberty. "The people" did not include Negroes. The prospect of a free black American was both unreasonable and unimaginable to the sage of Monticello. ❦

NOTES

1. Walter D. Mignolo, *The Darker Side of the Renaissance: Literacy, Territoriality, and Colonization* (Ann Arbor: University of Michigan Press, 2010).

2. Denise Ferreira da Silva, *Toward a Global Idea of Race* (Minneapolis: University of Minnesota Press, 2007).

3. See Mignolo, *Darker Side*, 264; Alexander Weheliye, *Habeus Viscus: Racializing Assemblages, Biopolitics, and Black Feminist Theories of the Human* (Durham, NC: Duke University Press, 2014), 24; and Sylvia Wynter, "Unsettling the Coloniality of Being/Power/Truth/Freedom," *New Centennial Review* 3, no. 3 (Fall 2003): 310.

4. Barry Bergdoll, *European Architecture, 1750–1890* (Oxford: Oxford University Press, 2000), 1–5.

5. For early examples, see Johann Bernhard Fischer von Erlach, *A Plan of Civil and Historical Architecture, in the Representation of the Most Noted Buildings of Foreign Nations, Both Ancient and Modern*, 2nd ed. (London: privately printed, 1737); and Julien David Le Roy, *The Ruins of the Most Beautiful Monuments of Greece*, intro. Robin Middleton, trans. David Britt (Los Angeles: Getty, 2004).

6. Fiske Kimball, "Jefferson and the Public Buildings of Virginia, II: Richmond, 1779–1780," *Huntington Library Quarterly* 12, no. 3 (May 1949): 303.

7. Da Silva, *Toward a Global Idea of Race*, 97.

8. Mark Wenger, "Thomas Jefferson and the Virginia State Capitol," *Virginia Magazine of History and Biography* 101, no. 1 (Jan. 1993): 82.

9. Thomas Jefferson, *Notes on the State of Virginia* (Richmond, VA: J. W. Randolph, 1853), 164.

10. Birgit Brander Rasmussen, " 'Attended with Great Inconveniences': Slave Literacy and the 1740 South Carolina Negro Act," *PMLA* 125, no. 1 (Jan. 2010): 201–3.

11. Fiske Kimball, "Jefferson and the Public Buildings of Virginia, I: Williamsburg, 1770–1776," *Huntington Library Quarterly* 12, no. 2 (Feb. 1949): 115.

12. Wenger, "Thomas Jefferson," 88.

13. William Hay and James Buchanan to Thomas Jefferson, 20 March 1785, folder 12, box 7, Capitol Square Data, vol. 2, Grounds (Original), 1776–1931, Archives and Maps Research Rooms, Library of Virginia (henceforth Library of Virginia Archives).

14. James Buchanan and William Hay to Thomas Jefferson, 18 October 1785, in *The Papers of Thomas Jefferson Digital Edition*, ed. Barbara B. Oberg and J. Jefferson Looney (Charlottesville: University of Virginia Press, Rotunda, 2008–16), https://www.upress.virginia.edu/content/papers-thomas-jefferson-digital-edition.

15. Hay and Buchanan to Jefferson, 20 March 1785.

16. Patrick Henry to Thomas Jefferson, 10 September 1785, in Oberg and Looney, *Papers of Thomas Jefferson*.

17. Richard Guy Wilson, "Thomas Jefferson's Classical Architecture," in *Thomas Jefferson, the Classical World, and Early America*, ed. Peter S. Onuf and Nicholas Cole (Charlottesville: University of Virginia Press, 2011), 102–3.

18. William Bainter O'Neal, *Jefferson's Fine Arts Library for the University of Virginia, with Additional Notes on Architectural Volumes Known to Have Been Owned by Jefferson, Issue 1* (Charlottesville: University of Virginia Press, 1956), 71–78.

19. Wenger, "Thomas Jefferson," 96–99.

20. Thomas Jefferson to James Madison, 20 September 1785, in Oberg and Looney, *Papers of Thomas Jefferson*.

21. Ibid.

22. Thomas Jefferson to James Buchanan and William Hay, 13 June 1786, in Oberg and Looney, *Papers of Thomas Jefferson*.

23. Jefferson to Madison, 20 September 1785.

24. Ibid.

25. Ibid.

26. Simon Gikandi, *Slavery and the Culture of Taste* (Princeton, NJ: Princeton University Press, 2014), 17.

27. Ibid.

28. Jefferson, *Notes on the State of Virginia*, 68.

29. I use the terms *Negro* or *black* rather than *African American* to encompass their ambiguous status at this historical moment, particularly since blacks were neither citizens nor were many of them Africans. Many blacks had descended from African and European families, who had lived in Virginia for two centuries; in many instances they were the product of white masters raping enslaved women. Additionally, there was a minority of freed blacks whose numbers had increased after the American Revolution.

30. Jefferson, *Notes on the State of Virginia*, 149.

31. Ibid., 145.

32. Suman Seth, *Difference and Disease: Medicine, Race and Eighteenth-Century British Empire* (Cambridge: University of Cambridge Press, 218), 212.

33. Jefferson, *Notes on the State of Virginia*, 151.

34. Ibid., 152.

35. Ibid.

36. Ibid., 148.

37. Ibid., 149.

38. Ibid.

39. Ibid.

40. Ibid.

41. Ibid., 155.

42. Ibid.

43. An ironic statement to make, since Jefferson would father six mixed-raced children (four survived to adulthood) with his enslaved concubine Sally Hemings, whom he took with him to Paris when she was fourteen years of age. Annette Gordon Reed, *Thomas Jefferson and Sally Hemings: An American Controversy* (Charlottesville: University of Virginia Press, 1998).

44. Jefferson officially freed Robert and James Hemings before he died. After his death John Hemings, Burwell Colbert, and Joseph Fossett, along with his sons with Sally Hemings, Madison and Eston Hemings, were set free. His two other surviving enslaved children with Sally Hemings, his son Beverly Hemings and daughter Harriet Hemings, left Monticello in 1822 without pursuit. See Lucia Stanton, *"Those Who Labor for My Happiness": Slavery at Thomas Jefferson's Monticello* (Charlottesville: University of Virginia Press, 2012).

45. Marie Tyler-McGraw, *At the Falls: Richmond, Virginia and Its People* (Chapel Hill: University of North Carolina Press, 1995), 65.

46. Thomas Jefferson to James Buchanan and William Hay, 13 August 1785, in Oberg and Looney, *Papers of Thomas Jefferson*.

47. Virginia Census and Tax List, Richmond, 1791, http://www.binnsgenealogy.com/VirginiaTaxListCensuses/CityRichmond/1791Personal/09.jpg.

48. Virginia Census and Tax List, Richmond, 1791, http://www.binnsgenealogy.com/VirginiaTaxListCensuses/CityRichmond/1791Personal/05.jpg.

49. "Sir there is due to Mr: Elliot," 12 September 1788, folder 1, Capitol Building and Receipts, 1786–1790, box 1, Capital Square Data Records, Library of Virginia Archives.

50. "Gentlmn, Please Pay to Robt Goode," 9 October 1788, folder 1, Capitol Building Vouchers, box 2, Capitol Square Data Records, Library of Virginia Archives.

51. Virginia Census and Tax List, Richmond, 1791, http://www.binnsgenealogy.com/VirginiaTaxListCensuses/CityRichmond/1791Personal/12.jpg. Virginia Census and Tax List, Orange, 1790, http://www.binnsgenealogy.com/VirginiaTaxListCensuses/Orange/1790PersonalB/16.jpg.

52. "The Directors of the Capitol to Dabney Minor," 27 February 1790, and "State of contracts made and executed in 1788 by the undertakers of work on the Capitol and paid for by the Directors viz.," n.d., folder 1, Capitol Building and Receipts, 1786–1790, box 1, Capital Square Data Records, Library of Virginia Archives.

53. "Explore Advertisements, Geography of Slavery" accessed 13 June 2017, http://www2.vcdh.virginia.edu/gos/browse/browse_ads.php?year=1794&month=9&page=0.

54. "Laborer Fortune waits for you," 2 July 1788, folder 15, box 1, "Dr. W. Samuel Dobie in Account," n.d., folder 1, box 1, and "Labr. Fortune work'd at clearing," October 1788, folder 1, box 1, Capital Square Data Records, Library of Virginia Archives.

55. Jefferson, *Notes on the State of Virginia*, 149.

THE ARCHITECTURE OF DEMOCRACY IN A LANDSCAPE OF SLAVERY

Design and Construction at Jefferson's University

LOUIS P. NELSON

As early as 1779 Thomas Jefferson offered a vigorous argument for widespread public education. In his unsuccessful "Bill for the More General Diffusion of Knowledge," he claimed that the best defense against the corruption of government was to "illuminate . . . the minds of the people at large." Years later, these fundamental convictions took the form of a new university, the final project of his life. The university's purpose was, in his words, "To form statesmen, legislators and judges, on whom public prosperity and individual happiness are so much to depend; To expound the principles and structures of government, . . . and a sound spirit of legislation, which . . . shall leave us free to do whatever does not violate the equal rights of another; . . . to develop the reasoning faculties of our youth, enlarge their minds, cultivate their morals, and instill into them the precepts of virtue and order." To that end he proposed ten professorships:

1. Ancient languages
2. Modern languages
3. Mathematics
4. Astronomy and geography
5. Physics, natural philosophy, chemistry
6. Botany and zoology
7. Anatomy and medicine
8. Government and history
9. Law and civics
10. Grammar, ethics, and the fine arts[1]

Adopting a commitment to the graduation of the liberally educated citizen, these ten professors were to live among the students in an "academical village." As the university began to materialize, Jefferson designed a campus that accommodated each those professors in one of the university's ten pavilions, five on each side of the Lawn (fig. 1).

The pavilions of the University of Virginia are among the most well studied designs in early American architecture.[2] Much of this stems from the unusually articulate intentions of their designer. The pavilions, in Jefferson's words, were to be "models of chaste and correct architecture, and of a variety of appearance, no two alike so as to serve as specimens for the architectural lecturer." To that end, they exhibited in three dimensions the various orders that served as the foundations of all classical architecture (fig. 2). This attention to detail included even the faces of Apollo that first appeared in interior friezes at Monticello, and then reappeared on one of the pavilions of the university (fig. 3). Jefferson intended the pavilions to be examples of ancient models in much the same way that he and Madison presumed that ancient models of government were the necessary foundations for a well-structured modern democracy. The Rotunda, which would serve as the library, was modeled directly on the Pantheon, which Jefferson would have known only through prints and architectural pattern books (fig. 4). The pavilions were designed "to improve the taste of my countrymen, to increase their reputation, to reconcile them to the respect of the world and to procure them its praise!"[3] Studying modern languages, anatomy, and astronomy among the architecture of the ancients was part of the collective project of graduating properly educated citizens who could with confidence stand on the world stage and defend their nascent democracy. Such a landscape, an academical village born from the pages of an ancient classical

Fig. 1. Benjamin Tanner, engraver (American, 1775–1848), *University of Virginia*, 1826 (from an 1824 drawing). Detail of the Böÿe Map of Virginia. Engraving. Jefferson Papers, University of Virginia

Fig. 2. Jacopo da Vignola (Italian, 1507–1573), *Les cinq ordres*, in *Regles des cinq ordres d'architecture* (Paris: Chez Jombert, 1764), plate 3. Washington University Libraries, Special Collections, NA2810.V62 1764

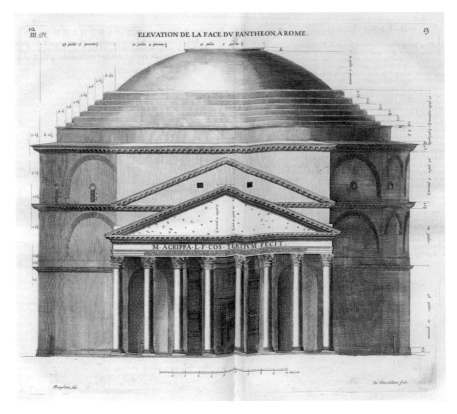

Fig. 3. Head of Apollo, architectural fragment from the north piazza frieze, Monticello. Lead. Thomas Jefferson Memorial Foundation at Monticello, Catalog # 001.210.0748

Fig. 4. Antoine Desgodetz (French, 1653–1728), Pantheon, front elevation, in *Les édifices antiques de Rome dessinés et mesurés très exactement* (Paris: Coignard, 1682), plate 3. Bound volume. Library of Congress, NA311.D4 1774, NA311.D4 1779, held in Sowerby 4198 Jefferson Coll fol. (LCCN 82466699)

tradition, was exactly the environment Jefferson presumed ideal for the inculcation of democratic and republican political values and the graduation of citizens prepared for global leadership. UVA was the architecture of democracy. But Jefferson's grand vision was beset from birth with a deadly cancer.

"All men are created equal, that they are endowed by their Creator with certain unalienable rights." These words framed a revolution, but they rang hollow for many of their hearers. The author of the Declaration of Independence was also the owner of 607 enslaved African Americans.[4] And while exploring Jefferson's complicated relationship with slavery is not the charge of this essay, it is my charge to offer a deeper understanding of the mechanisms by which UVA's architecture of democracy depended explicitly on a landscape of slavery. For they are inextricably linked, and to see one and not the other is the propagation of myth, not the writing of history. This argument will unfold in three short sections.

DESIGNING THE PAVILIONS

As imagined by Jefferson, the buildings on the Lawn were intended for faculty and students. The faculty were to live in the upper story of their respective pavilion and could connect with one another via the upper-story walkway; the students were to reside in the dormitory rooms between and take classes in either the Rotunda or the ground floors of the pavilions. In the preferred prospect of the university, captured best in a print from before it was completed, the academical village was represented as a white landscape (see fig. 1). Conversely, the ranges of the academical village, found downhill from each side of the Lawn, were dominated by "hotels," buildings where students took their meals in a common room and which also housed the large numbers of enslaved who cooked meals, cleaned laundry, and undertook all other domestic tasks. Enslaved domestic workers were hidden from view, expected to inhabit the basements of pavilions and hotels and the walled gardens behind. Jefferson's architectural designs separated education and work, free and enslaved.

Having already designed numerous private residences in Virginia, especially his own house on the mountaintop at Monticello, Jefferson knew that each of the pavilions would need a kitchen and some accommodations for the enslaved population. These were essential components of any antebellum Virginia household. Unusually, however, Jefferson placed the kitchen for each of the pavilions and hotels in the cellar (fig. 5). In the American South, kitchens were normally housed in exterior buildings in order to reduce the smell, smoke, and heat inside the residence, but also to reduce the risk of fire. By locating the kitchens in the cellars of the pavilions, Jefferson not only took advantage of the natural slopes on either side of the Lawn, he also thus hid both the people and the work to be done there partially underground, a strategy he had previously deployed at Monticello.[5]

Census data makes clear the large population of enslaved African Americans who lived in the academical village. Yet it is difficult to identify who they were or to obtain an exact count because institutional and state records are far from comprehensive. Virginia's decennial census numbers suggest that in any one year, the population of enslaved people was between 125 and 200. The vast majority of these people were owned by the hotel keepers who leased and operated the university's six hotels, which provided meals and cleaning services for all the students, but also by the faculty, who operated their pavilions in the manner of small-scale antebellum plantations. Students were forbidden from bringing any enslaved people with them to the university, although records make clear that students regularly broke

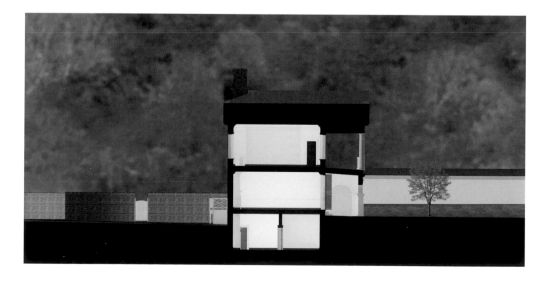

Fig. 5. Digital cross-section of Pavilion VII, Institute for Advanced Technology in the Humanities (IATH), University of Virginia

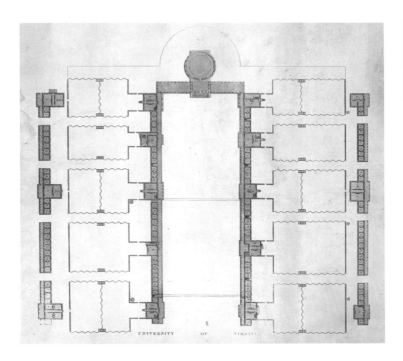

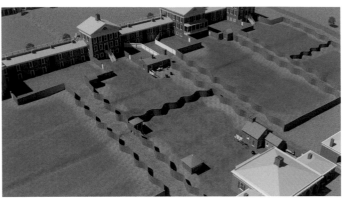

Fig. 6. John Neilson, draftsman (American, c. 1770–1827), and Peter Maverick, engraver (American, 1780–1831), University of Virginia ground plan, 1822, rev. ed. January–February 1825. Engraving. Special Collections, University of Virginia, Edwin M. Betts Collection, MSS 7073

Fig. 7. Digital reconstruction of the rear work yards between Pavilion VI and Hotel D, Institute for Advanced Technology in the Humanities (IATH), University of Virginia

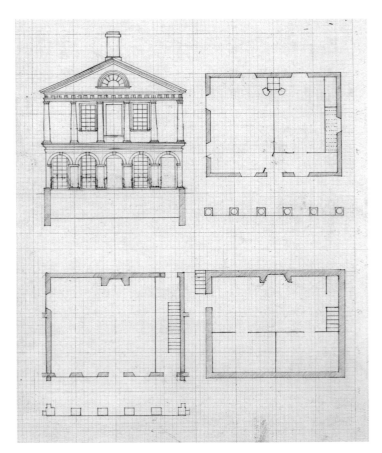

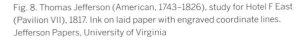

Fig. 8. Thomas Jefferson (American, 1743–1826), study for Hotel F East (Pavilion VII), 1817. Ink on laid paper with engraved coordinate lines. Jefferson Papers, University of Virginia

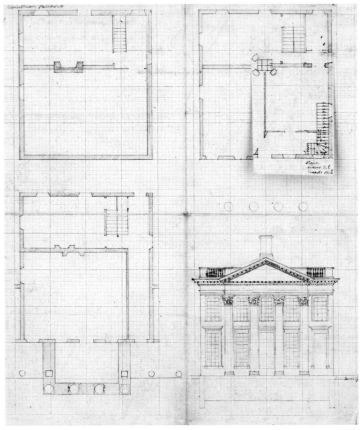

Fig. 9. Thomas Jefferson (American, 1743–1826), study for Pavilion III, c. 1818. Pricking, scoring, iron-gall ink on laid paper with engraved coordinate lines. Jefferson Papers, University of Virginia

that rule by housing them off grounds. If Jefferson used topography to hide the daily work of the enslaved in the pavilions, he used landscape features also to segregate the spaces beyond.

Unlike the more famous view, this early plan of the university helps to illustrate the university not as prospect but as spaces (fig. 6). In the plan, the gardens between the pavilions and the hotels are empty spaces bounded by serpentine walls. As reconstructed by the ladies of the Garden Club of Virginia in the late 1940s, today they are filled with geometric walkways and ornamental trees and shrubs, pleasure gardens akin to those at European estates. But these mid-century pleasure gardens were originally work spaces bounded not by serpentine five-foot garden walls but by eight-foot walls that worked to visually segregate students from the enslaved. Behind those eight-foot walls, African Americans grew food and prepared it, raised and butchered animals, washed laundry, chopped wood, and struggled to build lives and families (fig. 7). And it was no accident that the cellar spaces of the pavilions emptied directly into these rear gardens, making immediately adjacent the spaces of the kitchens and their work yards. But this ultimate solution was the result of an iterative process.

Although Jefferson had grand plans for his university, and especially for the designs of the pavilions, it was not designed in a single campaign. In fact, Jefferson turned his attention to the designs of the pavilions over the course of four years, from 1817 to 1820. This meant that as he was designing the later pavilions, he was able to learn from the occupation of the earlier pavilions. The likely use of completed pavilions as accommodations for builders and their teams meant that enslaved cooks and their kitchen workers were cooking in the cellar kitchens of the early pavilions before they were occupied by professors and their enslaved domestics. Not surprisingly, his designs for the cellars improved with time.

The construction of the university began in October 1817 with the laying of a cornerstone for Pavilion VII (fig. 8). Jefferson's plan for the building was concerned largely with the provision of a large classroom on the main floor and accommodations for the professor upstairs. In this first pavilion design, Jefferson paid very little attention to the design of the cellar, which included a kitchen and two chambers. He placed the cellar kitchen running north-south, with the cooking fireplace centrally positioned on the west wall. The only source of natural light in this space was the single southern door, which gave direct access to a work yard. But the limited natural light made available to the cook there was better than in the other two cellar chambers, which sat buried within the embankment. The only natural light for these two rooms would be through the exterior kitchen door, and then only when it stood open. The function of these two chambers is never made clear, but presumably Jefferson intended them for slave quartering, as they seem overly large for use as a pantry or storage.

Nearly a year later, in the summer of 1818, construction began on the second building at the academical village, Pavilion III (fig. 9). The plan differs markedly from that of Pavilion VII. In this design Jefferson made some improvements, especially in exposure to natural light. The north-south kitchen had an exterior door and two windows, one of which exploited the brighter, direct sunlight of a southern exposure. To provide more room for windows, the fireplace and hearth were moved to the interior cross wall. The creation of a northern stair hall reduced the width of the kitchen, allowing the fireplace to be closer to south-facing windows with far better natural light, while still centrally positioned in the room. The remainder of the plan is consumed this time by one very large chamber, likely a servants' hall. In 1833, this chamber would be described by then resident Professor Magill as "a comfortable room for servants" in his cellar.[6] Intended for a wide variety of uses by the enslaved community, the servants' hall accommodated sleeping, dining, children's play, and other realities of everyday life, but that use was still severely curtailed by the limited light streaming through the single small window. And furthermore, "comfort" might have been a stretch in this subterranean space; just a few years later, the university's committee on inspection resolved that the cellar of Pavilion V, just next door, was "to be made dry by draining the same."[7] These basement spaces were intended by Jefferson as kitchens and other accommodations for slaves, but their subterranean, dark, and often wet conditions likely resulted in frequent frustration, illness, and complaint among the enslaved population.

Fig. 10. Thomas Jefferson (American, 1743–1826), study for Pavilion I, c. early 1819. Pricking, scoring, iron-gall ink on laid paper with engraved coordinate lines. Jefferson Papers, University of Virginia

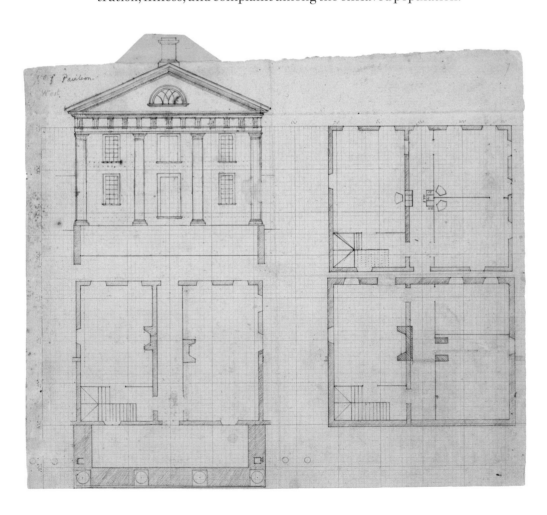

Early in the summer of 1819, Jefferson drew up plans for Pavilions I and V (fig. 10). While the exterior elevations were different on each, he used the same interior plan for both pavilions, including for the cellars. For these, his third and fourth pavilion designs, Jefferson made a few significant changes that would surely have been welcomed by the enslaved cook. The major shift was to rotate the kitchen so that it faced south, rather than east or west. This increased the potential for more light-filled south-facing windows. And while Jefferson's plans show only a single southern window illuminating the kitchen, that was changed during construction; as built, the kitchens have two south-facing windows. Preserving the close proximity of the kitchen and the staircase—to allow easier delivery of food from the kitchen to the dining room—the cellar stair hall occupies the southeast corner in these plans. Reflecting the organization of the spaces on the floors above, the cellar is subdivided by an east-west cross passage. This cross passage made more sense for the spaces upstairs; in the cellar it was largely wasted square footage. Opposite the passage from the kitchen are two chambers. Unlike the twin chambers in the cellar of Pavilion VII, these are both illuminated, but also clearly differentiated from each other. The larger space, much like the larger servants' hall in Pavilion III, has only a single window, but the smaller chamber to the west has both private access and two large windows, suggesting that this smaller chamber might have been reserved for the accommodation of the cook and their family. Such differentiation of spaces for more important or valuable slaves was not at all uncommon in other late-eighteenth-century or antebellum plantations in Virginia and across the South.

Just a few months after starting construction on Pavilions I and V, Jefferson began designs for the first pavilions on the east side of the Lawn. On June 15, 1819, he wrote that "it is but lately concluded to commence the Eastern range of pavilions & Dormitories I have not prepared the plans, nor shall I be at leisure to turn to that business till the week after the ensuing one, but those pavilions will vary so little from the dimensions last given & those of No. I, II, III the Western range that if the foundations are dug to that, that trimming them to what shape be the exact size will be trifling."[8] Soon thereafter he sat down to design a set of pavilions to stand along the east side of the Lawn.

The advances made by Jefferson in the cellars of Pavilions II, IV, and VI, all designed in the later summer of 1819, are best exemplified by the cellar of Pavilion II (fig. 11). In this plan he preserved the south-facing kitchen of his most recent designs, but he now worked to include even more light. Jefferson's design for the south-facing kitchen in Pavilion II included three windows along the south and two more to the east. But inspection of the building makes clear that when under construction, those three southern windows were all built as doors, giving extraordinarily fluid access between the kitchen and the southern work yard. In this plan Jefferson's intention to create a private chamber for the cook is even clearer. The fully private but small room with a single large north-facing window is immediately

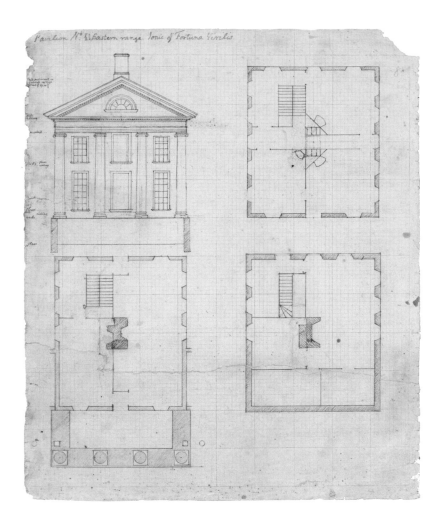

Fig. 11. Thomas Jefferson (American, 1743–1826), study for Pavilion II, June 1819. Pricking, scoring, iron-gall ink on laid paper with engraved coordinate lines. Jefferson Papers, University of Virginia

accessible to the kitchen through a door adjacent to the hearth. In Pavilion IV, the chamber that likely served as the cook's room even boasts a fireplace and is the first cellar room to be heated, excepting the kitchens, of course. In Pavilion II, the proximity of the kitchen to the staircase—so important in the pavilions on the west—is preserved. The distance here, however, is a bit more stretched, with the stair hall now located to the well-lit northeast corner. But the most important introduction in this phase of Jefferson's designs is his use of the entirely unlit zone of the embankment-buried portion of the cellar. In Pavilion II he reserved that zone for two long, narrow pantries with no windows and only a single door opening into the kitchen, very near the cooking fireplace.[9] With such limited access, both could have been easily securable. And so it would be that in his design for Pavilion II, in the summer of 1819, he capitalized on all of the various lessons and mistakes made in his designs for the west pavilions over the previous two years. As Jefferson designed his pavilions, he slowly came to recognize that his ideal vision for a university would necessarily include the labor of the enslaved. Largely inattentive to the labor of slavery at first, Jefferson gave increasing attention to the necessary work of providing for this academical village, revealing his gradual admission that his architecture of democracy depended on a landscape of slavery.

Zachariah was exhausted. He was strong, but the task was daunting. His owner, Luther M. George, had recently leased him to the University of Virginia, which had been under construction for two years. Soon after Zachariah arrived on-site, Mr. Henderson, the overseer for construction, directed him to dig the cellar and foundation for a hotel that stood behind and downhill from the first of the pavilions. Having lived and labored in Albemarle County most of his life, Zachariah had seen the firing of the massive kiln that produced the bricks for the first of the "academical pavilions" (now Pavilion VII). As he dug, he watched other black men working daily to level the larger worksite. The previous summer they had removed huge volumes of earth (records would report nearly one thousand cubic yards), forming what Mr. Henderson called "terraces." Zachariah watched as these men deployed shovels and barrows to slowly transform the gentle hillocks into the staged building sites for three more pavilions (now Pavilions I, III, and IV). Soon thereafter those same men dug foundations and cellars for the next two pavilions (Pavilions I and IV); Zachariah learned there were to be ten, five on each side of the terraces. Since only one building now stood completed, Zachariah and his fellow laborers slept on floor pallets in the upstairs chambers while the cook struggled to produce meals in the nearly unlit cellar kitchen. Zachariah's daily work excavating the hotel cellar moved quickly until he hit bedrock. For weeks he shoveled away the loose earth, all the while knowing that the substantial bedrock also had to be extracted. Once Zachariah began chipping away at the stone, his pace dramatically slowed, and Henderson became frustrated. Soon the earth-moving team from the pavilions was reassigned to work with Zachariah, and with the assistance of these others, the excavation was eventually completed.[10] The deep cellar of Hotel A and its attendant sunken yard are the work of Zachariah's hands (fig. 12). Yet, while he was digging, Jefferson and the board of directors were debating the appropriate sizes for the hotels. The sunken work yard Zachariah toiled so hard to excavate in 1821 was likely the result of a decision to shrink the building plan for the hotel *after* the cellar had already been excavated. And if that were not frustrating enough, the majority of Zachariah's earned money, more than $25, would go to his owner.

Enslaved laborers—both skilled and unskilled—played a critical role in the construction of the University of Virginia, yet few accounts from the period tell this story. We do not have a

Fig. 12. Digital reconstruction of Hotel A, Institute for Advanced Technology in the Humanities (IATH), University of Virginia

surviving journal from James Henderson, who was hired by the university proctor, Arthur Spicer Brockenbrough, to oversee the work of slaves like Zachariah. Were such a letterbook to survive, we might have Henderson describing the daily tasks and habits of Zachariah and other enslaved African Americans. As it is, one of our few options is to read between the lines of account books and to carefully piece together the working lives of slaves on the construction site through records never intended to be used that way. Zachariah's work, outlined above, comes to us with a bit more detail as a result of the frustrating nature of his task, the shifting of other laborers to the same task, and the resultant payments necessitated by the unforeseen bedrock.

The proctor's account book provides important insights into the everyday lives of the numerous enslaved African Americans who labored to build the University of Virginia. For example, on December 24, 1821, Proctor Brockenbrough made a draft to pay his slave Jack "for the waggonage of a Hhd [hogshead] of plaster from Milton & Lundy for kiln drying planks." The total was $2.[11] This entry is interesting in a number of ways. The first is the reminder that enslaved laborers—skilled and unskilled—were regularly leased to the proctor, as the agent of the university, to undertake work in the construction. For many large construction projects, it was common for enslaved people to be hired from local slaveowners. Sometimes laborers were hired for an entire year, or they might be hired for a particular project. In these leasing arrangements the earned money was usually paid to the laborer's owner, but occasionally, as in this case, enslaved workers were additionally compensated for accomplishing especially arduous tasks like digging the Hotel A cellar through bedrock or successfully completing unsupervised work like kiln-drying planks. The second is that Jack drove the wagon of hogsheads (large wooden barrels roughly four feet long and thirty inches in diameter) to the university construction site from Milton Farm, about eight miles away. Milton Farm was an important port on the Rivanna River and home to a lime kiln. This is a reminder that the construction of the university was a massive undertaking requiring the acquisition of huge volumes of building materials, many of which, contrary to common mythologies, were produced not on-site but in work yards all over the region or even across the state. Lastly, as the draft was made on Christmas Eve, perhaps the timing of this payment was related to the upcoming holiday, commonly the only week-long work break during the year, though it could simply be year-end accounting.

One of the slaves who appears most consistently in the construction record is Carpenter Sam, a well-respected artisan on the construction site who was owned by Proctor Brockenbrough. Sam first appears in the records when he is identified as the carpenter charged to begin the tinwork to cover the roof of the newly completed Pavilion VII in 1818, a task he later undertook for the roofs of Pavilion V and Hotels A, D, and F. By 1822, he was very active all around the site, contributing to the carpentry work on Hotels A and C and Pavilions V and VII. Either because he was an enormously well qualified artisan or because he was owned by Proctor Brockenbrough, Sam was among the most well paid of the slaves working on-site, usually drawing a salary for Brockenbrough of between $12 and $19 per month. We have no way of knowing, of course, if Sam received any of that money.

By 1824, as work on the pavilions and hotels was coming to a close, Sam built smokehouses around the site to meet the inevitable need for food preservation and storage once the pavilions and hotels were occupied. In this task, Sam supervised three other carpenters, Davey, William, and "young Sam," also owned by Brockenbough, and who may well have been the carpenter's son. Later that year, Carpenter Sam was identified as "old Sam" to differentiate him from the younger carpenter of the same name. In 1825, with the smokehouses complete, a team of three carpenters—old Sam, young Sam, and Davey—was set to the task of building stables, once again with old Sam in charge. Sam's services were retained through the opening of the university as the final tasks of construction dwindled to a close in 1827. Through the full decade of construction, Carpenter Sam was a prominent persona on the university's construction site, taking the lead on constructing many of the ancillary buildings necessitated by daily life at the university.[12] These thin details on Sam's life give us a better sense for his person than most slaves, who are remembered only by a single entry and often left nameless. Conversely, history has preserved for us a remarkable portrait photograph of Monticello's blacksmith Isaac Jefferson (see M. Wilson essay, fig. 16). This image was produced in 1847 after Isaac Jefferson was freed and took the name Isaac Granger.

As suggested by the payment to Mr. George for Zachariah's labor and to Proctor Brockenbrough for Sam's labor, many of the region's slaveowners tapped into the construction at the university as a means of generating personal income. The daybook records list at least sixteen different enslaved artisans who generated income for the proctor: Jack, old Sam, Davey, (young) Sam Jr., Henry, Ned, Dick, John, Aaron, Simon, Lee, Reubin, Burnly, William, Nelson, and Moses. Provocatively, the attic staircase installed in Pavilion I in 1832, when Brockenbrough was still proctor, bears a remarkable inscription scrawled in chalk: "Hurrah for Moses" (fig. 13). One wonders if that Moses might be the carpenter of the same name owned by the proctor, put to the task of building the staircase.[13] The vagaries of enslavement, of course, mean that we may never know. Again turning to the 1820 census, Luther M. George, Zachariah's owner, owned seven slaves in that year, a few years before he leased Zachariah to the university.[14] Of those seven, five were men between the ages of fourteen and forty-five. Another slave named Raphael was named in conjunction with Zachariah in the proctor's daybook associated with the digging out of the Hotel A cellar, so he may also have been owned by George.[15] George clearly felt that hiring out to the university was a worthwhile investment of slave time. And a number of the members of the board

Fig. 13. "Hurrah for Moses," chalk inscription, attic staircase, Pavilion I, University of Virginia

Fig. 14. Original steps from Rotunda, now installed at Bayly Drive, University of Virginia

of visitors, including former president James Madison, were also regularly paid for the labor of their slaves to build the university.

Few fragments are available today that allow us to name the artisan who produced some component of the early university. There is one important exception. In 1829 Proctor Brockenbrough purchased Thrimston for $600, one of the highest sums paid for a Monticello slave, and rented him to the university to complete the broad flank of steps that led up to the portico of the Rotunda at a much lower price than could be charged by free stonemasons.[16] Those stone steps were removed as a part of the 1930s Rotunda renovation, and some are currently installed as part of the retaining wall for Bayly Drive near the University of Virginia School of Architecture (fig. 14).

Carpenter Sam, Thrimston, and maybe even Zachariah became well-known personalities on the worksite and across the region, at least among builders. But reputations cut both ways; notoriety could also work against slaves if and when they decided to make an escape. Often through apprenticeships, enslaved laborers could become skilled artisans with identities that differentiated them from the majority. Under such conditions, they gained a degree of recognition, to the point that their owner's peers might even know their names and ask to hire their services. As a result, they had the capacity to earn money independent of their owner and, over time, the possibility to purchase their own or another's freedom. Running away was common. In 1822 the proctor directed James Harrison to track and find Willis, an enslaved man working at the university who had fled the work site for Louisa, about thirty miles away. Owned by planter W. Kelley, Willis had worked at the university for at least two years previous, having dug a cistern through rock in 1822 and helped to fire brick for five months in 1823.[17] He was named because he was well known. A few years later, when a slave named Jones fled the worksite, the proctor simply deducted the lost work from his payment to Jones's owner.[18] While there was very certainly a racial hierarchy at play, and also a clear hierarchy between skilled and unskilled laborers, the site was not so large that enslaved workers could not distinguish themselves and be known by name and reputation, which became a liability if any decided to attempt to secure their freedom.

From 1817 through the early 1830s, the University of Virginia was one of the largest building sites in the new nation. One result of that construction was the necessary production of a prominent male-dominated community of skilled and unskilled laborers—black and white, free and enslaved—who worked side by side, sometimes for years on end (fig. 15). Framed by the seasonal realities of construction, and animated by very real frustrations of unanticipated delays and the satisfactions of completion, this site witnessed the labor of hundreds of men through the decade, many laboring to erect buildings they would never be allowed to inhabit once complete. The academical village was the product of thousands of tasks and hundreds of projects undertaken by whites and blacks laboring together. Those enslaved who found themselves working there recognized that their situation differed from the more usual circumstances. They enjoyed a great deal more independence and freedom to travel than did their counterparts laboring in the fields of a plantation. And yet many of them, hired from far away, longed to return to their friends and families. Even so, recognition made all the more difficult the possibility of flight as they worked in a world ruled by whites motivated to foreclose any opportunity for freedom.

Fig. 15. Brick with handprint, architectural fragment, Monticello. Thomas Jefferson Memorial Foundation at Monticello

HOUSING THE ENSLAVED

One of the greatest shortfalls in Jefferson's transformation of the ideal "models of chaste and correct architecture" into functional houses for faculty was providing accommodation for enslaved domestics. Although Jefferson had by the later months of 1819 begun to design into his cellars a chamber reserved for the cook and his or her family, precious little space was allocated for the other enslaved laborers. As early as 1826, only one year after most of the pavilions were occupied and soon after Jefferson's death, the journal of the chairman recorded a series of requests submitted by the faculty for alterations to their pavilions. The chairman begged their patience and wrote that as soon as the funds would allow, the executive committee "will cause the necessary outhouses to be erected, & will consider the propriety of making the proposed alterations in their attics and cellars."[19] Just the year before, faculty had moved into their pavilions to find them equipped with cellar kitchens, some with pantries, others with a servant's hall, and some with a private chamber for the cook. But none of them provided enough quartering for their enslaved domestics. Consider for a moment the most extreme condition in the pavilions. The largest number of enslaved domestics was a total of seventeen owned by Professor John A. G. Davis, resident in Pavilion III in 1830. Presumably not all seventeen were sleeping in the "convenient" servant's hall described in the earlier section of this chapter; they likely slept in other chambers and passages of the house.

The faculty raised the issue of the dearth of accommodations or "offices" for their enslaved as early as 1826, but the situation had still not been addressed by 1828. In the summer of that year, Professors Emmet and Dunglison, in Pavilions I and X, respectively applied for the construction of separate living quarters for their slaves. Emmet had communicated that the cold and unventilated cellar chambers were causing his slaves to become ill.[20] The same was true of the hotels. The keeper of Hotel D, George W.

Fig. 16. McGuffy Cottage, University of Virginia

Spotswood, wrote that his cellar space "will always be unhealthy. Had I a cabin built for the reception of my servants, after they had done the dutys of the day to retire to, I should be in more comfort and my servants healthy."[21] As a result the proctor was directed by the board of visitors to construct "such buildings for the accommodation of servants," not to exceed $150 each. By September, both buildings were under construction. The following month, the board issued a policy expanding the offer to all faculty in pavilions and to the keepers of the hotels. The proctor was directed "to cause to be erected additional offices for the accommodation of servants in connection with the Pavilions and Hotels of the University, where they may be desired; not exceeding two apartments [each apartment of only a single chamber] to each hotel or pavilion." Numerous other faculty took advantage of this offer, so that by 1832 two-room quarters stood behind Pavilions I, III, V, VI, VIII, IX, and X.

Surviving building accounts suggest that these buildings ranged in size from 24 by 12 feet for a double apartment down to 15 by 12 feet for a single. Some of the records suggest that many of these included a garret accessible by ladder or stair, expanding the livable space of the apartment. In most cases the two main chambers would have been separated by a wall with a central chimney stack, so that back-to-back fireplaces could heat each of the two rooms. While many of these apartments were built, only one surviving example retains its early form, McGuffy Cottage behind Pavilion IX, which was built in the 1850s (fig. 16).

Close inspection of the attics of both Pavilions I and X has not yet produced any physical evidence that these spaces were regularly occupied by domestics as their accommodations, although the frequenting of these spaces largely by enslaved domestics is evidenced by the survival of "Hurrah for Moses," mentioned earlier. But the regular occupation and use of pavilion attics is suggested by the installation in the attic of Pavilion II of intentional series of nails on the collar beams near the front and rear windows. Of early-nineteenth-century manufacture, these nails are spaced in such a way as to accommodate the hanging of something light, possibly herbs for drying. This is an important indicator of the regular use of such marginal spaces, unprogrammed by Jefferson, as spaces of slave accommodation and labor.

It is worth recognizing that the requests for additional accommodations are greater among those faculty in the west pavilions than those in the east. One reason for this distinction is found once again in the landscape. The slope to the east is far more dramatic than it is to the west, and as a result the Lawn rooms to the east stand above chambers that serve as their foundations. As early as 1828, student Gessner Harrison communicated in a letter that washing and cooking could be done by "a woman who is the wife of a man who occupies my cellar."[22] As an attempt to minimize the potential of an epidemic, the proctor was required in 1832 to "have the Dormitories white washed, & the floors well scoured [and] to have such cellars as have been occupied also whitewashed," making clear the occupation of these spaces in the earliest years of the university.[23] And in 1840 the university approved "the cellar under the dormitory occupied as a study by Professor Bonnycastle to be fitted up for the accommodation of his Domestics."[24] Claims to use these spaces even became contested between faculty and students. The students living in the rooms to the south of George Blaetterman's pavilion inquired of the proctor "whether in paying rent of the dormitory, they had not a right to the cellar."[25] In so doing they wished to claim the rights to the cellar under their room that was being used by Blaetterman's slaves to house and milk a cow.

Physical investigation of these spaces across the academical village offers very clear evidence of this practice. The cellars below student rooms 10, 12, and 14 were occupied fairly early on by the enslaved domestics owned by Blaetterman, the resident of Pavilion IV just to the north (fig. 17). Physical investigation of these rooms shows clear evidence of early ceilings and whitewashed walls, evidence that these spaces had been at some point transformed from marginal leftover spaces into livable ones. The evidence is even clearer for the cellar under student room 22, which would have once opened onto the southern work yard of Pavilion VI. Here there is clear evidence

Fig. 17. Digital reconstruction of Pavilion IV work yard, Institute for Advanced Technology in the Humanities (IATH), University of Virginia

Fig. 18. *Lucy Cottrell Holding a Baby*, c. 1845. Daguerreotype, photographer unknown. Kentucky Gateway Museum Center, Maysville, Kentucky

for the postconstruction installation of a small chimney and fireplace. Similar but less clear evidence might survive for a working fireplace in the cellar chamber under student rooms 2 and 4, which would have opened into the southern work yard of Pavilion II. This is the same pavilion that once had three doors opening directly from the kitchen onto the same yard. For the cellar under student room 36, there even survives an 1850s plan of the basement that shows the cellar room communicating directly with the cellar under Pavilion VIII, visualizing the 1840 request for such an accommodation by Professor Bonnycastle. Documentary, visual, and physical evidence reveal a clear pattern. The cellars under the student rooms certainly appear to have been occupied by enslaved laborers and appear also to be associated most closely with the southern work yards of the pavilions standing immediately to the north. In a variety of ways, Jefferson's plan for his academical village failed to properly account for its dependence on slavery. There is no better evidence for this claim than the desperate scramble to rework his plans immediately after his death by the various faculty and hotel keepers who found themselves putting into action Jefferson's grand vision for a new university. While Jefferson's ideal vision could set slavery aside, in reality slavery pressed in at nearly every edge.

Let us conclude not with Thomas Jefferson but with a vignette that foregrounds the architectural experience of Lucy Cottrell (fig. 18). In September 1839 the students residing in Lawn rooms 10, 12, and 14 "complained . . . of very great nuisances created by the use of their cellar by Doct. B's [Blaetterman's] servants & of the yard embracing the cellar in which a cow was frequently penned & fed."[26] Awakened early each morning by the grunting and mooing of the cow being milked and then the stacking of milk pans, these students were annoyed by the work of Marshall and Ben, two enslaved young men who lived and worked in Pavilion IV, whose kitchen work yard sat just below the students' rear windows. Seen today, this yard space is a convenient parking lot for the pavilion, but this brief entry in the minutes of the university proctor opens a window for us into a very different set of conditions that once animated this marginal space in Thomas Jefferson's academical village. This lot was a work yard occupied by numerous enslaved laborers—and at least one cow—engaged in various activities throughout the course of the day to support the everyday life of a professor's family. This kitchen work yard was an extension of service spaces including the kitchen, pantries, and other chambers of Pavilion IV's cellar. By the opening of the university in 1826, the majority of the pavilions were occupied by professors who would bring with them or purchase in Virginia a cadre of enslaved domestics.

Pavilion IV's original cellar included five chambers: two smaller well-lit chambers to the east, an unusual north-south kitchen (the only such kitchen on the east side of the Lawn), and two fairly secure and unlit pantries to the west (fig. 19). As designed by Jefferson, the two more well lit eastern chambers were really quite distinct from each other. The northeast chamber included the staircase descending from the pavilion's first floor, but also the cellar's only exterior door. The chamber was clearly a nexus of circulation. The other chamber was a more secluded, even private, interior space with abundant southeastern light and the warmth of a corner fireplace. This chamber was likely occupied by Lucy Cottrell, her two adolescent sons, her mother, Dorothea Cottrell, and some other extended family, all purchased by Blaetterman from Jefferson's estate in various transactions between 1826 and 1829.[27] Lucy likely served the professor and his family as a cook, and her chamber had direct access to the longitudinal kitchen. Her poorly lit workspace was dominated by a large cooking fireplace and only two meager windows, one each at the north and south end of the room. As with the north-south kitchen in Pavilion VII, the significant distance of the single southern window from the cooking fireplace surely complicated the daily work of cooking. Insufficient light meant that Lucy often carried heavy iron pots to the window to more easily assess the progress of their contents. As cook, Lucy likely held the keys to the two unlit and unventilated pantries that opened onto the kitchen. The foodstuffs and other valuables stored in these rooms were surely of interest to Blaetterman's growing population of enslaved laborers.[28]

According to a pattern followed across all ten of the pavilions, the open yard to the south of Pavilion IV became a work yard for the various activities that were necessary for meal preparation and other support activities: butchering pigs, plucking fowl, milking cows, grinding grains, etc., activities that led eventually to student complaints. But a quick look at Jefferson's plan for the basement of Pavilion IV makes it clear that the southern work yard was entirely inconvenient to reach from the kitchen. Lucy had to pass from the kitchen and through the northwestern circulation chamber to the basement's only exterior door and then walk around the corner of the pavilion to step into the southern work yard. Something had to change, and it did. Sometime in the 1830s, Blaetterman consented to have a door opened between his kitchen and the cellar under student room number 10, ingeniously expanding the series of contiguous spaces of the basement and providing a direct route from the kitchen to the southern work yard, while preserving the valuable light

Fig. 19. Thomas Jefferson (American, 1743–1826), study for Pavilion VI, June 1819. Pricking, scoring, iron-gall ink on laid paper with engraved coordinate lines. Jefferson Papers, University of Virginia

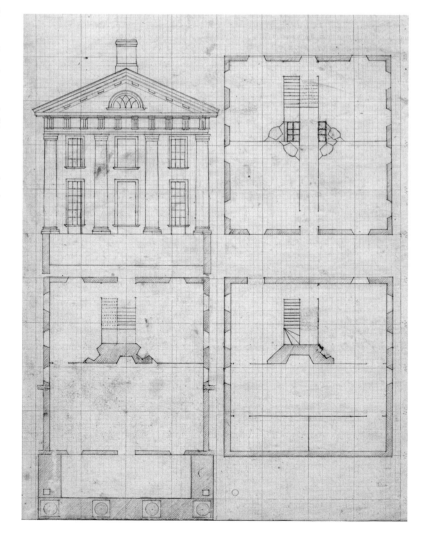

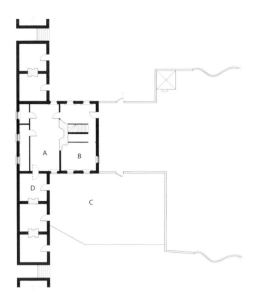

Fig. 20. Reconstructed plan of cellar of Pavilion IV communicating with work yard. Drawing by Nathanael Nelson

coming through the single southern window into the kitchen (fig. 20). Careful inspection of the wall between these spaces reveals a patch of brickwork where this opening was closed. Further inspection of the surviving original brick floor shows newly laid brick, presumably replacing heavily worn original brick, leading to this now-blocked door. The repair of a heavy wear pattern is further evidence of heavy traffic from the kitchen to the south yard through the cellar space under student room 10. And if the cellar under room 10 communicated with Cottrell's kitchen in Pavilion IV, those under rooms 12 and 14 likely served as additional quartering for Blaetterman's growing slave population and, for at least a season, the stabling of a cow. In this one change, largely invisible for the past century, we can begin to imagine Lucy Cottrell facing the hard work of her everyday life, cooking three meals a day for a man who probably threatened to beat her; Blaettermann was dismissed from the university for beating his wife, and if he beat his wife, he surely beat Lucy. Working to please her master while simultaneously avoiding him at every turn, Lucy additionally cared for her ailing mother and worked to raise her two sons in the hopes that her parenting might better equip them to navigate the landscape of slavery they already occupied. If opening a door to the work yard from her kitchen saved her a few minutes every hour, then that was worth the effort. Those reclaimed minutes could be added to the precious free time she might have with her family. That door was the closest, albeit insufficient, means she might have to her own declaration of independence. Her experience was shaped far more by the landscape of slavery than by the architecture of democracy. ❦

NOTES

1. "Report of the Board of Commissioners for the University of Virginia to the Virginia General Assembly, [4 August] 1818," *Founders Online*, National Archives, last modified June 13, 2018, http://founders.archives.gov/documents/Madison/04-01-02-0289. [Original source: *The Papers of James Madison*, Retirement Series, vol. 1, *4 March 1817–31 January 1820*, ed. David B. Mattern, J. C. A. Stagg, Mary Parke Johnson, and Anne Mandeville Colony (Charlottesville: University of Virginia Press, 2009), 326–40.]

2. Richard Guy Wilson, ed., *Thomas Jefferson's Academical Village: The Creation of an Architectural Masterpiece* (Charlottesville: University of Virginia Press, 2009); Joseph Michael Lasalla, "Thomas Jefferson's Designs for the University of Virginia," master's thesis, University of Virginia, 1992; Susan C. Riddick, "The Influence of B. H. Latrobe on Jefferson's Design for the University of Virginia," master's thesis, University of Virginia, 1988; Mary N. Woods, "Thomas Jefferson and the University of Virginia: Planning the Academical Village," *Journal of the Society of Architectural Historians* 44, no. 3 (October 1985): 266–83; Desmond Guinness and Julius Trousdale Sadler Jr., *Mr. Jefferson, Architect* (New York: Viking, 1973); William B. O'Neal, ed., "An Intelligent Interest in Architecture: A Bibliography of Publications about Thomas Jefferson as an Architect, Together with an Iconography of Nineteenth-Century Prints of the University of Virginia," *American Association of Architectural Bibliographers, Papers* 6 (1969): v–131; Frederick Doveton Nichols, *Thomas Jefferson's Architectural Drawings* (Boston: Massachusetts Historical Society; Charlottesville: Thomas Jefferson Memorial Foundation and the University Press of Virginia, 1961); and Fiske Kimball, *Thomas Jefferson, Architect* (Boston: privately printed, 1916).

3. "To James Madison from Thomas Jefferson, 20 September 1785," *Founders Online*, National Archives, last modified June 13, 2018, http://founders.archives.gov/documents/Madison/01-08-02-0191. [Original source: *The Papers of James Madison*, vol. 8, *10 March 1784–28 March 1786*, ed. Robert A. Rutland and William M. E. Rachal (Chicago: University of Chicago Press, 1973), 366–69.]

4. Lucia Stanton, *"Those Who Labor for My Happiness": Slavery at Thomas Jefferson's Monticello* (Charlottesville: University of Virginia Press, 2012); Lucia Stanton, *Slavery at Monticello* (Charlottesville: Thomas Jefferson Memorial Foundation, 1996).

5. Dell Upton, *Architecture in the United States* (Oxford: Oxford University Press, 1998).

6. Mary T. Magill, "Dr. Alfred Thurston Magill: A Memorial Sketch by His Daughter," *Alumni Bulletin of the University of Virginia* 4, no. 3 (November 1897): 77–84.

7. University of Virginia Board of Visitors minutes 1817–2007, July 4, 1845, and August 17, 1857, http://juel.iath.virginia.edu/resources (hereafter cited as Board of Visitors minutes).

8. Thomas Jefferson to Arthur Spicer Brockenbrough, June 5, 1819, Papers of the Proctor of the University of Virginia, RG-5/3, Special Collections, University of Virginia Library.

9. A room in much the same location in Pavilion VIII would later be called a pantry. "Minutes of the Faculty," July 8, 1853, http://juel.iath.virginia.edu/resources.

10. The vignette of Zachariah is pieced together from two entries in the proctor's account books: "Day Book, 1821–1828," 10/8/1821, p. 17, and "Day Book, 1821–1828," 11/25/1822, p. 107, RG-5/3/2/102, Albert and Shirley Small Special Collections Library, University of Virginia (hereafter cited as "Day Book"). The only major collected source on the subject of the construction of the university is Frank Grizzard, "Documentary History of the Construction of the Buildings at the University of Virginia, 1817–1826," PhD diss., University of Virginia, 1996.

11. "Day Book," 12/24/1821, p. 31.

12. Citations for Carpenter Sam are as follows: "Day Book," memorandum page; "Day Book," 1/30/1822, p. 36; "Day Book," 9/25/1822, p. 72; "Day Book," 11/25/1822, p. 107; "Day Book," 4/10/1823, p. 153; "Day Book," 9/16/1823, p. 210; "Day Book," 9/30/1823, p. 217; "Day Book," 12/29/1823, p. 239; "Day Book," 11/27/1824, p. 310; "Day Book," 6/27/1824, p. 271; "Day Book," 7/2/1824, p. 272; "Day Book," 9/18/1824, p. 298; "Day Book," 12/31/1824, p. 318.

13. For evidence of a carpenter by the name of Moses, see "Day Book," 5/14/1825, p. 345.

14. 1820 Decennial Census, Albemarle County, Virginia. *Fourth Census of the United States*, https://search.lib.virginia.edu/catalog/u2040113l.

15. "Day Book," 7/15/1822, p. 63.

16. Stanton, *"Those Who Labor for My Happiness,"* 140.

17. "Day Book," 1/25/1822, p. 35; "Day Book," 6/25/1822, p. 61.

18. "Day Book," 7/18/1825, p. 358.

19. Journal of the Chairman of the Faculty, October 2, 1826.

20. Board of Visitors minutes, April 3, 1826.

21. George W. Spotswood to James Madison, November 29, 1823, James Madison Papers, Library of Congress.

22. Gessner Harrison to Dr. Peachey Harrison, September 14, 1828, Papers of the Tucker, Harrison and Smith Families, 1790–1940, Box 2, Special Collections, University of Virginia Library.

23. Journal of the Chairman of the Faculty, August 1, 1832.

24. Board of Visitors minutes, July 4, 1840.

25. Willis H. Woodley to John A. G. Davis, Chairman, September 18, 1839, Papers of the Proctor of the University of Virginia, RG-5/3/1.111, Box 12, Special Collections, University of Virginia Library.

26. Ibid.

27. Elizabeth C. Blaetterman to Victoria, June 30, 1860, Papers of Francis Lee Thurman, University of Virginia Archives, Alderman Library, Charlottesville.

28. By 1850, Blaetterman owned eighteen enslaved African Americans, ten adults and eight children, who were divided between his pavilion and his small plantation near Keswick, Limestone Farm.

PLATES

JEFFERSON
AND HIS ARCHITECTURE

The last known portrait made of Thomas Jefferson is among the most classical, the portrait medallion in grisaille by the renowned Gilbert Stuart in 1805 (plate 1). The plaster bust of 1789, however, reflects the moment of Jefferson's Parisian sojourn, and belongs to a series of busts acquired by Jefferson of great American patriots sculpted in bust form, for his own home, by the key French Neoclassical sculptor Jean-Antoine Houdon (plate 2). Jefferson's home at Monticello has been called a portrait of Jefferson as well, because it so accurately reflected his person and ideas as they evolved over the two distinctly different designs he made, one before and one after his European experience. Compare the model of the house as it was when Jefferson left for France, a design derived straight from Palladio's *Quattro libri dell'architettura* (Four books of architecture), to the house as it stands today to understand how completely Jefferson had become his own original architect (plate 3). The aerial view (plate 4) of the building today shows how dramatically the profile of the house changed as the result of Jefferson removing the second floor and drastically expanding the house, adding a dome and single-story portico to the garden facade (plate 5) to create his own Pantheon in emulation of the Roman

temple that he and Palladio most admired. The most Palladian design he conceived was for the president's house in Washington, based closely on Palladio's Villa Capra "La Rotonda" near Vicenza (plate 6). The expansion of Monticello, meanwhile, proved inadequate to accommodate his many guests alongside his craving for privacy, and Jefferson built the smaller but exceptionally refined house at Poplar Forest, an estate he inherited through the family of his wife Martha Sayles (plate 7). Featuring the same structure of two opposing porticoes, this house also crowned a hill, but here Jefferson compensated for an incomplete wing using natural structures of a built-up berm and copse of trees in imitation of the missing architecture. Jefferson made many sketches and designs for friends. Barboursville (now ruined after an 1884 fire), near Charlottesville, repeated the domed portico of Monticello (plate 8). The most pure expression of Jefferson's admiration for the Pantheon in Rome was his design for the Rotunda at the University of Virginia, or his "academical village," the project that consumed his later years (plates 9, 10). Completing the campus fulfilled his dream of providing his Virginia with an educational institution in keeping with his Enlightenment ideals, but its design also provided a living architectural textbook, based heavily on Palladio's *Quattro libri*, that provided models of classical architecture for both students and the new nation.

Plate 1. Gilbert Stuart (American, 1755–1828), *Thomas Jefferson*, 1805.
Grisaille of aqueous medium on blue laid paper on canvas. Harvard University
Art Museum, Gift of Mrs. T. Jefferson Newbold and family, in memory of Thomas
Jefferson Newbold, Class of 1910, 1960.156

Plate 2. Jean-Antoine Houdon (French, 1741–1828), *Thomas Jefferson*, 1789.
Plaster. New-York Historical Society, Gift of Mrs. Laura Wolcott Gibbs, 1939.1

Plate 3. Designed by Simone Baldissini, constructed by Ivan Simonato, scale model of Jefferson's first design for Monticello (1:66), 2015. Wood, resin, and tempera. Palladio Museum, Vicenza

Plate 4. Thomas Jefferson (American, 1743–1826), Monticello, Charlottesville, Virginia, 1769–1809. Photo courtesy of Thomas Jefferson Memorial Foundation at Monticello

Plate 5. Thomas Jefferson (American, 1743–1826), Monticello, garden facade,
Charlottesville, Virginia. Photo by Martin Falbisoner

Plate 6. Designed by Simone Baldissini, constructed by Ivan Simonato, scale
model of Thomas Jefferson's entry for the 1792 White House design competition
(1:66), 2015. Wood, resin, and tempera. Palladio Museum, Vicenza

Plate 7. Thomas Jefferson (American, 1743–1826),
Poplar Forest, Bedford, Virginia, 1809–12

Plate 8. Designed by Simone Baldissini, constructed by Ivan Simonato,
scale model of Thomas Jefferson's Barboursville (1:66), 2015.
Wood, resin, and tempera. Palladio Museum, Vicenza

Plate 9. Thomas Jefferson (American, 1743–1826), University of Virginia,
Charlottesville, 1819–26. Aerial photograph courtesy of the University of Virginia

Plate 10. Rotunda, University of Virginia

VIRGINIA FOUNDATIONS

Jefferson's interest in nature and design was partly inherited from his own father, Peter Jefferson, a surveyor who published the first accurate map of Virginia in partnership with Joshua Fry (plates 11, 12). His father had surveyed the site of Virginia's Natural Bridge with a young George Washington as employee. Natural Bridge is a wonder of nature in the western part of the state, and one that proved to Thomas Jefferson that the arch form in architecture was derived from nature. It so inspired him that he purchased it from the British crown as a young man, prior to the revolution (plate 13). He praised it to his friend the English artist Maria Cosway, along with the spectacular junction of the Potomac and Shenandoah Rivers at Harper's Ferry in what was then still Virginia (plate 14). A British edition of another early American illustration of the Natural Bridge made a number of references to the injustices of slavery, another of the state's most distinctive features (plate 15).

Jefferson studied law at the venerable College of William & Mary in the state capital at Williamsburg, whose art collection gave him his first exposure to the broader history of art before his European trip. Matthew Pratt's copy of Guido Reni's *Jupiter and Europa* was typical of the fine copies after European masterpieces that were the most common form of art in the new republic, and the kind of paintings Jefferson acquired for Monticello as originals were too expensive (plate 16). He acquired his first version of Palladio's *Quattro libri* while still a student at the college, and as a true amateur would depend on his extensive, even exhaustive collection to develop his architectural designs.

The frontispiece to one of those volumes, the 1734 *Builder's Dictionary*, exalts the role of the amateur, showing a gentleman enlightened by means of its pages, then instructing a professional to proceed according to the latest principles they contained (plate 17). Jefferson and his contemporaries could learn about the details and history of classical architecture with exceptional sophistication. Roland Fréart's *Parallèle* specifically compared different ancient and modern versions of the classical orders of architecture, in this case pitting Palladio's design for the Doric column against that of his influential student Vincenzo Scamozzi (plate 18). Jefferson annotated his books in very direct fashion, in one instance cross-referencing this page with another book in his collection (plate 19). Once he was in Paris, however, the French draftsman and architect Charles-Louis Clérisseau persuaded him to examine actual Roman ruins rather than only Renaissance books, in order to learn the classical orders (plate 20), advice that profoundly influenced Jefferson's design for the Virginia State Capitol in Richmond. He continued to refer to his editions of Palladio's *Quattro libri*, however, as we see in his notes on his 1805 drawing for a hallway in Monticello (plate 21).

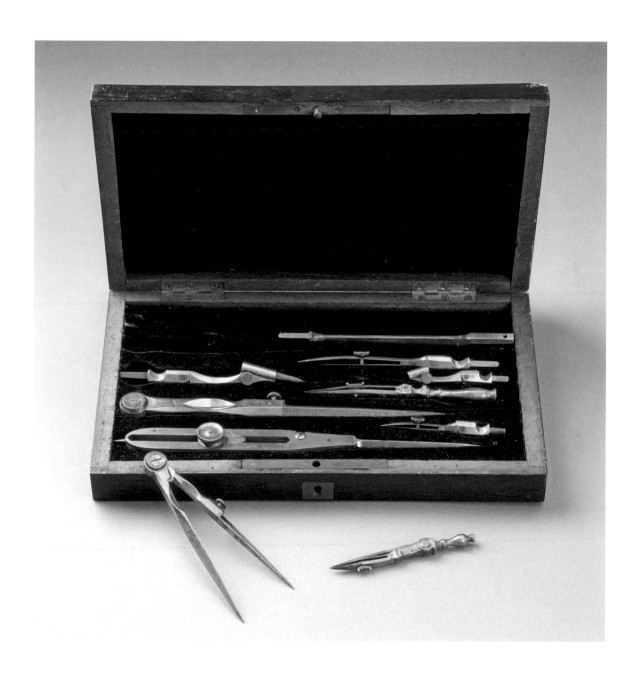

Plate 11. William Jones (English, 1762–1831) and Samuel Jones (English, 1770–1859), case with drawing instruments, 1786–1806. Brass and steel with mahogany veneer case and brass hinges. Thomas Jefferson Memorial Foundation at Monticello, Dr. and Mrs. Benjamin H. Caldwell Jr., 1992-9-2

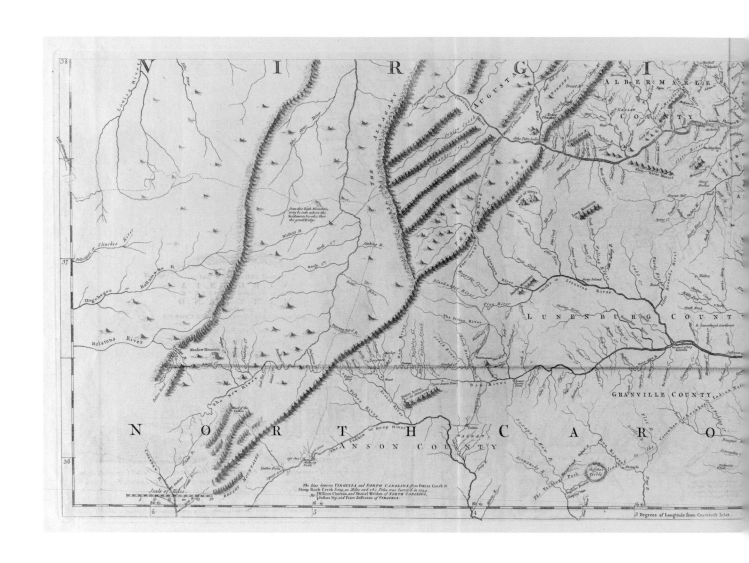

Plate 12. Joshua Fry (American, 1699–1754) and Peter Jefferson (American, 1708–1757), *A Map of the Most Inhabited Part of Virginia Containing the Whole Province of Maryland with Part of Pennsylvania, New Jersey & North Carolina*, c. 1775. Engraving. Chrysler Museum of Art, 55.11.3

Plate 13. Jacob Caleb Ward (American, 1809–1891), *View of the Natural Bridge, Virginia*, c. 1835. Oil on panel. Chrysler Museum of Art, Gift of the Norfolk Society of Arts, 2017.11

Plate 14. William Roberts (American, 1762–1809), *Junction of the Potomac and Shenandoah Rivers*, 1808–9. Watercolor on paper. Collection of the Museum of Early Southern Decorative Arts (MESDA), Gift of G. Wilson Douglas Jr. and Douglas Battery Fund, Acc. 3424.2

Plate 15. After William Goodacre (English, 1803–1883), published by
J. and F. Tallis, London, Edinburgh, and Dublin, *Natural Bridge over
Cedar Creek, Virginia*, from *History of the United States of America,
from the Earliest Period to the Present Time*, c. 1850. Engraving.
Chrysler Museum of Art, Museum purchase, 2018.13

Plate 16. Matthew Pratt (English, 1734–1805), after Guido Reni, *Jupiter and Europa*, 1770–71. Oil on canvas. Colonial Williamsburg, Partial Gift, William H. Cameron and Museum Purchase, 1992-45,a

To Face the Title.

T. Dewote inv.   Toms Sculp.

To build, to plant whatever you intend
To rear the Column or ỹ Arch to bend
To Swell the Tarras or to Sink ỹ Grot
In all, let Nature never be forgot.
                                        Pope.

THE
Builder's Dictionary:
OR,
Gentleman and Architect's
COMPANION.

Explaining not only the
TERMS of ART
In all the several
PARTS of ARCHITECTURE,
But also containing the
THEORY and PRACTICE
Of the
Various BRANCHES thereof, requisite to be known by

MASONS,	PLAISTERERS,	TURNERS,
CARPENTERS,	PAINTERS,	CARVERS,
JOINERS,	GLAZIERS,	STATUARIES,
BRICKLAYERS,	SMITHS,	PLUMBERS, &c.

Also Necessary Problems in
ARITHMETIC, GEOMETRY, MECHANICS, PERSPECTIVE,
HYDRAULICS, and other MATHEMATICAL SCIENCES.
Together with
The Quantities, Proportions, and Prices of all Kinds of MATERIALS
used in BUILDING; with DIRECTIONS for Chusing, Preparing,
and Using them: The several Proportions of the FIVE ORDERS of
ARCHITECTURE, and all their Members, according to VITRUVIUS,
PALLADIO, SCAMOZZI, VIGNOLA, M. LE CLERC, &c.

With RULES for the Valuation of HOUSES, and the EXPENCE calculated
of Erecting any FABRICK, Great or Small.

The Whole Illustrated with more than Two Hundred FIGURES, many of
them curiously Engraven on COPPER-PLATES : Being a Work of great
Use, not only to ARTIFICERS, but likewise to GENTLEMEN, and others,
concerned in BUILDING, &c.

Faithfully Digested from the most Approved Writers on these Subjects.

In TWO VOLUMES.

LONDON:
Printed for A. BETTESWORTH and C. HITCH, at the *Red-Lion* in *Pater-noster-Row* ; and S. AUSTEN, at the *Angel* and *Bible* in *St. Paul's Church-Yard.*
M.DCC.XXXIV.

Plate 17. Frontispiece, *The Builder's Dictionary; or, Gentleman and Architect's Companion* (London, 1734), vol. 1. Bound volume. Library of Congress, NA31.B82

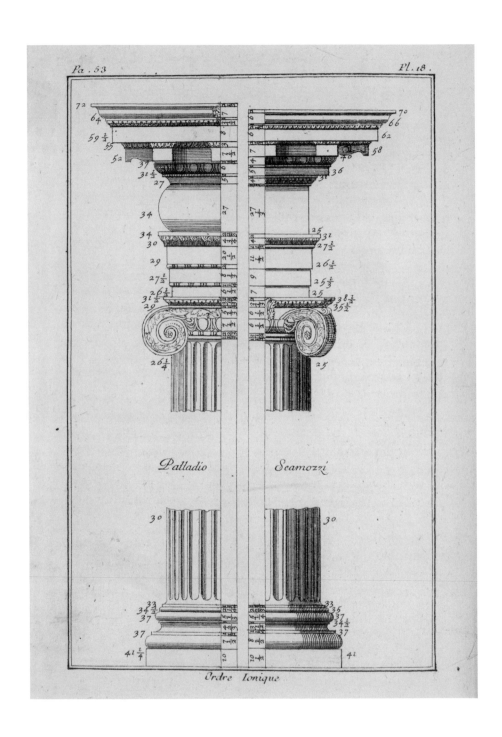

Plate 18. Roland Fréart (French, 1606–1676), *Parallèle de l'architecture antique avec la modern: Ordre Dorique: Palladio vs. Scamozzi* (Paris: Jombert, 1766), page facing 53, plate 18. Bound volume. Washington University Special Collections, NA2810.F87 1766

Autre profil tiré de quelques fragmens des thermes de
Dioclétien, *à* Rome. Planche 3.

C'étoit ici une des plus excellentes pieces d'architecture qui fû
dans les thermes de *Dioclétien*, & du meilleur goût, à ce q12
je puis conjecturer par un bon nombre d'autres esquisses que
j'en ai encore, lesquelles sont toutes dessinées d'une même
main, fort nettement & mesurées avec une grande étude, dont
quelques unes me paroissent assez licencieuses ; mais ce profil
est d'une si noble composition & si régulier, qu'il ne cede en
rien au précédent : enfin quoique les propriétés spécifiques de
cet Ordre soient d'être simple & solide, néanmoins les ornemens y sont si judicieusement appliqués sur chaque membre,
qu'ils conservent l'une sans blesser l'autre. Il peut suppléer dans
les occasions où celui du théatre de *Marcellus* ne conviendroit
pas, d'autant que la projecture de sa corniche est beaucoup
moindre : outre que la curiosité de voir les ornemens de ses
moulures attire l'œil à les considérer de plus près.

La proportion générale de ce profil n'est pas tout à fait con-
forme à celle de notre premier exemple, & leur différence me
fait juger que la colonne de celui-ci avoit huit diametres, c'est-
à-dire, seize modules ; car alors l'entablement, dont la hauteur
est de quatre modules, seroit exactement un quart de la colonne.

Ce qu'il faut considérer en ce profil, comme universelle-
ment observé par tous les modernes pour la hauteur de la
frise, c'est qu'en cette répartition des trois membres de l'entablement, la platebande qui porte le chapiteau des triglyphes
fait partie de la corniche, & n'est pas comprise dans la largeur
de la frise, quoique dans celui du théatre de *Marcellus* je l'y
aye fait entrer, pour demeurer dans les termes de la regle générale de cet Ordre, laquelle veut que la hauteur de la frise
soit d'un module & demi précisément, afin d'ajuster les in-
tervalles quarrés des métopes avec les triglyphes, ce qui est
une sujétion très grande, mais nécessaire. Au reste je ne veux
pas affirmer déterminément que la colonne de ce profil fût
sans base, car mon dessein ne m'en donne que l'entablement
& le chapiteau ; mais je puis aussi le croire, pour les raisons
que j'ai déduites ci-devant, & que j'ai amplement démontrées.

D ij

see an example of Doric with modillions Micali. Atlas. Tab. XIII.

Plate 19. Roland Fréart (French, 1606–1676), *Parallèle de l'architecture antique
avec la modern: Ordre Dorique: Palladio vs. Scamozzi* (Paris: Jombert, 1766),
page 27, with inscription below: "See an example of Doric with *modillions* Micali
Atlas Tab XIII." Washington University Special Collection, NA2810.F87 1766

Plate 20. Charles-Louis Clérisseau (French, 1722–1820), *L'ordre corinthien*, in or before 1768. Pen and gray ink and gray wash over graphite on laid paper. National Gallery of Art, Washington, DC, Mark J. Millard Architectural Collection, 1983.49.151

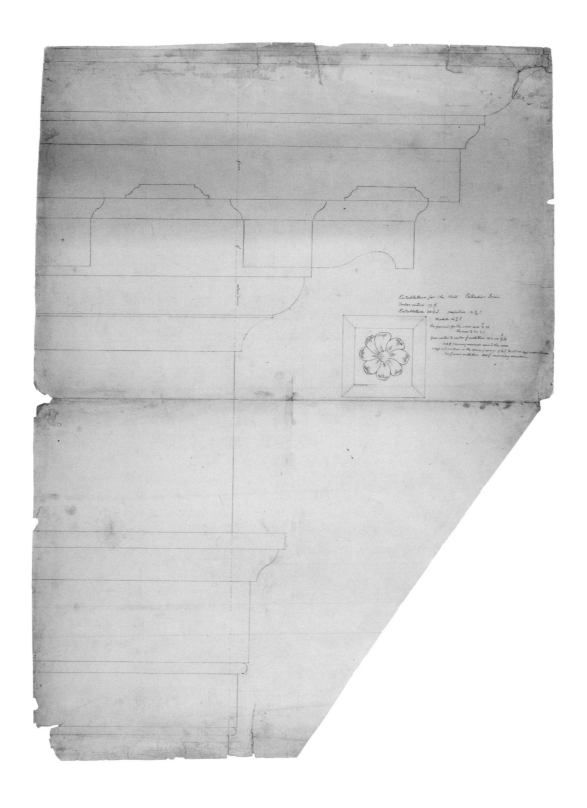

Plate 21. Thomas Jefferson (American, 1743–1826), Monticello, architectural
detail (hall), c. 1805. Pen and ink. Coolidge Collection of Thomas Jefferson
Manuscripts, Massachusetts Historical Society, N175; K160

ANDREA PALLADIO
AND PALLADIANISM

During his short stay in Italy in 1787, Jefferson was not able to reach Vicenza or Venice, the two cities in which Palladio spent nearly his entire career. The reputation of Palladio's work was spread not only through the manifold editions of his *Quattro libri* but also through the many paintings of his Venetian churches, paintings acquired by tourists to Venice in the 1700s. These favored paintings by Canaletto, like the c. 1750 capriccio that fictionally relocated the Rialto Bridge beside the iconic facade of San Giorgio Maggiore (plate 22). In another slightly earlier capriccio, the Venetian landscape artist honored Palladio's own design to replace the venerable Rialto Bridge according to classical principals, a design included in the *Quattro libri* (plates 23, 24). Palladio's architecture was based on his own extensive drawings of antique ruins like the Temple of Vesta, the best surviving round temple in Rome (plate 25).

Plate 22. Canaletto (Giovanni Antonio Canal; Italian, 1697–1768), *Capriccio: The Rialto Bridge and the Church of San Giorgio Maggiore*, c. 1750. Oil on canvas. North Carolina Museum of Art, 52.9.149

Plate 23. Constructed by Ivan Simonato, model of Palladio's design for
the Rialto Bridge in Venice, 2008. Wood and resin. Palladio Museum, Vicenza

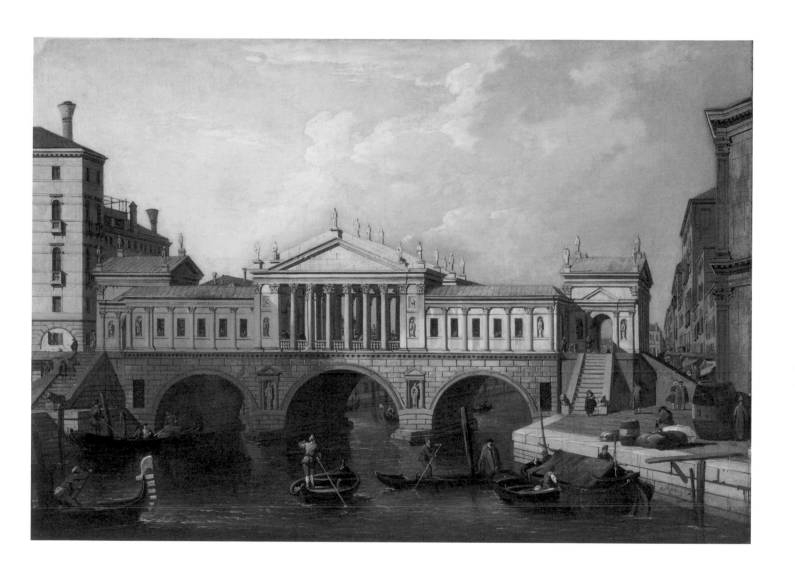

Plate 24. Copy after Canaletto (Italian, 1697–1768), *Capriccio with Palladian Design for the Rialto Bridge*, c. 1743–44. Oil on canvas. Philadelphia Museum of Art, Purchased with the W. P. Wilstach Fund, W1895-1-3

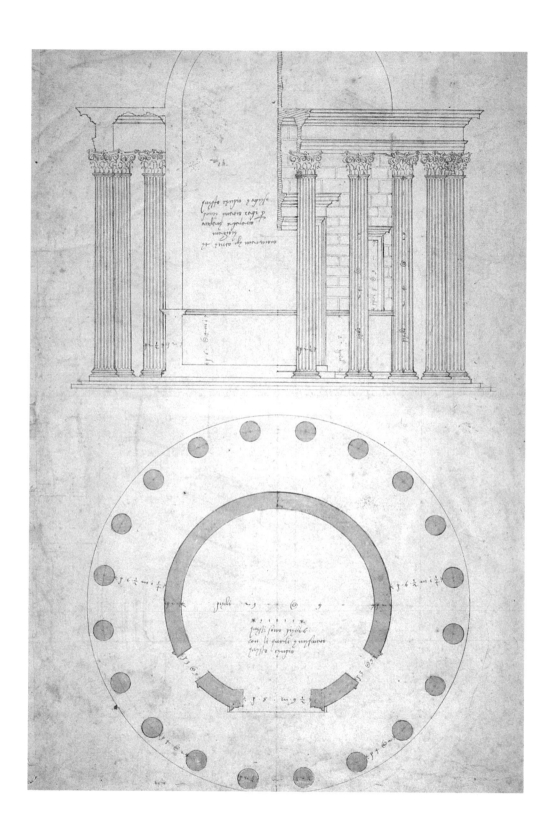

Plate 25. Andrea Palladio (Italian 1508–1580), *Circular Temple near the Cloaca Maxima, So-Called Temple of Vesta*. Pen and ink. Cornell University, the Carl A. Kroch Library, Rare Books, NA2517. P18

THE GRAND TOUR

Jefferson served as minister to France from 1785 to 1789, during an era in which gentlemen typically traveled to Italy to visit the sites mentioned in the books of their classical education. The elderly Charles-Louis Clérisseau persuaded Jefferson, who had hired him to assist on the design of the Virginia capitol, to visit the Roman ruins of Nîmes in Provence, such as the Temple of Diana illustrated in the frontispiece to his 1778 *Antiquités de la France* (plate 26). While in Paris, he saw the construction of the Hôtel de Salm, a building whose classical design, bowed facade, dome, and seeming single-story modesty enraptured him, and all influenced his second design and expansion of Monticello (plate 27). He met many other artists, including the neoclassical painters Angelica Kauffman and Élisabeth-Louise Vigée-Lebrun, whose *Portrait of a Young Woman Playing a Lyre* of a young lady in ancient Greek dress with a classical lyre captures the fascination with Greek and Roman antiquity that dominated Parisian culture at this moment (plate 28). While in Europe Jefferson also met the young American painter John Trumbull, who painted his portrait and whom he was able to influence toward classical ideals that are captured in his iconic *Declaration of Independence* (plate 29). Trumbull set the event in a Palladian interior and included the Paris portrait of Jefferson. Jefferson attended the Paris salons, as did artists including Angelica Kauffman. This celebrated woman artist painted her Neoclassical *Telemachus Returning to Penelope* in Paris shortly before she met Jefferson (plate 30). Although Jefferson was able to travel as far as Genoa and Milan on his own grand tour, Rome itself remained painfully out of reach.

Plate 26. Charles-Louis Clérisseau (French, 1722–1820), frontispiece, *Antiquités de la France, première parti: Monumens de Nîsmes* (Paris: Pierres, 1778). Bound volume. Library of Congress, LOC NA335.N5C6, LCCN 11034700

Clerisseau invenit.

Poulleau Sculp.

Plate 27. Laurent Guyot (French, 1756–after 1806), after François Martin Testard,
Vue de la maison de M le prince de Salm, située à la Grenouillère, in *Vues pitoresques des principeaux édifices de Paris*, 1787–89, plate 11. Engraving. Musée Carnavalet, Paris, G.3921

Plate 28. Élisabeth-Louise Vigée-Lebrun (French, 1755–1842), *Portrait of a Young Woman Playing a Lyre*, late 1780s. Oil on canvas. Cincinnati Art Museum, Gift of Emilie L. Heine in memory of Mr. and Mrs. John Hauck, 1940.981

Plate 29. John Trumbull (American, 1756–1843), *The Declaration of Independence, July 4, 1776*, 1832. Oil on canvas. Wadsworth Atheneum, Purchased by Daniel Wadsworth and members of the Atheneum Committee, 1844.3

Plate 30. Angelica Kauffman (Swiss, 1741–1807), *Telemachus Returning to Penelope*, c. 1770–80. Oil on canvas. Chrysler Museum of Art, Gift of Walter P. Chrysler, Jr., 71.665

PUBLIC ARCHITECTURE

Among Jefferson's most important projects was one
he designed with the help of Charles-Louis Clérisseau
while he was living in Paris: the Virginia State Capitol
in Richmond. Jefferson hired Clérisseau to assist him
in the design because of the older artist's immense
experience drawing the Roman ruins of France and
Italy (plate 31). Later Jefferson engaged Benjamin
Henry Latrobe to help construct another capitol
building, that of the United States in Washington, DC,
designed on the same classical principles (plate 32).
At this time Latrobe also drew a portrait of his friend
and fellow architect, one that captures the vivacity of
Jefferson and the tone of friendship between the two
men who forever changed American architecture,
making it continuous with the classical European
tradition (plate 33). John Trumbull sketched the interior of the old Maryland State House in 1783 for his
later painting *General George Washington Resigning
His Commission*, intended for the Rotunda of the US
Capitol, where it is still installed today (plate 34).

Plate 31. Charles-Louis Clérisseau (French, 1722–1820), *Roman Ruins with a Sepulchre*, n.d. Pen and gray ink with watercolor on laid paper. National Gallery of Art, Washington, DC, Gift of William B. O'Neal, in Honor of the 50th Anniversary of the National Gallery of Art, 1991.150.13

Plate 32. Benjamin Henry Latrobe (British, 1764–1820), *U.S. Capitol in the Course of Construction*, 1806. Pencil, pen, and ink. Maryland Historical Society

Plate 33. Benjamin Henry Latrobe (British, 1764–1820), *Sketch of Thomas Jefferson*,
1802. Graphite on white wove paper. Maryland Historical Society, 1953.73.2

Plate 34. John Trumbull (American, 1756–1843), *Sketch of Interior [Maryland State House, Annapolis]*, 1783. Graphite. Yale University Art Gallery, Gift of the Associates in Fine Arts, 1938.286a

VILLA IDEOLOGY

When George Washington initiated a competition for
the design of a new residence for the president in 1792,
Thomas Jefferson submitted an unsigned entry that
proposed a structure shockingly similar to La Rotonda
outside Vicenza, Palladio's crowning achievement
(plates 35, 36). It was not, therefore, a palace but a villa
that Jefferson proposed for the president, in keeping
with the approach Jefferson had taken to designing
his own house. Italian villas, like those of Roman
antiquity, were the centers of farming estates and
households as well as open and comfortable country
dwellings. Since Jefferson insisted on transforming
all of life through design, down to the furniture, he
commissioned the architect Benjamin Henry Latrobe
to create classical sofas and chairs for the president's
house based on ancient Greek designs. The house was
ultimately designed as a more palatial structure by
James Hoban (plates 37, 38).

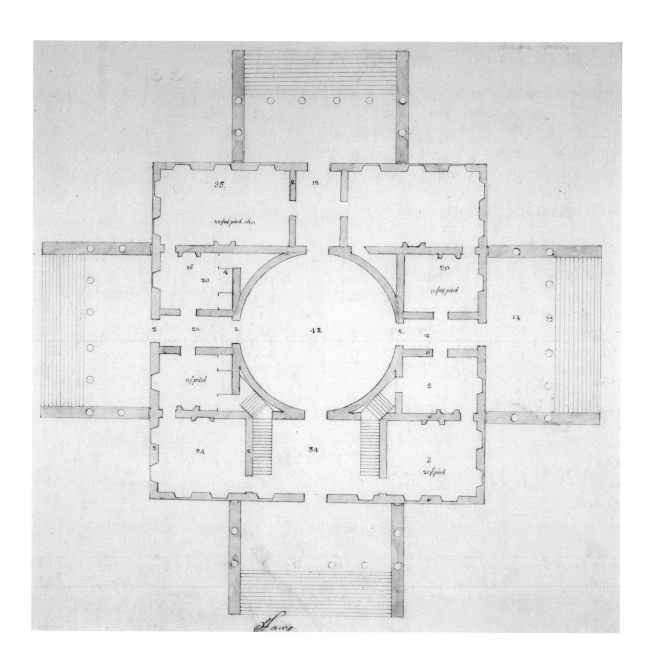

Plate 35. Designed and constructed by Timothy Richards, model of Palladio's Villa Capra "La Rotonda," Vicenza, 2015. Plaster. Photo courtesy of Timothy Richards

Plate 36. Thomas Jefferson (American, 1743–1826), president's house, first-floor plan, for the 1792 White House design competition. Pen and ink with gray wash. Maryland Historical Society, N399; K127

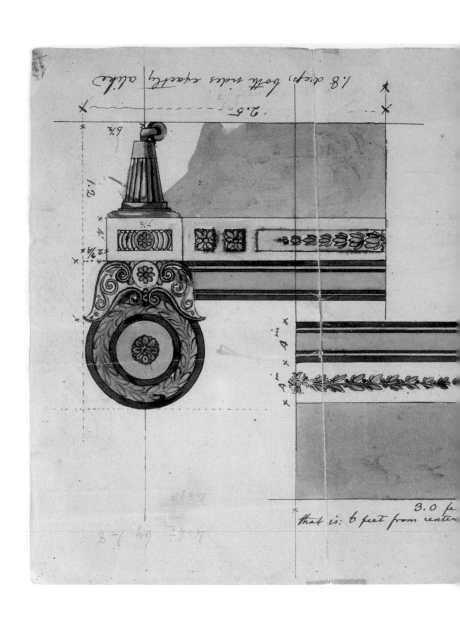

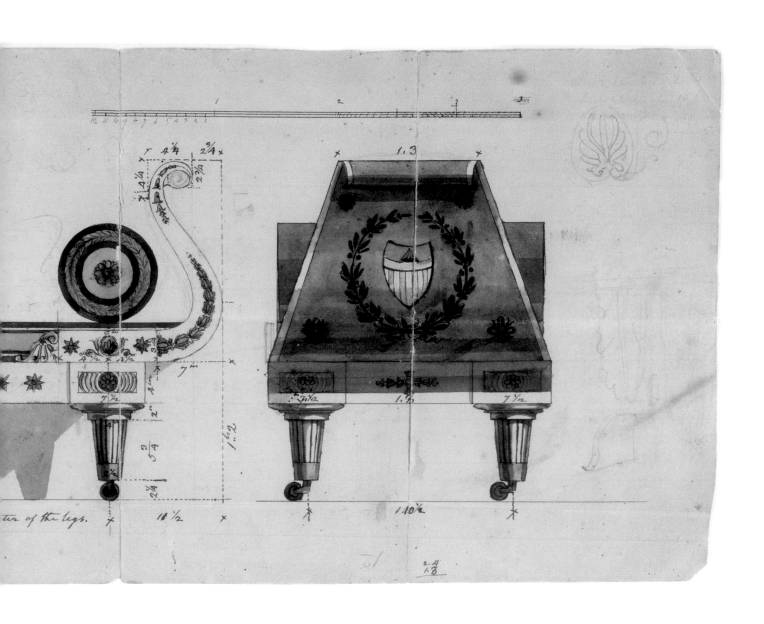

Plate 37. Benjamin Henry Latrobe (British, 1764–1820), drawing of a sofa for the president's house, 1809. Watercolor, pen, and ink on paper. Maryland Historical Society, 1960.130.2

Plate 38. James Hoban (American, 1755–1831), president's house, elevation,
for the 1792 White House design competition. Ink, wash, and watercolor.
Maryland Historical Society, 1976.88.3

MAKERS AND DESIGN

Jefferson insisted on designing a great many objects in his own house, from the obelisk form of his own tombstone to a clock mounted on twin obelisks. Although he never encountered an actual Egyptian obelisk on his travels in Europe, he certainly admired the ancient Egyptian form, which held funerary associations for him (plates 39, 40). He also asked John Trumbull to find replacements for the classically inspired candlesticks stolen from him in London, ones closely resembling a set at Colonial Williamsburg today (plates 41, 42). Skilled enslaved craftsmen like John Hemmings made doors, chairs, and Jefferson's more whimsical inventions at the joinery at Monticello, which was also a source of fine cabinetry for those on neighboring estates (plates 43, 47). He also designed several ancillary structures for Monticello that were never built, including an observation tower in classical style that would have allowed overseers to control the large enslaved population at Monticello more effectively (plate 45). He even felt compelled to conceive of a humble pigeon house in classical terms, as well as an octagonal pavilion that echoed the plan of several of his house designs (plates 44, 46).

Plate 39. Thomas Jefferson (American, 1743–1826), design for obelisk for the grave of Jefferson with his epitaph. Ink on paper. Library of Congress, Manuscript Division, Thomas Jefferson Papers, Series 1: General Correspondence, 1651–1827

could the dead feel any interest in Monu-
-ments or other remembrances of them, when, as
Anacreon says Ολιγη δε κεισομεσθα
                    Κονις, οστων λυθεντων
the following would be to my Manes the most
gratifying.
On the grave
        a plain die or cube of 3.f without any
    mouldings, surmounted by an Obelisk
    of 6.f. height, each of a single stone:
    on the faces of the Obelisk the following
    inscription, & not a word more
            'Here was buried
            Thomas Jefferson
    Author of the Declaration of American Independance
        of the Statute of Virginia for religious freedom
    & Father of the University of Virginia'

because by these, as testimonials that I have lived, I wish most to
be remembered. to be of the coarse stone of which
my columns are made, that no one might be tempted
hereafter to destroy it for the value of the materials.
    my bust by Ciracchi, with the pedestal and truncated
column on which it stands, might be given to the University
if they would place it in the Dome room of the Rotunda.
on the Die of the Obelish, might be engraved
            Born Apr. 2. 1743. O.S.
            Died ——   ,

Plate 40. Designed by Thomas Jefferson (American, 1743–1826) and Louis
Chantrot (active 1790s), obelisk clock, 1790. Marble, brass ormolu. Thomas
Jefferson Memorial Foundation at Monticello, 1985-43

Plate 41. John Robinson II (English, worked c. 1738–1773), candlestick, 1761–62.
Silver. Colonial Williamsburg, Museum Purchase, 1945-5.1

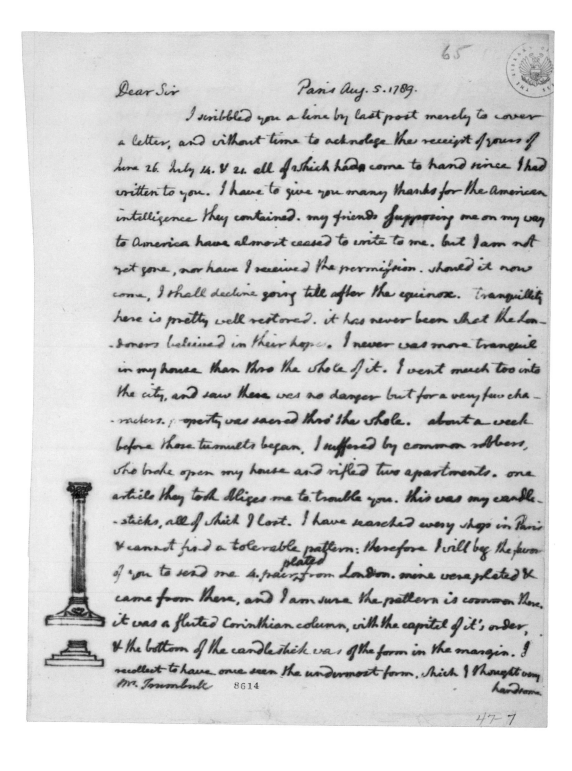

65

Dear Sir   Paris Aug. 5. 1789.

    I scribbled you a line by last post merely to cover
a letter, and without time to acknolege the receipt of yours of
June 26. July 14. & 21. all of which had come to hand since I had
written to you. I have to give you many thanks for the American
intelligence they contained. my friends supposing me on my way
to America have almost ceased to write to me. but I am not
yet gone, nor have I received the permission. should it now
come, I shall decline going till after the equinox. tranquillity
here is pretty well restored. it has never been that the Lon-
doners believed in their hopes. I never was more tranquil
in my house than thro the whole of it. I went much too into
the city, and saw there was no danger but for a very few cha-
-racters. property was sacred thro' the whole. about a week
before those tumults began. I suffered by common robbers,
who broke open my house and rifled two apartments. one
article they took obliges me to trouble you. this was my candle-
-sticks, all of which I lost. I have searched every shop in Paris
& cannot find a tolerable pattern: therefore I will beg the favor
of you to send me 4. pair plated from London. mine were plated &
came from there, and I am sure the pattern is common there.
it was a fluted Corinthian column, with the capitel of it's order,
& the bottom of the candlestick was of the form in the margin. I
recollect to have once seen the undermost form. which I thought very
Mr. Trumbull   8614   handsome

47-7

Plate 43. Attributed to Monticello Joinery, armchair, 1790–1815.
Cherry, webbing, linen, tow, hair, leather, brass. Colonial Williamsburg,
Museum Purchase, 1994-107

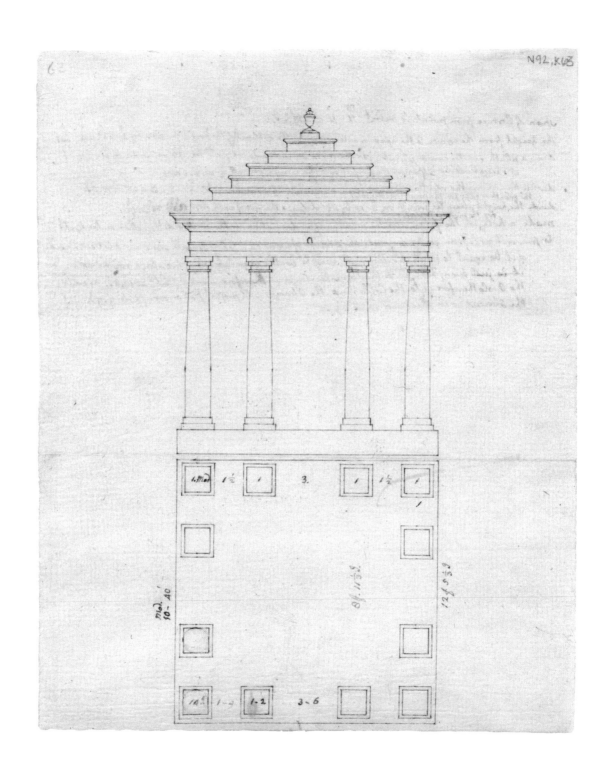

Plate 44. Thomas Jefferson (American, 1743–1826), pigeon house, Monticello, probably 1778. Pen and ink. Coolidge Collection of Thomas Jefferson Manuscripts, Massachusetts Historical Society, N92; K63

Plate 45. Thomas Jefferson (American, 1743–1826), observation tower,
Monticello, c. 1771. Pen and ink. Coolidge Collection of Thomas Jefferson
Manuscripts, Massachusetts Historical Society, N66; K39

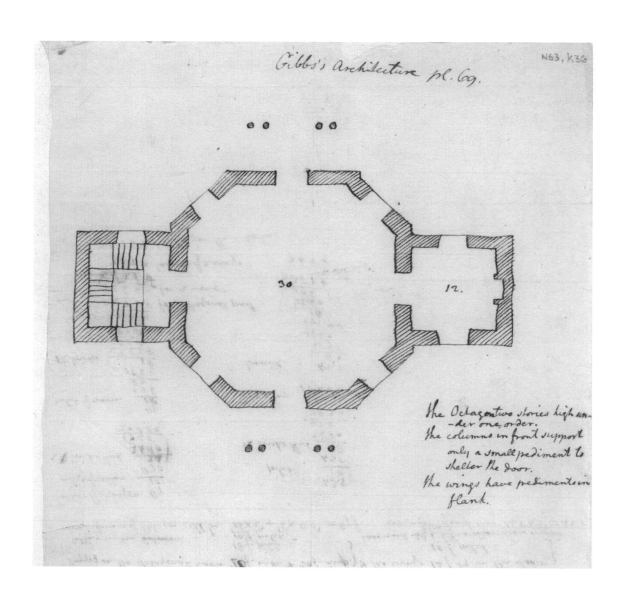

Plate 46. Thomas Jefferson (American, 1743–1826), garden temple, Monticello,
n.d. Pen and ink. Coolidge Collection of Thomas Jefferson Manuscripts,
Massachusetts Historical Society, N63; K36

Plate 47. John Hemmings (American, 1776–1833), Paneled door, 1809–19. Wood.
The Corporation for Jefferson's Poplar Forest, photo courtesy of Seth Trittipoe

UNIVERSITY OF VIRGINIA

The ancient Pantheon in Rome (113–25 CE), a temple Jefferson would have known very well through Palladio's images in the *Quattro libri* and through myriad other books in his library, was universally admired as an aesthetic as well as technical achievement. Tourists who had visited the building in Rome could acquire paintings like Hubert Robert's c. 1765–1800 *Landscape with a Temple*, which shows the Pantheon adjacent to the Colosseum and Roman Forum, a marvelous but illogical capriccio in the style of Canaletto (plate 48). The Pantheon first inspired Jefferson to combine a dome over a Greek temple-fronted portico at Monticello (see frontispiece). His Rotunda at the University of Virginia, however, was truer to its model, as it presented an entirely round structure to support the dome (plate 49).

Plate 48. Hubert Robert (French, 1733–1808), *Landscape with a Temple*, c. 1765–1800. Oil on canvas. Chrysler Museum of Art, Gift of Walter P. Chrysler Jr., 81.1

Plate 49. Designed by Simone Baldissini, constructed by Ivan Simonato, scale model of Jefferson's design for the Rotunda at the University of Virginia (1:66), 2015. Wood, resin, and tempera. Palladio Museum, Vicenza

ACKNOWLEDGMENTS

The Chrysler Museum of Art would like to thank a great number of people who have been instrumental in bringing this catalogue and exhibition to reality. Guido Beltramini, who developed the original exhibition at the Palladio Museum in Vicenza, helped us at every turn and dedicated the considerable resources of the Centro Internazionale di Studi di Architettura Andrea Palladio and the Palladio Museum, both in Vicenza, to the project. At the museum, Elisabetta Michelato and Ilaria Abbondandolo smoothly guided the loan of the precious models that are the spine of the exhibition. Without the newly corrected models developed by the museum, there would be no exhibition. Armando Varricchio, ambassador of Italy to the United States; Giulia Prati, head of the Cultural Affairs Office, Embassy of Italy; and her predecessor, Renato Miracco, have been steadfast supporters of this project. Howard Burns has been indefatigable in his support and labors on behalf of our project. Barry Bergdoll provided critical insight and assistance at an early stage of the project. We are grateful for the key contributions by Mabel O. Wilson of Columbia University and Richard Guy Wilson and Louis P. Nelson at the University of Virginia, as well as for the help of Matthew McLendon of the Fralin Museum of Art. Brian Hogg, Mark Kutney, and Ila Berman also assisted us at the University of Virginia; in addition, we thank Anselmo Gianluca Canfora at the School of Architecture, David Whitesell at UVA's Library, and Lauren Massari, Shayne Brandon, and Worthy Martin at UVA's Institute for Advanced Technology in the Humanities.

At the Thomas Jefferson Foundation in Charlottesville, Leslie Greene Bowman, Susan Stein, Ann Lucas, Gardiner Hallock, Emilie Johnson, and Lucy Midelfort generously assisted us. At Colonial Williamsburg, we gratefully acknowledge the aid of Ronald Hurst, Courtney Morfeld, Janine Skerry, Tara Chicirda, and Kate Teiken. Michael North, Eric Frazier, Rachel Waldron, and Giulia Adelfio helped us access the remarkable Jefferson collections of the Library of Congress. Jonathan Bober, Ginger Hammer, Rena Hoisington, and Mollie Salah welcomed us to the Prints and Drawings Collection of the National Gallery of Art. We also thank Ethan Lasser at Harvard Art Museums, Wendy Ikemoto at the New-York Historical Society, and Rebecca Rose and William M. S. Rasmussen at the Virginia Museum of History and Culture. In addition, we thank Bryan Clark Green, who provided information about the architect Thomas R. Blackburn. At Thomas Jefferson's Poplar Forest, Travis McDonald, Jeffrey L. Nichols, and Vincent Fastabend generously lent us their expertise and support. The Praxis Foundation was similarly generous. At the Massachusetts Historical Society, Brenda Lawson and Oona Beauchard helped us with the precious Jefferson papers, while at the Yale

University Art Gallery, Mark Mitchell and Rebecca Szantyr lent us their time and assistance. At the Wadsworth Athenaeum, Erin Monroe aided us, and at the Oak Spring Garden Foundation, Tony Willis provided generous assistance. We thank Mark Letzer and Alexandra Deutsch at the Maryland Historical Society, Brandon Brame Fortune and Beth Isaacson of the National Portrait Gallery, and Sue Ellen Grannis at the Kentucky Gateway Museum Center. At MESDA, Daniel Ackermann and Robert Leath helped our cause, as did Alex Nyerges, Michael Taylor, and Leo Mazow at the Virginia Museum of Fine Arts. At the Philadelphia Museum of Art, we salute Timothy Rub, Jennifer A. Thompson, Mark Tucker, Kathleen Foster, and Shelley Langdale for their aid.

We are very grateful for the support of Dominion Energy, the Wyeth Foundation for American Art, the National Endowment for the Arts, and the Embassy of Italy in Washington, DC. Funding for the models featured in the exhibition is provided by Roberto Coin. Support for the exhibition catalogue is provided by the Norfolk Society of Arts. Funding towards the exhibition has been provided by Joan P. Brock, The Goode Family Foundation, Peggy and Conrad Hall, Pamela and Bob Sasser, Susan and Dubby Wynne, Jim Hixon, Penny and Peter Meredith, Ashby and Joe Waldo, Duff Kliewer and Bruce Pensyl, Harry T. Lester, Charlotte and Gil Minor, Lelia Graham and Randy Webb, Meredith and Brother Rutter, Beth and Paul Fraim, Carolyn and Dick Barry, Virginia and John Hitch, Pam and Pete Kloeppel, Suzanne and Vince Mastracco, Patt and Colin McKinnon, Dixie and Jim Sanderlin, and Ashlin and Wayne Wilbanks. Programming for the exhibition was made possible in part by Virginia Humanities, Susan and Norman Colpitts, Kirkland Kelley, and the Docent Council of the Chrysler Museum of Art.

The staff at Yale University Press have been unflaggingly patient and professional. We would like to thank the great efforts of Katherine Boller and the editorial team, especially Kate Zanzucchi, Mary Mayer, Raychel Rapazza, and freelance copyeditor Miranda Ottewell, proofreader Carolyn Horwitz, indexer Krister Swartz, and designer Catherine Mills.

At the Chrysler Museum of Art, our project moved forward only through a huge team effort, but we would like to single out the dedication and efforts of Alison Bazylinski, Seth Feman, Debbie Ramos, Devon Dargan, Emily Zak, Kate Sanderlin, Kathleen Kaurup, Kate Wilson, Dana Fuqua, Clark Williamson, Susan Leidy, Anne Corso, Cody Long, Michael Berlucchi, Ed Pollard, Elizabeth Weir, Desi Mihaylov, Elise Duncan, Amanda Gamble, Cassie Rangel, Meredith Gray, Mark Lewis, and Allison Termine.

Lastly, we thank our boundlessly patient exhibition designer, Thom White, at WPA Architects in Norfolk.

INDEX

Frontmatter

Frontispiece: Collections of the Massachusetts Historical Society

Erik H. Neil | Introduction
Fig. 1. National Portrait Gallery, Smithsonian Institution
Fig. 2. © Thomas Jefferson Memorial Foundation at Monticello
Fig. 3. Photo Katherine Wetzel, © Virginia Museum of Fine Arts
Fig. 4. University of Zürich Libraries
Fig. 5. National Gallery of Art, Washington, DC, Mark J. Millard Architectural Collection
Fig. 6. Library of Congress
Fig. 7. Chrysler Museum of Art
Fig. 8. Library of Congress, Geography and Map Division, www.loc.gov /item/8864196/
Fig. 9. Palladio Museum, Vicenza
Fig. 10. University of Virginia Special Collections

Howard Burns | Thomas Jefferson, the Making of an Architect
Figs. 1, 26. Library of Congress
Figs. 2, 3, 4. Image in the public domain
Figs. 5, 7. Colonial Williamsburg
Fig. 6. Frances Benjamin Johnson, photographer. Library of Congress, https://www.loc.gov/item/2017891585/
Figs. 8, 11. Palladio Museum, Vicenza
Figs. 9, 13, 14, 19, 20, 30. University of Zürich
Fig. 10. Photo courtesy of Tom Weber
Figs. 12, 16, 22, 24. Collection of the Massachusetts Historical Society
Fig. 15. National Museum of American History, Smithsonian Institution
Figs. 17, 18. Getty Research Institute
Fig. 21. Photo courtesy of the Hammond-Harwood House
Fig. 23. Alamy Stock Photography
Fig. 25. University of Virginia Special Collections
Fig. 27. Bibliothèque de l'Institut National d'Histoire de l'Art, collections Jacques Doucet
Fig. 28. Universität Heidelberg, http://digi.ub.uni-he idelbert.de/diglit /becker1798/0001
Fig. 29. University of Virginia Special Collections, http://www2.iath.virginia.edu /wilson/cgi-bin/draw_filter.pl?id=N350
Fig. 31. Maryland Historical Society

Guido Beltramini | The Palladians
Figs. 1–9. Mediateca del Centro Internazionale di Studi di Architettura Andrea Palladio, Vicenza

Richard Guy Wilson | Jefferson and England
Figs. 1, 4, 5, 7, 8, 10. Courtesy of Richard Guy Wilson

Fig. 2. Greg Balfour Evans/Alamy Stock Photo
Fig. 3. Library of Congress
Fig. 6. © The Royal Collection Trust
Fig. 9. University of Wisconsin Libraries

Lloyd DeWitt | What He Saw: Thomas Jefferson's Grand Tour
Fig. 1. Yale University Art Gallery, Mabel Brady Garvan Collection
Fig. 2. Philadelphia Museum of Art
Fig. 3. University of Zürich
Fig. 4. © Thomas Jefferson Memorial Foundation at Monticello
Fig. 5. Library of Congress
Fig. 6. Photograph in the public domain, courtesy of Troy Owens
Fig. 7. Collection of the Virginia State Library and Archives, Richmond, Courtesy of the Virginia General Assembly
Fig. 8. Washington University
Fig. 9. National Gallery of Art, Washington, DC, Mark J. Millard Architectural Collection
Fig. 10. Österreichische Nationalbibliothek
Figs. 11, 14. Chrysler Museum of Art
Fig. 12. Virginia Museum of History and Culture, Richmond
Fig. 13. Palladio Museum, Vicenza
Fig. 15. Rijksmuseum, Amsterdam
Fig. 16. National Gallery of Art, Washington, DC
Figs. 17, 18. Photographs in the public domain

Barry Bergdoll | Books, Buildings, and the Spaces of Democracy: Jefferson's Library from Paris to Washington
Fig. 1. Musée Carnavalet, Paris
Figs. 2, 10. National Gallery of Art, Washington, DC, Mark J. Millard Architectural Collection
Figs. 3, 6–9. Bibliothèque Nationale de France
Figs. 4, 5. Heidelberg University

Mabel O. Wilson | Race, Reason, and the Architecture of Jefferson's Virginia Statehouse
Figs. 1, 2, 17. Maryland Historical Society
Fig. 3. National Gallery of Art, Washington, DC, Andrew Mellon Collection
Figs. 4–6. Huntington Library
Figs. 7, 10, 12. Collections of the Massachusetts Historical Society
Fig. 8. University of Zürich
Fig. 9. Bibliothèque Nationale de France
Fig. 11. Chrysler Museum of Art
Fig. 13. Palladio Museum, Vicenza, model 10
Fig. 14. National Gallery of Canada
Fig. 15. Library of Congress
Fig. 16. University of Virginia Library, Special Collections
Fig. 18. Courtesy of the Virginia Historical Society, Richmond

Louis P. Nelson | The Architecture of Democracy in a Landscape of Slavery: Design and Construction at Jefferson's University
Figs. 1, 8–11, 19. Jefferson Papers, University of Virginia
Fig. 2. Washington University
Fig. 3, 15. © Thomas Jefferson Memorial Foundation at Monticello
Fig. 4. Library of Congress
Figs. 5, 12, 17. Institute for Advanced Technology in the Humanities (IATH), University of Virginia. Courtesy of Louis Nelson
Fig. 6. University of Virginia
Figs. 7, 13, 16. Courtesy of Louis Nelson
Fig. 14. Photograph courtesy of James Zehmer
Fig. 18. Kentucky Gateway Museum Center, Maysville, Kentucky
Fig. 20. Drawing by Nathanael Nelson. Courtesy of Louis Nelson

Plates
Plate 1. Harvard University Art Museum
Plate 2. New-York Historical Society
Plates 3, 6, 8, 23, 49. Palladio Museum, Vicenza
Plates 4, 11, 40. © Thomas Jefferson Memorial Foundation at Monticello
Plate 5. Photo courtesy of Martin Falbisoner—Own work, CC BY-SA 3.0, https://commons.wikimedia.org/w /index.php?curid=56104432
Plates 7, 10. Alamy Stock Photography
Plate 9. University of Virginia
Plates 12, 13, 15, 30, 48. Chrysler Museum of Art
Plate 14. Collection of the Museum of Early Southern Decorative Arts
Plates 16, 41, 43. Colonial Williamsburg
Plates 17, 26, 39, 42. Library of Congress
Plates 18, 19. Washington University Special Collections
Plate 20. National Gallery of Art, Mark J. Millard Architectural Collection
Plates 21, 44–46. Collections of the Massachusetts Historical Society
Plate 22. North Carolina Museum of Art
Plate 24. Philadelphia Museum of Art
Plate 25. Cornell University
Plate 27. Musée Carnavalet, Paris
Plate 28. Cincinnatti Art Museum
Plate 29. Wadsworth Atheneum
Plate 31. National Gallery of Art, Washington, DC
Plates 32, 33, 36–38. Maryland Historical Society
Plate 34. Yale University Art Gallery
Plate 35. Photo courtesy of Timothy Richards
Plate 47. The Corporation for Jefferson's Poplar Forest, photo courtesy of Seth Trittipoe

LENDERS TO THE EXHIBITION

Carnegie Museum of Art
Centro Internazionale di Studi di Architettura Andrea Palladio
/ Palladio Museum
Cincinnati Art Museum
College of William & Mary, Earl Gregg Swem Library
The Colonial Williamsburg Foundation
Cornell University, the Carl A. Kroch Library
The Corporation for Jefferson's Poplar Forest
Harvard Art Museums/Fogg Museum
Kaufman Americana Foundation
Linda H. Kaufman
Library of Congress
Maryland Historical Society
Massachusetts Historical Society
Museum of Early Southern Decorative Arts
National Gallery of Art
The National Portrait Gallery, Smithsonian Institution
New-York Historical Society, Museum, and Library
North Carolina Museum of Art
Oak Spring Garden Foundation, Upperville, Virginia
Philadelphia Museum of Art
Private Collection
Thomas Jefferson Foundation, Monticello
University of Virginia School of Architecture
Virginia Museum of Fine Arts
The Virginia Museum of History & Culture
Wadsworth Atheneum Museum of Art
Washington University Libraries
Yale University Art Gallery